CW00669930

HAWKER VC

TO ALL THOSE
WHO CONSTANTLY FLEW AND FOUGHT
FAR OVER THE ENEMY LINES

HAWKER VC
RFC ACE

THE LIFE OF MAJOR
LANOE HAWKER VC DSO
1890-1916

TYRREL M HAWKER MC

Pen & Sword
AVIATION

First published in Great Britain in 1965 by
The Mitre Press

Reprinted in this format in 2013 by
PEN & SWORD AVIATION
An imprint of
Pen & Sword Books Ltd
47 Church Street
Barnsley
South Yorkshire
S70 2AS

Copyright © Tyrrel Mann Hawker, 1965, 2013

ISBN 978 1 78159 345 5

The right of Tyrrel Mann Hawker to be identified as Author
of this work has been asserted by him in accordance with
the Copyright, Designs and Patents Act 1988.

A CIP catalogue record for this book is
available from the British Library

All rights reserved. No part of this book may be reproduced or transmitted in
any form or by any means, electronic or mechanical including photocopying,
recording or by any information storage and retrieval system,
without permission from the Publisher in writing.

Printed and bound in England
By CPI Group (UK) Ltd, Croydon, CR0 4YY

Pen & Sword Books Ltd incorporates the Imprints of Pen & Sword Aviation,
Pen & Sword Family History, Pen & Sword Maritime, Pen & Sword Military,
Pen & Sword Discovery, Pen & Sword Politics, Pen & Sword Archaeology,
Pen & Sword Atlas, Wharncliffe Local History, Wharncliffe True Crime,
Wharncliffe Transport, Pen & Sword Select, Pen & Sword Military Classics,
Leo Cooper, The Praetorian Press, Claymore Press, Remember When,
Seaforth Publishing and Frontline Publishing

For a complete list of Pen & Sword titles please contact
PEN & SWORD BOOKS LIMITED
47 Church Street, Barnsley, South Yorkshire, S70 2AS, England
E-mail: enquiries@pen-and-sword.co.uk
Website: www.pen-and-sword.co.uk

Foreword

by

Air Marshal Sir ROBERT SAUNDBY,
K.C.B., K.B.E., M.C., D.F.C., A.F.C., D.L.

WHEN I was posted at the age of twenty to No. 24 Squadron, in July, 1916, I did not at first realize how lucky I had been. I knew, of course, that 24 was the first squadron to be fully equipped with fighter aircraft—the famous D.H.2,—and that the squadron had a very high reputation. But it was not until I met its Commanding Officer, Major Lanoe G. Hawker, V.C., D.S.O., that I understood.

Here was a leader of men who combined modesty with great courage, gentleness with a steely determination, and unselfishness with a most human understanding. At first I regarded him with an admiration and respect that amounted to awe; as I got to know him better my respect and admiration increased, but the awe diminished. It was replaced by a feeling that I can only describe as devotion.

Hawker taught me the meaning of leadership. Lord Trenchard has described him as one of the greatest war-time personalities of the Royal Flying Corps, and that is no exaggeration. In two years of war his influence on all who served with him was profound. He died young, at the height of his glory, and his death cast a shadow far and wide.

Whenever I think of him I am reminded of the tribute paid to Brutus in the closing scene of Julius Caesar:

> " His life was gentle, and the elements
> So mixed in him that Nature might stand up,
> And say to all the world, ' This was a man.' "

v

Introduction

by

Lieut. Col. A. M. WILKINSON, D.S.O. and bar, Royal Air Force*

I WOULD not have believed it possible to recapture so clearly the story of Lanoe Hawker's life, just as we in No. 24 Squadron knew him; it is perfect.

The author does not overstate Hawker's real genius for leadership; he had all the qualities—a high degree of intelligence, a great love for his fellow men, a tenderness which, like Nelson's, was almost that of a woman, combined with an implacable strength. His selflessness and his divine courage inspired his pilots and his men to achieve a standard which I venture to think was far above their normal.

He was the idol of all who knew him. Only those who worked with him, at times night and day, could really appraise his true value. Never before or since did we reach such heights of exaltation in the midst of horror and tragedy as we did in those amazing days in Hawker's Squadron. It was the happiest unit that anyone could have found in France; we were profoundly convinced that there was no other squadron in the same class, and every man thought himself extraordinarily lucky to be serving in it.

Hawker's influence spread far wider than he, or perhaps any of us, ever knew, and when they joined other squadrons his pilots took with them the Hawker spirit and the Hawker tradition.

* From the 1st April, 1918, till the 1st August, 1919, Air Force officers retained their military ranks.

Acknowledgments

I TAKE up my pen, well aware of my shortcomings as a writer, but who else could better describe my brother's life than I. with whom he spent more than half his days. I prepared the manuscript of his biography nearly thirty years ago, but for various reasons it has not been possible to publish it till now.

I have spared no pains in giving my readers a full and accurate account, and in this I have been fortunate in receiving the generous and enthusiastic help of many of his brother officers who survived the war, the permission of the Controller of Her Majesty's Stationery Office and the Air Force Department of the Ministry of Defence to quote from *The War in the Air,* the short histories of the Squadrons in which my brother served, many other official documents, some of them in my brother's handwriting and the helpful suggestions of Mr. H. A. Jones, M.C., the official historian and his staff and the staff of the Imperial War Museum.

I also acknowledge the generous permission I have been given to use extracts from *Flying Colours* and *No. 24 Squadron* printed privately, some two hundred of my brother's letters, carefully preserved by the recipients, many photographs taken before and during the war, including several supplied by the Imperial War Museum, information gained from the official history of the war on land, *Military Operations,* over two hundred books on the war, including both German and French, and copies of records supplied by the Reichsarchiv. Reference is made in notes to only a few of these works for fear of distracting the reader, but many quotations from them are included in the text.*

With all this care, I still fear that this biography may fall short of conjuring up a clear enough picture of the lovable, loyal and courageous companion, whose life was cut short at the very moment when his dearest wishes appeared to be on the point of realisation, his promotion imminent and his services as a leader in the air most needed by his country.

T.H.

* To reduce the number of footnotes, references to the official history *WAR IN THE AIR* are shown briefly in the text, V., C., A. and p. denoting respectively Volume, Chapter, Appendix and page.

Contents

Contents (contd.)

Part III

HAWKER'S SQUADRON

LIST OF ILLUSTRATIONS

INTRODUCTION TO 2013 EDITION

by

FLIGHT LIEUTENANT PHILIP MOBBS
XXIV SQUADRON, RAF

This new edition of Lanoe Hawker VC's life is much overdue. Originally written by his brother Tyrrel Hawker and published in 1965, it has been long out of print. The rather battered copy that resides in our Squadron History Room at RAF Brize Norton was a lucky find in a second-hand bookshop in the Belgian town of Ypres.

Anyone who has witnessed the Last Post ceremony at the Menin Gate and seen the large groups of school children from many countries, including our own, will know that the events of nearly one hundred years ago still feature large in the consciousness of the nations of Europe. As we approach the centenary of the start of the Great War there will be an even greater level of interest in the events of that horrific conflict. In 2015 XXIV Squadron will also celebrate the centenary of its formation at Hounslow Heath. Originally formed as a training unit preparing pilots for service in France it went on to become the first squadron in any air force to be equipped entirely with single seat fighter aircraft. It was fortunate to be commanded by Lanoe Hawker who was arguably the foremost pilot in the Royal Flying Corps at the time.

In 2010 XXIV Squadron was reorganised from an operational transport squadron to become the training unit for the Hercules C130J, effectively returning to its roots after ninety-five years. In the future XXIV will take on the training roles for other aircraft at Brize Norton, namely the C17 Globemaster and the A400M Atlas. Tyrrel Hawker's lament for the end of the squadron in this book, Death of a Fighter Squadron, may have been true for that role but 'Hawker's Squadron' has continued to serve and its future as Brize Norton's senior squadron seems assured.

When I joined XXIV Squadron in 2001 I was only dimly aware of Hawker and his legacy although his picture was seemingly everywhere in our HQ. It was not until 2009 when I first visited France on an exercise to retrace the steps of our predecessors from Hounslow Heath to Bertangle and then to the lonely farmland which was Hawker's final resting place that I really became familiar with his story. It was beside those fields where we laid a small cross to Hawker that I first conceived the idea of building a memorial to mark his burial place. The Hawker Memorial was finally unveiled in the village of Ligny Thilloy on 11 November 2011 on a cold and foggy day watched by almost the whole village as well as members of the Hawker family and representatives of the Luftwaffe's Richthofen Squadron who had come to pay their respects to a former opponent. One couple had even come all the way from the USA to be present.

The unfortunate consequence of the fog was that it prevented the flypast of the replica Airco DH2 that had flown all the way from Lincolnshire for the occasion. This aircraft, one of only two in the world and the only one in the northern hemisphere, is painted in the markings of the machine that Hawker was flying on his final flight. The difficulties and tribulations of that journey would make a book by itself and serve to remind us, if any reminder is necessary, of the dangers faced by those original pilots when they flew their fragile aircraft across the Channel to France. The weather smiled the following day and the DH2 was able to fly at last over the Memorial and the location where Hawker was buried, in the process also becoming the first of its type to fly over the Somme since 1918.

As this biography was written by Hawker's own brother, it could face an accusation of bias and of being a hagiography, particularly as the man that emerges from these pages has so many admirable characteristics and so few faults. Yet those that knew him, of which there are sadly none alive today, agreed with this view. But as Lieutenant Colonel A. M. Wilkinson wrote in his original Introduction, and he had served with Hawker in the Squadron, 'The author does not overstate Hawker's real genius for leadership…He was the idol of all who knew him. Only those who worked with him could really appraise his true value.'

The inscription that we chose for Hawker's Memorial was copied from the original Foreword to this book written by Air Marshal Sir Robert Saundby. As Lieutenant Saundby, he had accompanied Hawker on his last patrol and said that, whenever he thought of him, he was reminded of the tribute paid to Brutus in the closing scene of Julius Caesar:

> "His life was gentle, and the elements
> So mixed in him that Nature might stand up,
> And say to all the world, 'This was a man'."

PART I

BORN TO SERVE

1

Hawker

IT was already dark as I rode over the railway crossing, the clouds behind me but faintly lighted by the flicker of the guns on the Somme.

The nearest of three big sheds loomed up ahead and, beside it, a crack of light streamed out from a squat little hut, " the office ". A grimy sergeant saluted smartly and took charge of my horses and batman. I walked towards the mess, pausing in front of the big sheds in turn. The sentry saluted, adding a friendly grin of recognition. Inside each shed a group of " airmen " (mechanics, fitters, riggers) worked almost silently in the glare of a lamp; each was intent on his work and it needed no officer here to urge them on, for they were bitten by an intense spirit of keenness which far out-stripped in value any external pressure.

The machines looked sinister in this half-light, their blunt nacelles thrust up and out beyond the planes, a perilous looking perch for the pilot, but giving him a wonderful view; the vicious snout of a machine-gun peeped out in front. These were the famous D.H.2 Scouts; infamous too, for many a good pilot had been killed by their vices.

There was no difficulty in finding the officers' mess, for shouts of laughter seemed to shake the oblong hut. Through the half-closed door I could see about twenty-four young officers on either side of a long table, at the far end of which the Major tilted back his chair, a glass in his hand. Everyone was talking and laughing at once; evidently this was one of the ecstatic celebrations of another defeat of the once dreaded Fokkers, and No. 24 had invited, for this lively occasion, the pilots and observers of the neighbouring squadron, whom they escorted and protected on their slow and perilous task of photographing the enemy's elaborate trench system.

I pushed my way in to shouts of welcome, and joined these hilarious officers in an excellent dinner, accompanied by plenty of whisky. The pilots recounted, in comic form, their hair-raising encounters with the Fokkers, often adding advice to others, much of it facetious, leading to hot arguments and further roars of laughter.

Then the guests from the neighbouring squadron made some intentionally provocative remark, and, in an instant, chairs were flung back, the table pushed aside and all heads were down in a whirling, shouting scrum, pushing and struggling till the offenders, fewer in number, were thrust against the side of the hut, which, hingeing outwards from the top, allowed them to be ejected in a struggling heap on to the grass outside. With whoops and hunting calls, they rushed for their Crossley tender, for though their quarters were but half a mile away, they never dreamt of walking there.

Laughing and breathless from romping, the Major hooked his arm in mine. " Bed time, old chap," he said and led me to his quarters in a clearing in a nearby copse, where stood a canvas-walled hut divided into three compartments, bedroom, sitting room and square alcove for the tub-shaped bath. Cane armchairs, table with cloth and writing materials, curtains, pictures, flowers, carpet, an extra camp bed; compared with a dug-out in the front line, these were luxurious quarters indeed. Were we really at war? Through the curtained window, that sinister flicker in the east was a constant reminder of the endless agony in the trenches.

The major sat quietly on his bed undressing, his brown hair on end from the scrum, large square head, large round eyes, well-shaped nose, neat moustache, large ears, large sensitive mouth, firm square chin; his features were on a generous scale, in the Kitchener mould; he was of average build and height. As I watched him, his eyes took on that familiar fixed stare of concentration; of what was he thinking now? Yet another invention or some new tactical scheme for " strafing the Hun "?

Soon he was asleep, but I lay wondering what it was that had gone to make this remarkable and famous squadron, Hawker's Squadron, which had swept the Fokkers from the sky, which had done so much to establish on the Somme front a supremacy in the air never equalled before, and, as it turned out, never to be equalled again. Here in this hut slept their leader, Hawker himself. What were the magic ingredients that made such a leader?

Lying awake I tried to answer that question.

2

Ancestral

HAWKING is a sport of great antiquity, and the hawker watches keenly the flight of his bird as it dives upon its prey. Though he hunts by proxy, as it were, his nerves are taut with the excitement of the chase, imagining himself in the place of the hawk. This hunting instinct passes down through many generations.

From hawking for kings it was no great step to serving in the king's armed forces in times of war, and the Hawkers, without the omission of a single generation, held commissions in the army from the days of Queen Elizabeth.*

The junior branch of the family held commissions in the navy, the only break in this line being the Hon. G. C. Hawker, who migrated to Australia in 1840, served with distinction in parliament for 25 years and as Speaker in the House of Assembly. Of his 16 children, Harry held a commission in the navy and in 1879 married Julia Gordon Lanoe, the younger daughter (the elder daughter, Marie, was the authoress Lanoe Falconer) of Major Peter Hawker of Longparish House, thus uniting the two branches of the family. On retiring from the navy Harry Hawker settled in Longparish, where was born his fifth child, Lanoe George, the subject of this biography.

On the army side Colonel Peter Hawker, born in 1785, was not only a noted sportsman, author of *Hawker on Shooting* and a well known sporting diary, the manuscript of which now lies in Yale library, but also an inventor of great ingenuity. This versatile ancestor may well have passed on some of his natural gifts to his great-grandson, Lanoe.

* See " Burke's Landed Gentry," 1911.

3

Longparish

IF you happen to be travelling between Andover and Whitchurch, the road that turns south at Hurstbourne Priors will lead you along the Test through Longparish. The pretty thatched cottages are neatly kept and soon you will come to a large white Georgian house standing in a park by the riverside. This is Longparish House, the ancestral home of the Hawkers. Further on you will notice a quaint wishing well, a little church with low square tower, and then on the right a charming gabled brick house surrounded by lawns and gardens, then named " Homecroft ", where Lanoe was born on the 31st of December, 1890. It is difficult now to conjure up the tranquil country life of those happy days, undisturbed by aeroplanes, motor cars, loudspeakers and foreign affairs.

Lanoe was a fine baby, but when only a few months old nearly died of pneumonia owing to the carelessness of his nurse during his parents' absence in Egypt, where his father was convalescing from an accident which had cost him his left eye.

At six months Lanoe could already speak a few words. He was devoted to a baby cousin though she bullied him, and was distressed when she left, but recovered his spirits on the arrival in this world of his younger brother, Tyrrel, in September, 1892.

As a small child Lanoe had a large head, high forehead, large, round eyes and large ears. His manner was serious and enquiring. When two years old he took a great liking to *Strewel-Peter* and persuaded " grown-ups " to read passages from it, always pointing to the words with a finger for him to follow : he memorised some of the stories and repeated them as he pointed to the words himself. The family doctor was horrified to find this very small child apparently reading nursery rhymes, and proposed that he should be kept in a darkened room !

In search of knowledge as he grew older, Lanoe asked endless questions in a slow, deliberate voice, many of them difficult or awkward to answer. As soon as he learnt to read he consulted *Encyclopaedia Britannica,* and gathered from it a mass of information, sometimes on the strangest subjects. He had an annoying way of questioning " grown-ups " and then subjecting their answers to criticisms from what he had learnt in the Encyclopaedia.

When about four years old he owned a small tricycle which he left in the verandah near his uncle, Major Charles Main-waring. On his return, noticing that it was faulty in some respect, he stationed himself before his uncle and said in his deliberate voice : " Uncle Charlie, have you been riding my tricycle ? " " No of course not, my little man," replied his uncle, startled at such an absurd idea.

" All I can say, Uncle Charlie is that it is very peculiar. No one else has been here but you, and my tricycle was quite all right when I left it."

Uncle Charlie somehow felt horribly guilty without the slightest cause and decided, that in future, he would not condemn any of his men brought before him, just because they looked guilty. Later Lanoe admitted that he had hoped that his implied accusation would induce Uncle Charlie to mend his tricycle for him.

As soon as he could manage a crochet hook Lanoe set about making a woollen shawl, buying pieces of bright coloured wool with his Saturday pennies. When his little fingers grew tired, he would dump the work in the lap of a grown-up and silently look up with large pleading eyes, which were irresistible. At last the proud day came when Lanoe made a birthday present of the many-coloured shawl to his mother. It was one of the gifts she treasured most, and was always given a place of honour in her room.

Lanoe, who had little fear of the concrete things in this world, imagined strange terrors in a shadow on the sky-light, or a towel hanging against a cupboard in the half-light. Also he walked in his sleep, and, waking suddenly, would rouse T. with his screams, but his fear left him the instant he felt his brother by his side. Before going to sleep, he was in the habit of leaning out of his bed and looking beneath it to make sure that there was nothing horrible lurking there. On one such occasion he was met by the stare of two large green eyes. His terrified screams brought the family running into the room, as Masters, the big ginger cat, scurried out of it.

He was always an early riser, and in winter would sometimes go out before dawn to play in the garden. His leadership led to some rather doubtful adventures. Once he got T. up at about 4.30 a.m., dressed him and took him out to assist in purloining, from the neighbour's high wall, some coping stones he required for tunnel construction in the sand pit. Somehow he was detected, and a polite note arrived, asking that the coping stones should be replaced when he had finished with them.

He also discovered some loose cash in a desk drawer in the drawing room and together with T., helped himself occasionally when no one was looking. The proceeds were spent on new bread, salt butter and cheap sweets, not an approved diet for small boys.

Repetitions of these thefts led to discovery and beatings by Daddy with a dog-whip. These punishments were accepted as a sporting risk, and only made the thieves more cunning and cautious. It was the distress caused to their mother that finally put an end to these depredations.

Like all small boys, these two had their quarrels, but if it came to fisticuffs, Lanoe was sure to get the best of it; his large eyes flashing with anger and his square chin thrust forward, he advanced with both fists punching hard, made no attempt to protect himself, and disregarded any blows he might receive. T.'s nose always seemed to get in the way, and the fight had to stop for fear of making too much mess with the blood that flowed freely from it. Unable to hold his own with fists, T. took revenge with dream tales. " I dreamt I met a bear in a dark wood and I took a stick and hit it, but Lanoe ran away crying." " I didn't," shouted Lanoe, indignant at the slander.

A neighbour, Mrs. Mitchell, arrived with her nephew, Rex, who was brought up with the intention that he should be a soldier; she told tales of battles to give him a martial spirit, and he responded bravely, saying what he would do with his sword. One day she described to the three small boys a terrible battle, in which most of the combatants fell bleeding to the ground. " And what would you do, Lanoe? " she asked. Lanoe grunted incredulously. " And what would you do T.? " " I think I'd go indoorth," he lisped with good sense. " Now Rexie, tell them what you would do," she said with proud expectation, " you're going to be a soldier." " Well Auntie," he replied meekly. " I'd no idea it was so dangerous."

Lanoe was one of those small boys who could always be trusted with a task. One of his favourite jobs was the filling of honey tins for his father; at each closing of the tap the drip was wiped off with a small finger, which was cleaned in the mouth, a legitimate reward for patient work; more than that he would not take.

Instead of being brought up by nursery maids or governesses, the little boys had the great advantage of the devoted care of Nettie Baldie, their mother's cousin. Much of their knowledge and progress in later life was due to her long-sighted and gentle management of their early years at Homecroft.

Sister Sally, about eight years older than Lanoe, and musically inclined, taught him the words of " Gaily the Troubadour " and also to play the accompaniment on the piano, but he had absolutely no ear for music and sang right off the note. Sally gave up the attempt to teach him anything else, but much later, we shall hear more of this song.

Mr. Bishop, the gardener, known locally as " Old Bish ", had a permanent shake to his head, which was tilted to one side, giving him a knowing look. With his limited energy, he guarded the fruit as best he could from all depredators, but the straw-berries were inadequately protected by dilapidated netting from either birds or boys. The latter assumed the law of Divine Providence by which the tasting and sampling of ripe fruit is not stealing but, even so, must be indulged in with caution and circumspection. One day, noticing that the boys were heading in the direction of the strawberries, Bish took a devious route, hoping to catch them red-handed, but they were too wary for him, and he found them standing with hands in pockets, and mouths wiped clean, contemplating the strawberry bed. Bish looked at them suspiciously, with much head-wagging.

" A lot of my strawberries 'ave been took," he said accusingly. Lanoe, looking the picture of injured innocence, replied reproachfully :—" Oh Bish ! The birds can get in anywhere through that netting and take them."

Old Bish, with his head on one side, looked very wise. " I

reckon I know them birds," he said. "Them be two-legged birds, them be."

A welcome addition to the household was Bogey, an Aberdeen terrier mongrel, a most faithful and intelligent companion and a great ratter. The little boys ranged the countryside, over water-meadows, across the parapets of railway bridges, up lofts, over walls and wherever they went Bogey had to go too; he was their inseparable companion.

One day, when Lanoe was romping with Bogey on the lawn, T. threw a stone along the ground to attract the dog's attention. Just at that moment Lanoe dived forward and the stone hit him on the temple, making a nasty cut which bled profusely. He made no fuss, but went indoors and had the wound bathed and bandaged, explaining that he must have fallen against a brass spike on the dog's collar. Terrified of the consequences of his rash act, T. was relieved to hear this explanation, but confessed his guilt to Lanoe, who quietly replied:—"I knew that, but I wasn't going to get you into trouble."

Most of the boys' pocket-money was spent on mechanical toys which Lanoe, with exceptionally sensitive fingers, took to pieces to see how they worked, and then carefully put together again. One of his earliest and greatest joys was a bicycle on which, having learnt to ride almost immediately, he then taught T., with great anxiety for his new machine. In the winter there was skating on a pond at Longparish House and tobogganning at Southside Hill. Lanoe showed early presence of mind on one of these occasions; the two little boys were given a turn by themselves in a Canadian toboggan, but their light weight failed to break the frozen crust on the snow, with the result that the toboggan, gathering unexpected speed, made straight for a partly frozen pond near the bottom of the hill. Realizing the danger in time, Lanoe had the pluck and sense to turn the toboggan over, resulting in a nasty spill, but averting a dangerous accident.

Preparatory to going to school the boys were coached by a local tutor. Lanoe took great interest in his work and made good progress; he was eager for knowledge and anxious to please his teacher, but one day, in a moment of impatience, the latter boxed his ears. Lanoe was not the type of boy to be treated in this rough manner; grey with fury, he retired to the far side of the table, and in steady, biting words reproved his tutor for his bad temper and his unauthorised act.

Early in 1900 Lanoe saw his father leave for the Boer War, not as an officer, for his naval rank did not entitle him to a commission in the army, but as a trooper in the Australian Light Horse, in which regiment the disability of his age and the loss of an eye were passed over. Such a patriotic example made a deep impression on the nine-year-old boy, who was proud of his family traditions.

A few months later both boys left for Geneva. Poor little Bogey was the chief one to suffer by their absence; he wandered round the house whimpering dismally, suddenly rushing to the sound of a voice that might be theirs, only to be disappointed. At last he fell ill, and out of kindness was sent to the " happy hunting ground " where he would pine no more; he left behind him a memory of devotion and loyalty that never faded. Not often did Lanoe weep, but on the news of Bogey's departure he was unable to restrain his tears.

4

Geneva

BUSTLING and packing for a great journey to a distant land, jog-trot in the dog-cart, rumble in the train, Dover, paddle-steamer, hot-smelling engines, cold wind and spray, misery of a rough crossing, strange blue-smocked, gesticulating, noisy porters, rumbling and clanking for hours across a strange land, slowly through a dripping tunnel, Geneva at last; clatter of cab on cobbled and hilly streets, on to the Rhone bridge, and suddenly there, hanging in the sky like fairy castles, pale and detached from this world, glowed pinkly in the afternoon sun the snow-clad Alps. On through narrow streets and a fine public garden ("you can come and play in these gardens") up hill to a tall white building, up three flights of stairs, warm corridor, welcoming voices, Miss Stable ("like a picture of Queen Victoria"), the journey had ended. The two little boys spent many happy days in the capable and loving care of this charming and kindly old lady.

Geneva held a surprise for the young sons of England, for the Swiss had been carefully led by German and French propaganda to believe that the English had no other object in the South African War than to steal their country from the Boers. Fortunately the Genevese were a gentle and highly civilized people, with a regard for fair play, showing little sign of Germanic influence, and the clashes between English and Genevese children were devoid of bitterness or cruelty, but their antagonism was not lessened when these young foreigners boasted that their father was fighting the Boers.

The boys arrived in Geneva, dressed in their hideous Norfolk tweeds, which were the fashion at that time in England, but very different from anything worn by small boys on the Continent. In consequence, when they walked the streets, they were mobbed by a dozen stocky urchins, about Lanoe's size and probably a little older, who shouted in chorus "Ongleesh Bocken! Ongleesh Bocken!" Lanoe did not know the meaning of Bocken, but he

11

did not like the sound of it, and greatly resented the effrontery of these foreigners daring to insult the English, so he planned with T. a place and moment where they could be trapped and punished. It did not occur to him that they were 12 to 2; he never counted nor even considered the odds. At his signal, he and T. rushed upon the noisy urchins, banged their heads together and otherwise dealt out retribution. He would show them that the English could not be insulted with impunity. Shouting with pain and indignation, they ran out of arm's reach and then made the mistake of throwing stones, for this was T.'s favourite weapon, and with a swift and accurate fusillade, he soon scattered them well out of range. Lanoe's temper cooled at once and he laughed at their quick discomfiture and flight.

On return to the flat, he asked Miss Stable the meaning of " Bocken ". A Swiss woman guessed it at once and said in French that what these urchins had read on the shop windows and were shouting was " Ongleesh Spocken ". Poor little wretches! It was doubtful if they knew the meaning of " English Spoken ", and the brothers felt ashamed at having treated them so roughly on a hasty misunderstanding.

The happy sequel was a shopping expedition with Miss Stable, who gave them the treat of choosing Swiss summer outfits. They settled for wide straw sailor hats, for it was very sunny, and striped blue and white Swiss sailor suits, a joy to wear and lightning quick to don in the morning, accompanied by lightning quick if inadequate ablutions. No more were they mobbed by urchins shouting " Ongleesh Bocken ".

The boys first went to a large day-school, where Lanoe made use of his few words of French to enter a class of Swiss boys of his own age. T., using an ill-pronounced " comprend pas," started at the bottom of the school, and as an occupation was given Genevese comic papers to cut out and paste in a scrap-book. To Lanoe's indignation he found that these papers contained crude illustrations of Boer, Swiss and English, in which the latter always took an undignified part.

" You ass," he said angrily to T., " can't you see what you're doing? " T., ashamed, cut the figures out of the pictures, and re-arranged them to his own artistic taste, which turned out highly offensive to Genevese pride. There was no rule against sneaking in this Swiss school, and soon the teacher and pupils were shouting their indignant protests. T. was punished and the scandal spread throughout the school. The next morning, as the pupils filed into the main hall for prayers, both English boys received sundry pinches, kicks and prods from behind. A minor form of frightfulness had started, but Lanoe was the last person to put up with it tamely.

" Next time kick down and back," he advised, giving a vigorous demonstration, and on the following morning the entrance to prayers was marked by howls of agony and a clear space round two innocent-looking English boys. During the morning recreation the Genevese boys took their revenge, trapped their victims in an ambush at the doorway, and frog-marched them to the fountain where their heads were cooled. It was useless to struggle in the hands of so many; Lanoe sub-mitted silently, but when released, unable as yet to tell his tormentors in French what he thought of them, he thrust his hands deep in his pockets and, with touseled and dripping head held very high, looked at the hooting crowd with an obvious expression of intense scorn. They could not fail to admire his pluck and his forebearance, exceptional in their school, in not complaining to the masters. He despised them for their sneaking and would never stoop to such a level.

In spite of these reprisals, T.'s insulting pictures continued, the scrap book was confiscated and a fresh ambush set, but this time it was anticipated, and by a counter ruse was made to fall upon an astonished master, who punished the offenders. Con-stant scuffles, resulting in bruises and torn clothes, led to a change from this school to one attended by both sexes, under the direction of Mlle. Pantard, whom Lanoe grew to love and respect.

Each Saturday the children of this school marched round the classroom singing, to the same tune as " God Save the Queen ", what the English boys mistakenly supposed to be " Hosana Dépendant "; they joined in with gusto. This zeal was surpris-ingly unpopular, and Mlle. Pantard decided to teach them the words of their own national anthem. For this they were kept back for five minutes of the morning break.

Coming out to play, they found that war had been declared to avenge the insult (it was only some 25 years later that the writer discovered that the correct words of the song were " Aux

Monts Indépendants ", parodied by the Swiss children into
" Aux ânes indépendants " !), and the Swiss boys had collected
ammunition dumps of pebbles behind the trees on the playground. Lanoe was unafraid; he picked up a huge stone, too
heavy to throw, but with threatening gestures advanced unflinchingly on the defenders of the main ammunition store: T.,
gathering a few stones quickly, darted round to a flank and sent
a well directed stream of pebbles amongst their legs. With
shouts and screams the enemy broke and ran. At this crucial
moment Mlle. Pantard, hearing the uproar, appeared upon the
scene. Not only did these English boys disturb the peace of her
classes, but they must needs turn the playground into a battle
field. Her patience was such that she did not immediately eject
this turbulent element from her school; she had taken a liking to
Lanoe, and the boys' punishment was a light one.

Many minor encounters followed, the Swiss children relying
on superior numbers, but Lanoe was an unsatisfactory opponent
and never gave way. He went into the fight with one cry,
" England," and then silently ploughed his way into the middle
of the screaming mob, punching hard with both fists and disregarding any blows he might receive; always he ended by
putting his opponents to flight and then, his anger melting
quickly, he gave a merry laugh, rippling up and ending on a
high note. His sturdy fighting in the forefront gave confidence
to T., who learnt to give a good account of himself.

The Genevese children soon contented themselves with shouting " Je m'en fiche ", and then running out of range. This
happened so often that Lanoe understood " Je m'en fiche "
to mean " I'm going," or " I'm off," with unfortunate consequences, for one day he arrived late in class carrying his stilts,
and when told by Mlle. Pantard to put them away, replied,
" Je m'en fiche" (" I don't care a d———") as he turned his back
on her to carry out her order. The school was aghast; such
scandalous behaviour had never been known.

Lanoe was horrified when he learnt the real meaning of his
words; not for anything would he have been rude to Mlle.
Pantard, but his French was now so good that it was difficult to
excuse his ignorance, nor for the sake of discipline could his
crime be overlooked. He shed bitter tears at the thought that
the mistress he now loved should disbelieve his innocent intention

and refuse to forgive him. As punishment he was kept in on the next holiday instead of going for a trip to the mountains.

The sequel was typical of Lanoe's ability to turn misfortune to advantage. T. spent a miserable afternoon wandering about disconsolately outside the school, whilst Lanoe, giving free vent to his passion for questions, spent an interesting and enjoyable time with Mlle. Pantard, discoursing on many subjects, and establishing an affectionate understanding with her, which remained unruffled during the rest of his time at the school.

Miss Stable's sister-in-law, Annie, was responsible for running the domestic side of the flat and she managed the kitchen. One day Lanoe strayed in there and did something which annoyed her. Impatiently, she grabbed him by the ear, but he twisted himself free, nipped round the table and shaking with rage shouted at her, " You have no right to touch me. I am in Miss Stable's charge, not yours, and anyhow my Mother says no one is to pull my ears; they are too big already." Annie took this as astonishing impertinence from a small boy, shouted at him and chased him round the kitchen. Miss Stable, hearing the uproar, appeared on the scene, stood up for Lanoe and, later no doubt, told Annie to keep her hands off him. She, herself, never punished the boys, was far too tender-hearted to chastise them, and certainly was not going to let Annie do so.

Lanoe submitted meekly to recognised authority, but became furious at any unauthorised interference. He would not speak to Annie that day, not even look at her. She was not unkind, and probably had grown fond of Lanoe, but she was quick tempered. At supper-time, seeing Lanoe's gaze averted from her, she said quietly, " Lanoe, I am sorry. I won't touch you again." Lanoe slipped off his chair, went round and kissed her, returned to his place, and when she looked up at him, he smiled brightly at her.

One night when the boys had gone to bed, T. heard Lanoe crying and sobbing, so he too started to cry, rather noisily. Lanoe sat up in bed and asked testily :—" What are you crying about? " T. replied, " I'm crying because you are crying." Lanoe said angrily, " You don't know what you are crying about, so shut up and go to sleep." But T. was not satisfied. " What are you crying about? " he asked. Lanoe replied in a mournful voice, " Queen Victoria is dead, my Queen". To which T. replied, " She's my Queen too, and I have as much right to cry for her as you have ". With that he turned over and went fast to sleep.

With the accumulation of several cash presents T. bought a small Swiss four-wheeled cart, known as a ' charette ', large enough to hold both boys back to back. Lanoe sitting in front steered with his feet, a taste of the future, whilst T., with his long legs, propelled the cart when the slope was insufficient to maintain speed. In hilly Geneva, Lanoe quickly developed dexterity in steering the charette down the winding streets and paths.

Up in the mountains, during the summer vacation, he again showed great presence of mind and quickness of decision when the charette was heading for a precipice. Without hesitation he turned the cart over on the stony hill, and to T.'s howls of indignation, replied by pointing silently to the danger avoided.

The boys soon made friends amongst their Genevese school-mates. T. selected a rosy-cheeked little girl, Gerda, and boasted that he kissed her, which Lanoe disbelieving, he demonstrated satisfactorily. Lanoe, put on his mettle, kissed his plain-faced Marcelle, who rewarded him with a sound slap. " She's not pretty," Lanoe admitted ruefully, " but she's sporting." Perhaps he was right, for henceforth Marcelle fell tigerishly upon anyone who tried to tease Lanoe.

The boys attended a gymnasium, swimming-bath and a riding-school. At the first of these, Lanoe was put to box the principal's son, a stocky lad of fourteen, against whom he stolidly held his own without much result on either side ; Lanoe ignored punishment, the Swiss boy avoided it, and in so doing kept too far off to do much damage.

The years spent in Geneva were very happy ones, full of adventure and interest. The boys stuck together, and between them there grew complete confidence and understanding. When in July, 1902, Lanoe left for an English school, it was a sad day for T. who realised, when he had gone, what a bright and jolly companion he had been, also both spearhead and shield in every encounter with the Swiss boys. However, T. looked forward to the time, in a few months, when he might rejoin Lanoe at school in England. Strange trick of fate ; the brothers were never again at school together.

5

The Navy

LANOE was sent to Stubbington House, a delightful, well-managed school on the Solent, with an enlightened treatment of the boys far in advance of its time; the school specialized in preparing boys for the navy.

By some mischance Lanoe's school clothes were not ready in time, and, rather than arrive late, he was sent to school in his Swiss sailor suit. In any case new boys came in for a good deal of teasing, but here was an ideal victim in his striped blue cotton suit of quaint foreign cut, on whose large square head the little round school cap looked ridiculous. Amongst all these teasing boys Lanoe suddenly felt lonely without the companionship of his brother. He, who had always been so jolly and sociable, now walked alone, his hands in his pockets, his head in the air, feigning indifference; but he was always sensitive as to his appearance, and suffered acutely without knowing how to reply, for he had been told that fighting was strictly forbidden. His mother, realizing how inarticulate boys are, had invented a code of two simple signs by which he could indicate if he were happy or not, and upon receiving a negative sign in his first letter, she went and saw him and advised him to stick up for himself, with fists if need be. "Oh may I?" said Lanoe brightening up, for he had felt obliged to obey the rule against fighting. The next week, visiting the school again, she was greeted by her son with a wide grin and a black eye. He seemed perfectly happy now and, watching the other boys on their way to church, waved cheerfully to one who also showed the scars of battle.

Lanoe took his work seriously and made excellent progress. Soon his jolly nature won him many friends. He was small for his age, and was not brilliant at games, but made up in good will and pluck for what he lacked in size and skill. On his own initiative he took up fencing; the quick co-ordination of wrist

and eye, his instinct for immediate attack, were assets in this
sport which he turned to good account.   He did not grow
physically strong, as he should have done, nor did the removal
of his appendix and tonsils prove to be the remedy.   He had a
deviation in the bone of his nose, which obstructed his breathing,
but this escaped notice for some years.

On half-holidays the boys were allowed to roam the countryside, but too often abused this privilege and indulged in forbidden
mud fights with the village lads, which Lanoe thought foolish.
Instead he walked down to the cliffs, and lying there watched
the hovering gulls, the fascinating ease with which they controlled
their flight.   If only he could fly!   What boy has not at some
time sighed for a pair of bird-like wings?

On his return a year later from Geneva, T. had hoped to
join Lanoe at Stubbington, but by a misunderstanding was sent
to a little school in Reading, where he was unhappy and half
starved.   Lanoe told him of the wonderful food at Stubbington,
the comfortable quarters, the greater freedom, the ideal surroundings.   T. was to enjoy this paradise, but only after Lanoe had
left.

During the holidays at Longparish a few hours each day were
spent with John Collins, a clever little Cambridge graduate, from
whom Lanoe gained a mathematical foundation that was of
great value to him later.

The boys were sometimes joined by Peter Ryves Hawker, the
cousin at Longparish House, a year older than Lanoe, and this
lively trio, calling themselves " The Invincible Three ", ranged
the countryside.   No barn nor orchard in the district was so
well locked or guarded that they could not penetrate it somehow.
Owing to Lanoe's level head, the mischief done was of small
consequence, but many a farmer must have sighed with relief
when the school term started.

Always mature and responsible for his age, Lanoe decided
to enter the navy, and in March, 1905, he was nominated by
Prince Louis of Battenberg, and in July successfully passed into
Britannia Naval College.   He revelled in the life at Dartmouth,
which he took very seriously.   He was a most promising cadet,
and by his pluck and keenness attracted the attention of Captain
Goodenough, the commandant.   To his brother's amazement
and amusement Lanoe was chosen to sing in the college choir,

for though he had a clear treble and a liking for music, he had no ear and sang " yards off the note ".

" I'm quite all right," he retorted indignantly. " I have a chap singing each side of me, and I keep in between."

Owing to his small size and his reliable disposition he was chosen to cox the college boat. As a sport he followed the beagles with too much energy ; the obstruction in his nose proved to be a serious handicap. He was not robust, first contracted a chill, then jaundice, and stoically refusing to report sick till too late, ended by straining his heart. He was given sick-leave so that he might recover his strength, but this entailed loss of seniority, which appeared prejudicial to his career. Wisely though sadly, he finally decided to retire so that he might regain his full strength under conditions less strenuous than in the navy. Captain Goodenough was sorry to lose him and wrote, " He's as plucky a little beggar as you could wish and always trying, but not over-strong." It was a hard blow to Lanoe, for the life had appealed to him, and he had made good friends at Dartmouth.

Service for his country had become his ambition, but he bore his disappointment with characteristic fortitude. At times his eyes took on a troubled look, his mouth a firmer line, his chin a forward set ; he carried his head high. He never complained.

6

The Army

In the summer of 1906 the family moved to Broxwood Court, a large country house in north Herefordshire. There Lanoe quickly recuperated. At first he took up stamp-collecting, but as he regained his strength he was soon able to enjoy an active outdoor life, shooting, fishing, bathing, playing tennis and hunting on a grey pony. On one occasion the hounds checked after a fast run; Lanoe sat still on his pony near a thick hedge, and, as something moved, his brother pointed. " Hush," said Lanoe, " he's dead beat," and the hounds casting wide, moved on. Lanoe enjoyed the gallop across country, but he had too much sympathy for living creatures to wish them killed.

He broke his forearm riding and, instead of taking part in a tennis party, was compelled to walk about with his arm in a sling, but proudly wore his naval cadet uniform. His smart diminutive figure attracted the gushing admiration of the ladies, which he received with quiet condescension. As soon as his arm was better he was out on his grey pony again.

It was at Broxwood that Lanoe started experiments with kites and primitive model aeroplanes. One of his kites was an excellent imitation of a hawk, and whilst his father was watching him fly this over the home covert, a shot rang out and the kite came fluttering down. An amusing moment followed when Lanoe and his father met the head game-keeper in the covert collecting his " bag ".

After long and tiring shooting parties Lanoe watched his father on a winter's evening warming his feet by the fire in the lofty hall, whilst the gramophone played the appealing strains of Ave Maria, sung by Melba. To Lanoe this melody meant more than the enjoyment of music; it was the symbol of the loving family life in the peaceful surroundings of the English countryside. This scene remained ever vivid in his memory.

Lanoe grew strong enough to start work again, but he was past public school age. He had not relinquished his ambition to serve his country and now decided to be a sapper (Royal Engineers). After a few months at Orleans to polish up his French, he went to a coach at Richmond where he studied for the " Shop " (Royal Military Academy, Woolwich). Gentlemen cadets at Woolwich became sapper or gunner officers, the former requiring a high standard of mathematics.

Lanoe understood the threat of war coming from Germany, which his father pronounced inevitable. The Germans were a proud and ambitious people, who believed that their military efficiency entitled them to dominate the world, and their motto was clearly "might is right". So it was then; so it will be for centuries to come.

With this inner urge Lanoe worked hard, attended Sandow's institute to build up his physical strength, continued his riding at a school at Earl's Court, and when dissatisfied with the progress of his studies, asked that he might again work with Mr. Collins. His far-sighted parents arranged for this clever tutor to take a small house at Cricklewood, where Lanoe could combine his special studies with his attendance at Sandow's and the riding-school. Here he was joined by T., and the boys spent many happy days together. Mr. Collins, with great enterprise, installed chemical and physical laboratories which included an electric generator, X-ray tube and a pair of two-way wireless (coherer) sets. Thus the boys had much scope for their enquiring minds, were continually carrying out experiments and manufactured, amongst other things, miniature searchlights, guns and their ammunition.

At a cinema in Cricklewood Broadway the boys saw, for the first time, a film of the Wright aeroplane in flight. How can one explain today, when flying is commonplace, the thrill of that first realization that we could fly? The next demonstration of flying came in April, 1910, when Graham-White passed overhead on his attempt to reach Manchester before Paulhan. During the summer holidays that year the boys attended their first aviation meeting at Bournemouth on the 13th of July. The Hon. C. S. Rolls had been killed in an accident the previous day. Was it this challenge of the air that determined Lanoe to learn to fly? It was certainly from this moment that he became intensely interested in aviation. Trips were made to Hendon, but as yet little flying took place except at rare moments of dead calm, or during aviation meetings.

The boys now spent their spare time and cash in making model aeroplanes. Lanoe, consulting weighty books on the subject, drew up the plans. T. produced the materials, and the two set to work to build small gliders. A new language came into use, camber, dihedral, warp, pitch and other terms unknown till then. Lanoe standing on the lawn below, looking up with anxious face, gave instructions to T. how to launch the glider from the upper window. After the first successful experiments the planes were fitted with elastic motors. There were accidents, repairs, modifications, fresh plans, control gadgets, which altered rudder and elevator. Running beneath the aeroplane in flight, Lanoe watched closely the effect of these devices. The models required much time to make and repair, and often the boys worked till after midnight so that their latest machine might be ready to fly on the morrow. Without a doubt Lanoe gained much information from these experiments that was useful to him later. Everything was new and had to be thought out; special materials and plans were not available in the market. Lanoe refused to be beaten by any obstacle, and he showed remarkable ingenuity in getting round apparently insurmountable difficulties. At times his thoughts were so concentrated that he became oblivious to his surroundings, nor was it easy to bring him out of his isolation without shaking him, but he strongly resented being touched. Even in the middle of a meal he sometimes became motionless, staring vacantly whilst his brain struggled with some problem. Occasionally by intuition, or by guess, T. supplied the answer to his thoughts, and then Lanoe suddenly came to life, amazed that his mind had been read.

To reach the high standard of his ambition Lanoe spent long hours at his work and this, coupled with the lack of outlet for his enthusiasm for flying, put a strain on him that led to occasional fits of irritation over trifles, but it was not in him to be ill-humoured for long. When he was suffering from these moods T., with deliberate clowning, made him laugh in spite of his attempts to keep a glum face. Then Lanoe became furious at his own inability to restrain his laughter, a really comic mixture of emotions.

He not only worked hard to pass his examinations, but took a great interest in all branches of science far outside the syllabus for the " Shop ". In this way he failed to get the highest marks in examinations, but later surprised his brother officers and his seniors by the breadth of his knowledge and the fertility of his inventive genius.

7

Growing Wings

LANOE entered " the Shop " in February, 1910. Rough though the life was, he found it greatly to his liking, and felt at home in the service of his country again. He was proud of his uniform, and held himself very straight on parade. There was plenty to occupy his active brain and, though he had made up his mind to become a sapper, he took much interest in gunnery; his knowledge of this subject was of great use to him later. As always, he asked questions, intelligent ones, but fewer now. His steady, frank look caught the attention of his instructors, who found something arresting in his smart, soldierly bearing, his large enquiring eyes and his square firm jaw. This cadet would certainly make a very good officer, possibly a great military leader.

The obstruction in Lanoe's nose was noticed by the medical officer; he underwent an operation to have it removed, and soon grew much stronger. He took up fencing again and won his colours for this sport; he was an enthusiast at the revolver range, played squash rackets and tennis. He soon made friends amongst those cadets who were also striving for sappers, amongst them Gordon Bayly, Ian Gourlay and David McMullen.

From time to time dances were held in the gymnasium, to which the cadets invited their lady friends and relatives. At one of these dances Lanoe met for the first time Gordon Bayly's sister, Beatrice. To her he was just one of the " boys ", one of Gordon's friends, but to Lanoe this meeting was the beginning of romance. Beatrice was a beautiful girl, spiritually and physically; she would have made a perfect model for a Rosetti picture. Lanoe danced with her on several occasions, both at Woolwich and later at Chatham, sometimes to " Destiny " and " Ecstasy ", his favourite waltzes. Steadily his love for her grew, though she remained unaware of it.

As a reward for his success in entering Woolwich, Lanoe was given a Triumph motor-cycle. On this machine he rode 15 miles each way through London traffic to spend the week-ends with T., who was still at Cricklewood, also preparing for his entrance to the " Shop ". Lanoe took him on the pillion of his motor cycle on many a jolly jaunt, both during these week-ends and in the holidays. He had an exceptionally fine sense of balance and speed ; the brothers covered thousands of miles, both through traffic and in the country, without a single accident.

At Cricklewood the model aeroplane experiments continued, Lanoe bringing with him fresh plans, which T. carried out during the week. Time passed quickly during these happy, busy days. Both boys joined the Royal Aero Club as founder members in June 1910, which entitled them to free entry at all times to Hendon aerodrome. During fine week-ends they went there on the motor-cycle, and spent their time on the aerodrome or in the hangars. Lanoe talked to the flying men and the mechanics, some of whom were French and welcomed this lad who could speak their language ; again his well pointed questions and his large enquiring eyes proved irresistible. No one had the heart to send him out of the forbidden hangars. At last he managed to beg a joy-ride from Mr. Barber on one of his Valkyries, a strange, spider-like monoplane.

Up on the little flat seat beside the pilot, with his feet on a rail and nothing to keep him in, the peak of his cap to the back, his eyes sparkled with excitement. The machine lurched and rumbled a long way before it lifted cumbrously into the air, but once off the ground Lanoe felt the exhilaration, the power, the ecstasy of flight. Much more important than this, he realized at once the military significance of the aeroplane, its invaluable use for reconnaissance ; everything could be seen from the air. How had this vital fact escaped the notice of our military leaders ?

Back to earth again, with his eyes streaming from exposure, he was quivering with eagerness and excitement. Then and there he determined to learn to fly so that he might join the Royal Flying Corps. The first step was to join a school so that he could obtain his pilot's certificate, and for this he needed parental authority and £50. He found that both these requisites would be forthcoming if he could convince Nettie Baldie, of

Longparish days, that flying was safe. He took her to see the " Valkyries ", the huge front booms of which gave a superficial impression of security on landing. Lanoe made the most solemn promises that he would not take undue risks, and obtained consent to join Mr. Barber's school.

In the meantime he had done three terms, a year and a half, at the " Shop ", the last term with the customary rank of corporal, and he " passed out " in July, 1911. The last day at the " Shop " was always a pretty hectic one, ending with a dinner for the corporals at which port was placed on the table *ad. lib.*; as a result most of the participants drank more than their custom and became a little excited. After dinner there was the traditional rag; on this occasion a dozen lively spirits started a bonfire, added some cadet's furniture to it, and then suggested fetching Lanoe's furniture to put on top; instead of protesting uselessly, he joined joyously in the fun, but noted carefully the ringleaders, and suggested that their furniture should also be burnt; the hilarious mob brushed aside the owners' protests and soon produced what Lanoe described as a most satisfying blaze.

He was given his commission in the Royal Engineers on the 20th of July, 1911, and was posted to the School of Engineering at Chatham. With him went his friends Gordon, Ian and Mac. These were days of great enthusiasm and high adventure. The course of instruction included military duties, tactics, building construction, roof projections, field works, road making, electricity, workshops and railways. The young officers also went on a surveying course in Wales and a bridging course at Woldingham. Here were many subjects that proved of great value to Lanoe. Roof projections and road making may not sound exciting, but, as will be seen, he turned them to excellent account in later years.

Before he had made much progress with his flying instruction, an army pilot got into a spin in a Valkyrie and was killed. The machine proved too dangerous for anyone but its designer to fly, and in consequence Mr. Barber closed his school. For the moment Lanoe's flying lessons came to an end.

At about this time Lanoe acquired one of the earliest G.N. sports cars, which had a belt drive and a primitive, even brutal gear change. He worked out a differential belt drive with gradual change of gear, operated by increasing or decreasing the effective diameters of the belt pullies. This device, which seemed to solve the problem, and for which he quickly took out a provisional patent, turned out, on calculation, to put too great a strain on the belts then in use and he discarded it, blaming himself for being too impetuous in patenting the device before he had worked out the practical side.

His next invention was even more ambitious. This consisted of a radial hydraulic pump, mounted on a sliding bed and driven by the car's engine. By sliding the pump on its bed he could, by eccentric action, gradually increase or decrease to nothing or even reverse the flow of the liquid. He proposed to pipe this liquid to hydraulic rotary motors, one fixed to each wheel, so that the car could be driven in an infinite variety of gears without clutch, gear box or differential gears of any kind. Moreover the motors on the wheels could be used as powerful, synchronised and well controlled brakes by restricting the flow of liquid from them. Lanoe was still working on this invention when the war broke out in August, 1914, and then he shelved it.

Sometimes at week-ends, now that T. was no longer at Cricklewood, Gordon invited Lanoe, amongst others of his comrades, to his home at 45 Rowan Road, Hammersmith, where he found a most sympathetic friend in Mrs. Bayly. She appreciated his fine character, and was always glad to see him. On one occasion he promised to take her for a ride in his side-car, an offer which caused great merriment amongst his brother officers, who considered him a reckless driver; but they were mistaken. Lanoe had a remarkable control over his machine, and did many spectacular stunts on it, but he never took risks with others, and above all was exceptionally careful where children, old ladies or animals were concerned. Certainly Mrs. Bayly had no cause for alarm, and greatly enjoyed her ride. Later Lanoe bought a roomy car and took Beatrice and her mother for many enjoyable rides and picnics.

In the spring of 1912 Lanoe arranged to continue his flying instruction at the Deperdussin school at Hendon. Gordon and Mac, sharing his enthusiasm, joined the Ewen school at the same aerodrome, and a friendly rivalry sprang up between these young officers. The method of learning was a tedious one; the pupil taxied across the aerodrome till his wheels left the ground, then landed before gaining dangerous height, repeating this process, lengthening each hop, till at last he had sufficient feel of the controls to venture a complete circuit of the aerodrome. What excitement that first circuit was, and Lanoe, of all people revelled in the sensation of flight, but however keen he might be to make rapid progress, he kept his promise and never took undue risks. It was a slow business, as practice could only take place when there was a dead calm, a rare occurence in England, and the pupils had to await their turns on the few machines available. The instructors gave little instruction, each had his own ideas on flying, and it was often a matter of chance if the pupil did the right thing in an emergency.

T., who was now at the " Shop ", also asked to be allowed to learn to fly, but Lanoe opposed his wish on account of the danger. His veto was decisive, and on the plea that his mother could not be expected to endure two of her sons in the air at once, T. was persuaded to withdraw his request. Lanoe had reason later to regret his decision, for nothing would have pleased him better than to have had his brother by his side.

In the summer of 1912 McMullen formed a camp at Hendon, to which he invited Lanoe and Gordon. The calmest moments in the air were just after dawn, and by being on the spot the boys seized every opportunity and learnt more quickly.

By this time the family had moved to south Dorsetshire. During the Christmas holidays Lanoe joined his father in the hunting field, the latter declaring that he was getting too old for shooting, and when he heard someone pointedly express sympathy for an elderly friend who had broken his neck out hunting, asked if anyone could wish him a more pleasant way of leaving this world. A few weeks later he suffered the same fate. Always gay, jolly and sporting he took more risks than younger men, rode young horses, choosing his own line, till one day his horse fell at a high bank, throwing him heavily. For a few days he lived on, uncomplaining, a stoic example to his soldier sons. A great sportsman, loved by all who knew him, he left this world just at the moment when his boys could appreciate him most. Lanoe, now head of the family in England, took charge, nor would he allow T. to share with him the painful formalities.

He wrote to Beatrice in reply to her letter of sympathy, and with his New Year's greetings he sent her a brooch of two inter-locked rings of garnets. Beatrice was taken aback at Lanoe's modest present, and would have returned it, but her mother asked her not to do so at this moment of Lanoe's sorrow, though she did not wear it then. Lanoe was happy that she kept it, and in years to come he was to see it again.

On the 4th of March, 1913, Lanoe and Mac succeeded in passing their flying tests at Hendon, consisting of two figures of 8 and a climb to about 400 feet. Lanoe had got his " ticket " at last, which meant that he was now eligible to be selected for the Royal Flying Corps. Shortly afterwards the Deperdussin company went into liquidation, and he was chaffed for having " broken " two schools to obtain one " ticket ". A fortnight later Gordon also obtained his " ticket " and the boys were very happy at their united success.

At Whitsuntide Lanoe was on leave in Weymouth, and motor-cycled to Moreton, where his father had been buried. He had a great love of the English countryside. He wrote :—

> " Whitsuntide, 1913.
> The country was glorious ; the young fresh green of the trees contrasting against the deep colour of the firs ; the light green of the water meadows against the brown and purple of the heather, with brilliant splashes of yellow from the gorse and that strange brown green of the sprouting oaks. Moreton is a lovely spot and I enjoyed my ride immensely."

In June the young officers went into camp at Woldingham for a course of bridging. Lanoe, Gordon, Ian and Mac were a happy, healthy band of young enthusiasts, leading a hard, clean life. In the autumn Lanoe was sent to Portsmouth and Gosport on a course of searchlights and telephones. Then came the passing-out examinations ; he was disappointed with the results, and yet he gave his mind to so many subjects that he could hardly expect to compete successfully with those who took care to specialize. All but the first few sappers on the list were sent abroad, and Lanoe found himself posted to Cork. He hated leaving England and his friends, above all he knew that he would miss those happy days at Hammersmith, the moments he spent with Beatrice. On the 1st of October he was promoted lieutenant.

Before leaving for Ireland in November he asked Beatrice to marry him. His proposal came as a surprise and a shock to her. She looked upon Lanoe as Gordon's friend, one of the boys, but marriage had not entered her thoughts. To his sister, Siola, who was in his confidence, Lanoe wrote :—

> "Now I ask you, can you imagine my feelings when, on my declaring my emotions, acute distress spread itself over the face of the one person I would do anything to shield from pain, worry or trouble?"

Lanoe managed the situation with courage and tact, so that his relations with Beatrice remained unstrained. He was prepared to wait, ready to give without exacting anything in return, willing to play his part manfully. A few days later he wrote to Beatrice asking her to use his christian name, but she felt unable to do this then. Perhaps they were a little old-fashioned and formal, but there was courtesy, unselfishness and sincerity in their intercourse. Lanoe's love was deep and generous, and he was confident that destiny would ultimately bring him the reward he so ardently desired.

8

Ireland

ALTHOUGH Lanoe was sad at having to leave England and take up routine work, which was dull and uninspiring compared with his ambition to join the Royal Flying Corps, he did not allow his disappointment to depress his spirits or impair his work. The 33rd (Fortress) Company, R.E., to which he was posted, was responsible for the searchlights at Cork Harbour and carried out ordinary training and routine work. He was soon on good terms with his company commander, Capt. Palmer, who noticed his keenness on flying and appreciated his " very attractive personality ". He was fortunate in being able to spend Christmas at home, but wrote :—

> " What a pity to have a lock-out so near Xmas ! It will mean many a scanty meal instead of cheerful Xmas fare, and nothing to spare for the bairns."

His letters on many occasions show his sympathy for those who suffered. Not only in words, but in deeds, he showed his kindness and concern for others, and especially for the men who served under him ; in this way he won their devotion, which greatly added to the efficiency of his command.

Back at Cork after Christmas leave, Lanoe settled down to work his hardest as an antidote to yearnings, for his thoughts kept turning to those he loved in England and to the Royal Flying Corps. He wrote :—

> " 15.4.14.
> My car is sitting outside the mess now and my thoughts wander and I do so long to drive over and take you all out for one of those delightful trips through the country—I never realised how much I really did enjoy them till I found how much I missed them.
> I feel a trifle homesick at times, home now includes

45, Rowan Road [Hammersmith]. I am being very energetic and go on parade every day at 7.30 a.m., dance or no dance.

Ordinarily we take duty in turns and only rise twice a week, but it agrees with my constitution, gives me more time and is a good habit to cultivate."

Siola wrote cheering letters, to which he replied humorously :—

" 16.5.14.
I don't know what is happening the other end but I have been upset by the most persistent emotional storms. I tried medicine without result; that uncomfortable feeling above the tum-tum on the left side usually yields to this treatment, but hasn't this time. But it is a long time since I was in Hammersmith."

Lanoe was living an active life, making new friends, going to dances, dinners, tennis parties and above all working hard.

" R.E. Office, Cork, 22.6.14.
Dear Hawker,
I went down today to inspect the Shawnbally Camp and was very much pleased with the way you had made all the arrangements. It does you great credit.
                           Yours sincerely,
                               J. E. Vanrennen."

Thus his colonel appreciated his efficiency.

At the end of May, Gordon had joined the Central Flying School and Lanoe, who had hoped to pass the course with him, was disappointed to find that his application had not been granted. However, at the end of June he received orders to join the school in September, and this was very happy news, for it meant that he would soon be back in England, soon be flying again. He asked Siola to bring Beatrice over for a ball at Fermoy, but this could not be arranged.

Amongst the gramophone records in the mess he turned on " Destiny " and Ecstasy ", which evoked happy memories of his dances with Beatrice.

" 7.7.14. Crosshaven.
We had a lovely dance at Fermoy which I enjoyed thoroughly. I should have loved to have had you and Siola there.
My car has gone and done it again. Coming back she went

Crash—h—h—.

I'm full of good health and good spirits just now—I do get the most awful dumps now and then."

Lanoe was sent to Kinsale for a week to put the casuals through their musketry course. The mess, the quarters, the barracks and the ranges were all miles apart, entailing starting at 5.45 a.m., and much marching in hilly country. He found the officers there very depressed, but he had a charm which was infectious, a magnetism which drew others into his happy moods. Without knowing why, they found themselves feeling cheerful again, catching his optimism, echoing his rippling laugh. He wrote to Beatrice :—

" 15.7.14. Kinsale.

I found everyone very much in the dumps, but was feeling very cheerful myself and passed it on to the others.

Dr. McCall has very kindly lent me a quaint little single cylinder 6 h.p. de Dion two-seater, B.C. 1902. It looks peculiar but climbs these hills remarkably well. We should have been lost without the ' Grunter '.

Gordon says he is working hard at wireless telegraphy. He seems to have had an exciting time on a Henry [Farman aeroplane] in a cloud at 4,000 ft.

How I long to get up in the clouds too, literally that is, as I am continually being ragged about " being in the clouds " from a " day-dream " point of view.

Which reminds me, do you like Destiny and Ecstasy? I love them and they send me off into day-dreams—Somehow I always associate them with you."

At this time Mr. Asquith was handling the Irish question with remarkable incompetence, which unfortunately led to some of the officers allowing their political feelings to come to the surface. Not so Lanoe; when asked what he would do under certain awkward contingencies he cheerfully replied with Mr. Asquith's famous words : " Wait and see," but there is little doubt that he would have obeyed orders without question.

His next orders were to take over the command of Bere Island on the 30th of July, but Germany's ambitions had suddenly brought Europe to the brink of war. The " precautionary period " came into force on the 29th, so Lanoe took with him 24 men in full war kit. The following morning a telegram arrived for him; tension was high, and an official telegram must contain something important. For a moment his usual calm left him; he tore open the envelope, then his eyes glittered with excitement, and he pushed forward his chin in characteristic manner.

"Report at once at Central Flying School."

At last! At last he was to fly, and what was more he would soon be within reach of those he loved, back in England again. A hurried packing of a few essentials, quick settling of mess bill and other minor matters, a few hasty farewells and within half an hour he was on the way. To the beat of the wheels clattering on the rails, he went through all he had learnt at Hendon, all he had read up with such enthusiasm. His heart thumped with excitement and he realized now how much, how very much he had been longing for this order. To be left in Bere Island with a war on would have been terrible.

Central Flying School; he had seen photographs and read descriptions of it. Now he was on the way; he had got what he had asked for, what he had longed for, what he had prayed for. Not a moment would he lose, not a chance would he miss of learning how to fly and fly well, better if possible than anyone else had ever flown before.

PART II

WAR

9

Soaring

GERMANY'S military leaders assumed that any conflict must involve her and Austria with both Russia and France, and her war plans were designed by Count von Schlieffen to hold off the Russian armies whilst Germany concentrated her greatest strength in a rapid drive through Belgium to sweep round the left flank of the French armies, which would then be rolled up southwards and destroyed.

To carry out this plan it was essential that the passage of the German armies through Belgium should not be delayed by the fortresses on the frontier, and to this end Germany's precautionary period of mobilization included the seizure of Liège. This automatically brought England into the war if we were to honour our treaty guaranteeing the neutrality of Belgium. It was hardly to be expected that, after our efforts and wars during the last two centuries to prevent this small but strategically vital country from falling into the hands of a major European power, we would now tamely surrender it to our most dangerous potential enemy.

Germany discounted Britain's small army as being insignificant (the popular word is "contemptible"), and counted upon eliminating France before we could intervene effectively. Thus when Germany pulled the trigger of her war machine, she committed irrevocably the major European powers to the flames of war. But at the end of July, 1914, it was not apparent that our peace-loving Government would act in time to save France from the disaster which threatened her, and if France were crushed, our turn would come soon.

Lanoe's joy at returning to England and at being posted to the Central Flying School was somewhat tempered by his anxiety as to whether Mr. Asquith's government would stand up to England's promises. He felt that the country's honour was at stake, as well as her vital interests. He was under no illusion as to German might and the horrors of a fratricidal war between civilized peoples, but as he wrote : " those two great aggressive powers that have so often nearly precipitated a war in the past " must now be squarely faced and, if need be, fought. There was no hesitation in his mind, neither was there exultation at the prospect of war. Dishonour would be worse than destruction, not that he had any doubt that the British Empire would win through, for he had great faith in his countrymen's character, and was ever a steadfast optimist.

On the 1st of August Lanoe arrived at the Central Flying School, one of a batch of pupils replacing those who had been posted to their squadrons (including Gordon to No. 5) and was posted to ' D ' Flight under the capable command of Captain O'B. Hubbard. He started his instruction on a Maurice Farman " Longhorn," the front elevator of which gave a feeling of balance and security, but he was soon flying a " Shorthorn ", and then a Henry Farman. In these biplanes the pilot sat in a nacelle well in front of the wings, the rotary engine and the propeller being immediately behind him ; in consequence he had a splendid view in all directions except behind. Between the planes was a network of struts and wires, which screamed like a thousand witches when the machine was diving steeply. He wrote : —

> " 1.8.14. C.F.S. Upavon.
> We are going to have a strenuous time—no such luxuries as week-end leave—and work on Sundays into the bargain !
> But it is good to be back in England and you do not know how much I am longing to come up to Hammersmith again."

> " 5.8.14. C.F.S. Upavon.
> Like you, all of us here passed thro' an anxious time, till we knew that our rulers were living up to our great traditions. Now everyone is much calmer and there is not the same eagerness for news—news—news.
> ' What are we going to do? ' was on everyone's lips—not that the majority wanted ' war at any price ' but only that we should live up to our obligations.
> Yours is indeed the hardest task, the uncertainty, without our action, that occupies our time."

Mr. Bayly, who had been in failing health for some time, passed away on the 4th of August, and on hearing that Gordon had to return to duty, Lanoe obtained leave to attend the funeral, went home with Mrs. Bayly and Beatrice, and in his quiet and sympathetic way was the greatest comfort to them. He said very little; he had a perfect understanding with those whom he loved, and words were unnecessary.

Describing to Gordon his return journey he wrote:—

"8.8.14. C.F.S. Upavon.
I started out at 10 p.m. (moonlight again) and I had the ride of my life, blinding for all I was worth—most exciting and good training for my nerves—I nearly came an awful toss over loose stones. Unfortunately I broke a belt fastener—no spares—so I cut up the foot piece of my pump—good tip— and made a hook that brought me here without trouble.

I will push for No. 5 as much as I can. Hope to join you soon but I've only done 35 minutes up to date!"

"9.8.14. C.F.S. Upavon.
I was talking to the naval pay fellow last night—we join a reserve squadron as soon as we leave here, which presumably will feed the squadrons at the front, no personal applications would be considered, it is just a matter of luck which squadron I went to.

The thing is to guide that luck and I suggest you get your major to drop a line to whoever runs the appointments asking him to 'give me Hawker' and I will do what I can my end.

Weather is beastly and it is sickening having done nothing yet but it won't be for want of trying if I don't get on. I'm doing morse code and photography and I am going to try and find out all about a machine-gun. Zeppelin hunting on a gun-bus with you would be too good to be true.

As you know I would go anywhere and do anything with you with implicit confidence—and I should think we would make a good pair."

One could hardly imagine a finer pair of young officers, both soldiers to the marrow of their bones, the pick of the young brains of the army, eager to join together in whatever enterprise might come their way. Lanoe's dream was not destined to be realised in this world.

"11.8.14. C.F.S. Upavon.
At last, I've done my first solo and so am feeling more content—I was so wildly impatient.

It was a great joy to find myself free in the air once more, without the instructor shoving the controls about."

Everything seemed to be moving rapidly except flying instruction. Machines were few and those ancient. Untrained pilots in their eagerness constantly damaged them. It was exasperating to one so keen on action to be delayed at the outset by this shortage of aeroplanes. Lanoe never missed an opportunity of flying or of gaining some fresh knowledge of the accessory subjects such as wireless signalling, photography, machine-guns and so on. There was never sufficient to occupy his keen brain.

Between the 11th and 15th of August the H.Q., R.F.C. and Nos. 2, 3, 4 and 5 Squadrons departed overseas taking with them all serviceable aeroplanes. On the 17th T. left with the 1st Division, and Lanoe began to feel that he would soon be following them.

On the 14th of August he wrote to Beatrice telling her how much she meant to him, and sending her an engagement ring he had bought for her some time ago; he asked her to keep it for him in case he should not return.

"23.8.14. C.F.S. Upavon.
I had several more trips on the M.F.—the official abbreviation for Maurice Farman—and took to descending in steep spirals.

I did my first cross country trip—Bulford to Amesbury and back—on Monday and flew back at 3,200 feet just over here, wondering if Mum and Tolie [his sister Siola] had arrived, and then descended in a proper spiral—i.e. using the elevator as a rudder, pulled hard back and spinning so hard that I was being thrown forward by the centrifugal action.

Next day I was due to go up on the H.F. [Henry Farman] but they suddenly exchanged me into 'C' Flight and I am now on a B.E. As usual it felt a bit strange at first, but after an hour's instruction I got the hang of landing and was sent up alone to do two circuits and my first solo landing. More by luck than anything else I made a "stunt landing" in very excellent fashion in front of my instructor—most sensible—my other landings were not nearly so good.

I'm not at home in the air yet tho'. I feel like being on a young horse that is just about all I can manage and if I don't give it my whole attention I go 'slithering round corners' to use my instructor's expression, owing to not banking enough or else I dive and find myself travelling nearer 90 than 60 m.p.h. She is, of course, ever so much faster than the old MF and faster even than the HF.

Do let me have any news you get of Gordon.

T. departed on Sunday and was last heard of in a rest camp at Southampton, very indignant at being kept waiting."

Lanoe had already covered most, if not all, of the theoretical work taught at the C.F.S., and found many of the lectures elementary and boring, though undoubtedly essential for beginners. Up before dawn so as not to miss a chance of flying, he found it hard by the evening to keep awake during lectures, and occupied himself anticipating the instructor's questions and writing down the answers ahead.

At the end of a tiring day he fell fast asleep during a lecture. The instructor, looking over his sleeping shoulder, read out the answers to a number of questions, so far unasked, much to the amusement of the other pupils, and all agreed that Lanoe might as well be allowed to sleep on. After the lecture, however, some of the students persuaded Lanoe to coach them in these subjects which they had found difficult to understand, but which he " could do in his sleep ".

Lanoe was very sensitive to the feelings of those he loved, and would be plunged into moods of anxiety and depression when they were in trouble. Towards the end of August he suffered from an exceptionally heavy mood of this kind. He seemed to have some premonition that disaster had overtaken his best friend. He would fight against these moods, but they troubled him greatly. A letter from Beatrice was always of help to him. He wrote to her :—

" 1.9.14. C.F.S. Upavon.
Very many thanks indeed for your nice long letter, which cheered me up at the right moment, I have quite recovered now.
Yes I am sure you were glad to hear from Gordon as we were from T."

Gordon's letter was posted in Maubeuge on the 18th of August. On the 22nd he failed to return from a reconnaissance and after some delay was reported missing; there was a chance that he had been taken prisoner. Though it was not known at the time, he and Lieut. Waterfall were shot down at 11.10 a.m. near Enghien in Belgium, the first war casualties suffered by the British Expeditionary Force. England and the Royal Flying Corps lost one of its most promising, courageous and enterprising

young officers, and Lanoe lost a true and loyal friend. He had
counted on joining Gordon and flying with him. He had set
his heart on this ideal combination. Now he realized with
anguish that it could not be accomplished in this world. The
shock was a terrible one, his own grief profound, but his first
thoughts were of Mrs. Bayly and Beatrice, and their suffering
hurt him terribly; he did all he could to comfort them, obtained
leave, hired a car and took them to Alverstoke where Mrs.
Bayly's sister lived.

When Lanoe returned to Upavon Beatrice wrote to him, and
for the first time used his christian name, as he had asked her
to do nearly a year before, and gave him permission to use hers.

> " 22.9.14.   C.F.S.   Upavon.
>
> My dear Beatrice,
>
> Very many thanks for your charming letter. I am more
> touched than I can say, as you give me the one privilege I
> felt I really did want, but did not like to ask.
>
> I am so glad if I have done any good, as my greatest
> pleasure is to do things that would earn Gordon's approval.
>
> I am one with you in appreciating Gordon's splendid
> character. Never has anyone 'made good' like he did;
> never have I met such cheering optimism in face of any dis-
> appointment, an influence that will never depart from my
> life."

These were not idle words and Lanoe lived up to them. He
added a postscript to his letter :—

> " Had two nice long flights of an hour each today. No. 1
> before breakfast, a cold, dull day. I climbed to the clouds
> and got thro' them at about 4,000 ft. Never have I enjoyed
> such a lovely morning, blue sky, warm sun, an unbroken vista
> of lovely white clouds. I went on climbing up to 8,500 feet
> in all. I stopped my engine and planed down gently to this
> beautiful sea of clouds.
>
> Underneath I had a cold bumpy journey back to the
> aerodrome. It was simply glorious up there all alone."

To Lanoe this adventure of flight was pure ecstasy, to be
free from the clogging clamour of this world, free in the warm
sunshine and pure beauty of the skies above the cloud-damped
earth. His thoughts soared with the power of flight and gave
him renewed energy and inspiration.

He had been disappointed at having missed the previous course, which might have enabled him to accompany Gordon to France, but now he felt some consolation in having been able to help Beatrice and her mother, especially as they were moving house to High Wycombe; he constantly thought of them and of their great sorrow.

" 2.10.14.

To us Gordon will always be very much alive. This catastrophe—I refer to the war—will, I think, revolutionise thought; it will leave a world in mourning, for few will escape, but I think it will bring the ' other side ' very much closer.

In my disappointment at not getting the previous course, I consoled myself with the thought of what a good time we would have when we got to the same squadron. Now it is postponed, perhaps not for long, to the far greater happiness when I do join up with him."

On the 3rd of October Lanoe passed out of the C.F.S. with a perfect confidential report that any young officer might envy :—

" 3.10.14.   Central Flying School.
Confidential Report.

Lieut. L. G. Hawker, R.E.

V.G.   B.E.2.
V.G.   H.F.
V.G.   M.F. both types.
V.G.   Cross country flying.

A very keen and zealous officer with plenty of initiative. Time in the air at C.F.S. 25 hours."

When General Rawlinson's force was sent to attempt the relief of Antwerp, Lord Kitchener decided that a squadron should be ready in 48 hours' time to go with it. On the 5th of October No. 6 Squadron received orders to bring its establishment up to strength for this duty, and Lanoe was one of the flying officers posted to it.

Lord Kitchener had great faith in the value of aircraft, and foresaw their importance in war more clearly than any other English statesman of that time.

No. 6 Squadron left Farnborough on the 6th of October :—

Commanding Officer	Aeroplane flown
Major J. H. W. Becke	B.E.2a No. 667

Flight Commanders

Capt. F. J. L. Cogan	B.E.2b No. 646
Capt. A. C. E. Marsh	B.E.2a No. 492
Capt. C. L. N. Newall	B.E.2a No. 488

Flying Officers

Capt. G. H. Cox	B.E.8. No. 636
Capt. A. Ross-Hume	Henri Farman N. 440
Capt. W. Lawrence	Henri Farman No. 680
Lieut. P. Rawson-Shaw	B.E.
Lieut J. B. T. Leighton	B.E.8. No. 632
Lieut. L. G. Hawker	Henri Farman No. 653
Lieut. C. Y. McDonald	Henri Farman No. 669

N.C.O. pilot

Sergt. C. Gallie	B.E.2a No. 470

Eight aeroplanes arrived safely at Dover on the same day. The other four were delayed by engine trouble, but soon rejoined the squadron, except Leighton who was replaced by Lieut. W. C. Adamson.

" Tuesday, 6.10.14.   Grand Hotel, Dover.

As you see by my address events are moving.

I arrived at Farnborough on Saturday.   The colonel told me, ' you needn't think you'll be rushing off to the front at once '; and I proceeded on week-end leave and spent a restful Sunday at Wycombe.   Monday morning I was told I was to learn on a Bleriot as a stepping stone to a Morane Saulnier monoplane and in the meantime while the weather was a bit rough, I could continue on a Henry which I had been flying last at the school.

About 11.00 things began to hum at headquarters and I was warned to be all ready to take a Henry to the front ' tomorrow ' i.e. Tuesday.

During the afternoon machines appeared from all quarters —including several old friends from the school—and various pilots summoned in haste.   We left Farnborough for here this morning.

I'm awfully glad to get off at last but wish it hadn't been so rushed.   We don't know where we are going yet."

" 7.10.14.   Dover.

Just a hurried note to say I've had a good night's rest, the weather is beautiful, so I hope we'll cross today."

On the 7th of October, 1914, No. 6 Squadron flew across the Channel without mishap, bound for Bruges.

10

Winter Comes

WITH a small amount of kit and a few tools stowed on the observer's seats, for the pilots were crossing the channel without passengers, the eight machines climbed to 5,000 feet so as to have gliding height in case of engine failure, an uncomfortable contingency, possibly leading to a fatal landing in the sea. Lanoe noticed beneath him two narrow grey destroyers, the only signs of war, spread their wake on either side of the cross-channel boat, no longer the familiar but unpleasant little paddle steamer which he knew too well. How quick the crossing in the air, how simple it was, how delightful! He could already see the cliffs at Gris Nez. He turned his machine to have a last look at the country he loved, safe-guarded from invasion by that narrow strip of water which he crossed so easily and, he thought, might as easily be crossed by an enterprising enemy one fine day.

England! There she lay, her line of white cliffs and beyond them the green fields and woods fading into the haze, and in that haze those easy-going, peace-loving people who obstinately closed their ears to all warnings, exasperatingly complacent at times, and yet he loved them for their kindness, their good nature, their courage and their cheerfulness when the emergency was upon them.

Turning again he passed up the coast to Ostend and from there to Bruges, where he landed on the little race-course, inconveniently surrounded by tall poplars. The eight pilots gathered together with mutual congratulations at their successful crossing, for not one had failed to land safely at the appointed place, an achievement unequalled for over two years (according to " Sefton Branker," p. 221).

The transport had not arrived, there were no mechanics, no petrol, no oil, no kit and no orders; in fact nothing but a field

46

with the aeroplanes standing in it. It was a strange feeling this arrival in a foreign country, which was being rapidly over-run by a relentless and powerful enemy, who might appear on the scene at any moment. The pilots pegged down their machines, and took a little petrol and oil from some of the aeroplanes, and put it in the tanks of two others. Soon Major Becke was in touch with the H.Q. of Rawlinson's Force, but it was too late to set out that evening, and a reconnaissance was ordered for the morrow. The pilots slept under the wings of their machines that night, ready to destroy them should the enemy arrive before daylight.

" 14.10.14.
It's very cold early in the morning and also the first night when we slept under our machines before our valises arrived! I had to get up about 2 a.m. and run about to get warm."

With Marsh as pilot and Lanoe as observer the first reconnaissance of No. 6 Squadron set out at 7.10 a.m. on the 8th of October, followed at 7.40 a.m. by Cogan and McDonald. This was a new sensation of excitement and tension, flying above the diminutive enemy. Lanoe realized the extra strain on the nerves of the pilots and observers, but the adventure held an irresistible fascination for him. The evacuation of Antwerp was commenced this day, and No. 6 Squadron moved to Ostend in the afternoon, where it shared the race-course with the Belgian flying corps, and was joined by its transport. Lanoe got out his camera and took several snapshots of the machines. There were no tents nor hangars, and the aeroplanes were pegged down in the open.

Such was Lanoe's keenness, that he was again the first up on the the 9th of October, piloting his Henry Farman with Cunningham as observer. He took Kinnear up on the 10th for two hours, and Capt. Dowding early on the 11th for the same period. He had been up each day, and out of the 11 reconnaissances made by the squadron, he had taken part in four, but he was soon to find that neither the engine nor the aeroplane would stand the strain of such heavy work.

" 11.10.14.
As we were not pleased with our landing ground we came on here next day, nice place, but rather hard to get out of.

We've been pretty busy, on the whole, as I've been out regularly every day, sometimes early, sometimes late, for 2½ hours at a time."

" 12.10.14.
We have to be ready to go out if required at any moment. T. may come my way any day now so I hope I may get a chance of seeing him."

On the 12th the squadron was ordered to retire to St. Pol aerodrome near Dunkirk. Our troops were leaving Ostend and it was getting late, but Lanoe volunteered to set out at 5 p.m., with Kinnear as observer, to find the way to the new landing ground. Over Dunkirk they saw three Taubes, as the German monoplanes were called, and fired five ineffective shots at one of them. This was Lanoe's first encounter with the enemy, who promptly made for home. It was dark when he landed at St. Pol.

The next day was foggy, the Germans were approaching Ostend. No. 6 Squadron transport was sent off by road and it began to look as if the machines might have to be burnt and abandoned, but Lanoe returned in his H.F. and led the other machines along the coast. He had discovered that it was possible to find the way, despite the fog, by flying low over the breaking waves on the beach, and all arrived safely at St. Pol after an anxious moment.

On Wednesday, the 14th, a detachment of No. 6 Squadron, including Lanoe and Kinnear, was sent to Ypres and spent a disturbed night there, as the German cavalry, somewhat scattered and often behind our lines, came into contact with our outposts and mopping up parties.

" 14.10.14.
We struck fog and came down to see if there was anything doing. We saw transport—ours we thought—and then a burning house, and then cavalry dismounted and started firing so we concluded we were mistaken as to nationality and cleared out quickly as we were only 1,500 feet."

On the 15th and 16th the squadron assembled at Poperinghe and came under the orders of the G.O.C., R.F.C. Lanoe went up as observer with Marsh whilst his machine was being overhauled.

" Friday 16.10.14.

Quite well personally but machine on sick list. Engine showed signs of giving out—not over the enemy thank goodness—so had it changed for a new one, testing which, some ass left a spanner so that it fell on the propeller and gashed it badly—no spare, but it's being patched up to carry on with.

Some excitement Wednesday night as we were only just inside our outpost line and were ready to rush and destroy our machines if necessary—woods infested with Uhlans left behind, and they were being caught at odd moments all over the place. A Taube lost its way in the fog and flew over the town rather low—like we did the other day— terrific fusilade and it was brought down and drivers captured unhurt, to say, nothing of a lovely engine."

There was a French squadron at Poperinghe and Lanoe was soon on friendly terms with the pilots, who were glad to find an English officer who could speak their language. They gave him some of their steel darts, and he rigged up a box under his machine from which he could release them by pulling a string in the nacelle. They also gave him a large incendiary bomb to try out, which he hooked on somehow.

The weather being cloudy he took his bomb over the lines with the intention of testing it on a German encampment he had seen, but on arriving there he was surprised to find that the bomb had already released itself from his improvised rack, and he wondered who had received it. On his return he learnt that one of our squadrons had reported that a strange aeroplane had emerged from the clouds, dropped an incendiary bomb on its aerodrome and popped back into the clouds again. The bomb had failed to explode and had been identified as of French make. Lanoe immediately flew across to the squadron in question to apologize, and discover the reason for the bomb having failed to ignite. The young pilots swarmed round his Henry, and one of them pulled the string, letting all the darts out on to the ground. Lanoe gathered them up and put them back, but before he could get his machine going someone else pulled the string. When this happened a third time his angry look became so menacing that they left his gadget alone. After taking off Lanoe circled low over the tarmac, and waved to these jolly fellows, but to his surprise they had taken cover, and all he could see were their boots protruding from under the lorries.

It annoyed Lance to be shot at from the ground without means of retaliating, and he took with him what bombs and grenades he could when going over the lines. In the alphabet, which the R.F.C. made up at this time, " B " stood for " Bomb in which Hawker delights."

The 19th of October marked the opening of the First Battle of Ypres. Besides strategic reconnaissances, that is reporting on the position and movements of the enemy well behind the lines, the squadron was now called upon to do tactical reconnaissances, that is report the position of the enemy's trenches, gun positions and so on, which was made more dangerous and difficult by both sides firing impartially at every aeroplane, friend and foe alike.

On the 20th, hearing that the First Division was on its way to Ypres, Lanoe sought out the billeting party of T.'s battery, which arrived ahead and included the sergeant major mounted on T.'s second horse, a conspicuous light blue roan. Lanoe borrowed the horse, certain that T. would recognize it even in the dark, and in this he was not disappointed.

> " 25.10.14.
>
> I heard that T.'s division was due to pass thro' our town and hunted up his battery. He got the surprise of his life when I rode alongside him in the dark ! He was looking very well and happy and must have been in action the next day."

Lanoe's joyous laugh was indeed enough to make T. change his thoughts to happy ones. The battery had lost its kindly major, and the fussy captain would neither offer Lanoe dinner, nor grant T. a few hours leave to dine with the squadron.

It was already dark and a fine drizzle was falling. Military traffic streamed past as the two brothers, arm in arm, talked in the squalid street on the outskirts of Poperinghe. The captain stood white and naked in the glimmer from the doorway of the crowded little billet, whilst his servant poured buckets of cold water over him, his way of taking a bath. A number of ragged and dirty children stared in amazement, wondering if this was some form of field punishment, or just another case of English lunacy. Along the far side of the road the last of the refugees, old men, women, little children, all heavily laden, all terribly tired, unable to obtain shelter in overcrowded Poperinghe, struggled painfully, slowly, silently away from the enemy, who knew not the meaning of pity.

T. longed to join Lanoe in the R.F.C. and get away from the stagnant mud, and Lanoe was anxious to help him, but regular officers with a technical training were not easily spared from the artillery, and T.'s 6 feet 5 inches were looked at askance by the R.F.C.

On the 21st No. 6 Squadron changed places with No. 4 at St. Omer, and Lanoe's machine underwent a further overhaul, whilst the weather made flying almost impossible. On the 24th and 28th Lance did strategic reconnaissances with Cunningham as observer. The machines were now under almost constant fire over the German lines, not only from the infantry, but from " Archie ", the nickname given to anti-aircraft artillery.

" Wednesday, 28.10.14.

I was out last Saturday and again today—both times dodging Archie with some success, tho' this time we could hear and see them bursting behind us. When they get the range, a horrid metallic sort of noise like a short burst of a powerful klaxon followed by a metallic bang, leaving a yellow puff from high explosive, the more usual, or white, from shrapnel. Some of them are very good and put shells all round the machines, most alarming when the concussion shakes the whole machine.

It is quite an unusual thing for a machine to come in without a bullet or two—I got five today—the planes cover such a large area, but it is very rare that the vitals are injured and it takes quite a lot to damage the planes.

We feed in luxury here; it is really very extraordinary. As long as we are here we might not be at war, while in under an hour we are in the thick of it, and then back again in calm and peace before another two hours are up."

Lanoe's machine had been so much exposed to the weather that it had seriously deteriorated, and would not carry him with an observer to a reasonably safe height. In addition, the strong west wind caused the machine to hover almost motionless in the air when trying to regain our lines. In contrast the German machines were not often seen over our lines, and could quickly escape down wind from our fire.

" 25.10.14.

Two Taubes came over this morning. Great fun watching our Archie have a go—very bad shooting, but then it is their first attempt.

I saw a lot of artillery fire against our lines including the Black Marias. No mistaking them either, great big black clouds of smoke on burst.

I regret to say we see plenty of fires on our trips; whole villages on fire, shell fire does it I think, very bad luck on the unfortunate inhabitants.

They haven't seen any Germans in this town and it is remarkable how far less cordial they are—all the petits Belges would do anything they could to help us, but we are billeted in a house where they wanted to refuse to have us and are very unpleasant in consequence."

" 31.10.14.

We saw streams of refugees moving away from the battle-fields—no fuss or crying or lamenting, the nation is so stunned but it was a pitiful sight, and brought home the horrors of war far more than anything else—wounded soldiers, burning houses or bursting shells."

On the last day of October, Lanoe had his first encounter with a hostile machine whilst flying solo, that is without a passenger. It was a strange experience flying close up to the enemy aeroplane, and banging away at it whilst the German pilot and observer looked at him with mixed feelings of curiosity, astonishment and alarm.

" 1.11.14.

I met a German biplane yesterday afternoon and fired six shots at him with my revolver—no good of course, but he took fright and made for home.

Had a dull time lately as my machine won't take a passenger tho' I had an amusing time today when I went out twice solo; we heard that the Kaiser was expected in a little town today so four of us called on him and left cards, I left three, one weighing 16 lbs. and two about 8 lbs. each.

I dodged one Archie that had given us a bad time yesterday, but ran into another instead and got a piece thro' my wing.

Again this afternoon five of us went out on a little raid and I got rid of four more and some smaller grenades."

Lanoe had no great belief in the material effect of dropping bombs haphazard, but he felt the moral effect was good, and he liked the Germans to know that he could drop a bomb on them any time he liked. He had two uncomfortable experiences on these trips. On one occasion a bomb he had hooked on under his machine became wedged, and refused to drop when he pulled the release, nor could he shake it free by stunting his machine. He was obliged to land knowing that a jerk might free the infernal thing and blow him up. He made the smoothest of many smooth landings, and the bomb remained wedged. On another occasion somewhat later, Lanoe was handed some Mills grenades to take over the lines. They were new to him, and when near his target he " prepared " them by pulling out the safety pins. To his horror he found that he had on his lap several smoking grenades with the time fuses burning; he dumped them only just in time.

"8.11.14.

I'm having a very dull time just now, while my machine is being tuned up.

It is a week since I 'took the air' and I am bored beyond description. A week's rest sounds inviting, but I hate inaction, and find it far more tiring than hard work. The weather is perfect, considering the time of year, for my present occupation, i.e. sitting or lying about the aerodrome waiting for the next meal. But a fog hangs over the low-lying marshes and makes our efforts of no avail—this is distinctly annoying for most people, but is some small consolation for those unfortunates who have no chance of sallying forth to brave the atmosphere—to say nothing of Archie."

"11.11.14.

My luck is out and I'm having a horrid dull time. My machine was finished yesterday and I hoped my days of boresome inaction were over—there is nothing so tiring as being bored—the weather was horrid, wind and rain, but I took it out for a short trip to see if all was O.K. It showed promise of being quite a success but required minor adjustments. This morning, however, it was blowing a gale, so I couldn't try it again and while I was down at lunch the brute broke loose and was completely wrecked. So I'm worse off than before, which is most annoying as I've been bored to tears this last week and was looking forward to getting into harness again.

However, I did good work during the month I had it, covering 2,500 odd miles."

Although Lanoe was sad at the destruction of his Henry Farman, it was really no great loss. At its best it was so slow and climbed so badly that it made little headway against the strong west winds, and hung too low in the air, an easy target for Archie which it could not avoid, and within effective range of the German infantry.

He would have felt far less bored if he had not been kept uselessly hanging about on the aerodrome by routine. He was always eager to visit neighbouring squadrons, batteries in action, the infantry in the line, learning how best to co-operate with them; anything would have been better than enforced idleness. In time he developed a more cheerful philosophy.

> " Thursday, 19.11.14.
>
> It's snowing at the moment and looks like keeping it up. We're very lucky to be in a nice warm billet, sitting round the fire.
>
> I've given up worrying when things I can't help don't turn out right or as nice as they might have, as it invariably turns out for the best in the long run and so now I always expect it to turn out for the best.
>
> The weather has been so bad I haven't missed much and I still hold the record for most flying—46½ hours in one month, tho' it's over two weeks now since I've been out."

On the 24th Lanoe rejoined the squadron which had moved to Bailleul and took what opportunity he could of going up as observer. The aerodrome was in a field at the back of Bailleul lunatic asylum, the inmates of which had been removed " pour faire place aux Anglais ". On the 30th the squadrons were organized into wings, Nos. 5 and 6 forming the Second Wing under the command of Colonel Burke, a rugged, capable and courageous pioneer of aviation.

> " 2.12.14.
>
> The troops take it in turn now to come back for a spell of well-earned rest, so several of our people have been able to visit their regiments and they bring us back tales of what's been happening in the trenches. The endurance and courage of our fellows is almost beyond belief, and French's praise is well earned. Apparently one of the great amusements of the fellows in the trenches is watching our aeroplanes being shelled

—amusement if you please—and a lot of betting results as soon as an aeroplane is sighted.

One man won the field with 60 shells fired at one unfortunate aeroplane!

We think this must have been the man who returned with hundreds of bullet holes; the mechanic had one through his helmet and the pilot his chin cut and the back of his neck grazed!"

Lanoe's admiration and sympathy for the infantry was constant and sincere. For them he would go up cheerfully in any weather and take any risk.

On the 3rd of December the squadron was inspected by H.M. the King.

As Christmas drew near Lanoe found something rather cynical in his activities.

"6.12.14.

How time does fly, another two weeks and Xmas will be upon us.

And what a Xmas! I shall probably be doing my best to kill someone with bombs—last time it was All Saints—and someone will be doing their best at me with an Archie!

And then I'll come home and eat plum-pudding, open some Xmas card about "Peace and Good Will". What a blessing when a real peaceful Xmas comes round again, but it will be such a sad time for so many poor people."

On the 12th Lanoe was back at St. Omer hoping to be allotted a reconditioned B.E. His constant complaint was inaction, but on the 18th he got his machine and was given the task of training newly joined observers, whilst he attended signalling classes in the evenings. Christmas soon arrived, and both officers and men had a good dinner. Lanoe described the menu and added:—

"It somehow failed to be Xmasy but it is the first I've spent away from home.

Pity I couldn't get near T. but even when I'm 'forward' we are far apart."

On the 28th there had been another gale in which the R.F.C. lost many machines, Lanoe's being badly damaged. He had good cause for feeling depressed. He had lost his best friend, the first British casualty of the war; and now his active brain was cramped by enforced idleness. His first aeroplane had been destroyed and his second damaged. He had tried without success to get T. posted to the R.F.C.; he longed to have him by his side; the brothers had never been bored when together; now the short distance that separated them was made impassable by strict orders. But Lanoe had learnt to be patient and philosophical, and, despite all his disappointments, he was always good company. His comrades of those days remember his jolly laugh, but have forgotten his moods of depression, if he ever showed them.

Forced inactivity was painful to Lanoe, and he made the most of the small opportunities offered him, hoping that soon he would be fully employed again. Although at the time he did not know it, the last day of 1914, his 24th birthday, was also Lanoe's last day of boredom.

11

Steady Work

THE armies on the Western Front had settled down to trench warfare with all the advantages on the side of the Germans. They occupied the higher ground dominating our positions. They held the interior lines, which enabled them to concentrate on whichever front suited them. They had a marked superiority in machine-guns, artillery and shells, especially of the heavy types, of aeroplanes, engines and of trained officers and men.

To compensate in some degree for these advantages on the German side, our airmen were more enterprising, and carried out their work over the German lines. Many of our pilots showed an aggressive spirit, which set a standard for the future. Those early pilots, who attacked without hesitation every German machine they came across, decided from the outset who should dominate in the air on the British front, and by their example rendered a service to the army and to their country which it would be difficult to exaggerate.

In 1914 there had been few opportunities of fighting in the air, but as the weather improved in the spring and summer of 1915, and as our aeroplanes became better armed, combats were more frequent and decisive.

Lanoe was one of the first pilots to make an invariable practice of attacking every hostile machine he saw, and there were no conditions or reservations to this policy of his. He attacked his enemy, fearlessly disregarding his own safety, and concentrated his whole effort on striking his quarry down. Early in 1915 he could make little impression with his comparatively slow two-seater and primitive weapons. His chief duties were reconnaissance, artillery ranging and photography. Fighting at this time was incidental to his work, but he showed a strong instinct for attack, and by his fine example established a precedent, which our air service followed till the end of the war.

Before becoming the leading fighting pilot of his day, Lanoe had to pass through a hard apprenticeship, carrying out a great variety of duties with unfaltering courage. He used initiative and ingenuity to reduce the risks to which he was exposed, but never avoided them at the expense of his work. On the contrary, as he became experienced he seemed to welcome the more dangerous tasks, and faced them with cheerful optimism.

If 1914 ended on a depressing note for Lanoe, 1915 started on a high note of expectation and eagerness.

"1.1.15.
I'm just off to the front again this very minute at ½ hour's notice. Happy New Year."

At a moment's notice he was ordered to join 'B' Flight of No. 6 Squadron at Bailleul, and given a new B.E. to fly. This machine had a speed of about 72 m.p.h., compared with his Henry Farman's 59, and it climbed twice as fast and could fly twice as high. Lanoe was delighted at receiving these orders; at last he was to be in action again; away with boredom! It never entered his mind to count the risk of flying over the enemy's lines under fire from Archie, whose shooting was improving with practice and better equipment.

After the bitter experience of having one of his machines destroyed and the other damaged by gales, Lanoe determined to make a suitable shelter for his new B.E. that would protect it from the weather. He had not forgotten the roof projections and other building work which he had studied so industriously at Chatham, and he quickly designed an efficient shed, which, with Marsh's help, was made from the hop-poles found near the aerodrome. This shed was so satisfactory that the sappers were requested to make more of the same pattern, and by the end of the year similar shelters were common on all aerodromes. (V. II, p. 186.)

In spite of the bad weather, Lanoe was quite cheerful, glad to be with his comrades again, and taking an active part in the war. In the comparatively fine intervals he did artillery registration, using an unreliable lamp, the only means of signalling available to him at that time. He also made some early attempts at photographing the German trenches, and sketching their shape, and took up young officers who were attached to the squadron for instruction.

On the 25th there was great excitement, as it was reported that the Kaiser would review troops in Lille on the 26th, the eve of his birthday, and every squadron spent the night fitting up the machines to carry bombs to celebrate the occasion. Lanoe made an early reconnaissance on the 26th with the object of finding out if there were troops in Lille, but saw nothing on account of fog. The party was cancelled owing to the bad weather, much to everyone's disappointment.

On the morning of the 28th he spent an hour up in a gale and snowstorm, an indication of the improvement in his flying ability. The appearance of the countryside was completely transformed by its covering of snow whilst he was in the air. He continued this strenuous work both morning and afternoon; it was bitterly cold, but Lanoe never complained so long as he was kept occupied.

Seven days leave was due to him, and he tried to arrange to take it at the same time as T., but owing to several postponements this was not possible. Lanoe finally left on the 30th and spent his leave quietly, dividing it between Beatrice and Mrs. Bayly at High Wycombe and his mother at Pinhoe near Exeter.

"Sunday. 7.2.15. The White House, S. Farnborough.
Much to my joy I found a telegram waiting for me telling me to report here as a B.E.2c was ready for the expeditionary force."

He wrote describing this Channel crossing, which was an anxious one owing to a defective engine and, as he struggled towards the French coast, constantly losing height, he could see "the waves reaching up hungrily to devour me", but he just managed to stagger in to the coastal aerodrome and, after essential repairs, flew on to St. Omer.

Lanoe only reached Bailleul after several forced landings. He started a diary from which extracts are given below.

Diary :—

"Monday 15th. The trouble has been engines, four different ones all giving trouble. Sick of staying here, [St. Omer] a fortnight's mails waiting for me at Bailleul, I've only one change of cloathes (*sic*) here, so hope to goodness I do get off tomorrow.
Tuesday, 16th February. I flew to Bailleul. I found great

alterations in the aerodrome, new hangars up, covered-in drains dug and the 'tarmac' of ashes finished.

The sheds are really splendid. They are built by the sappers, copied with adaptations, from the experimental shed designed by myself out of hop-poles with Marsh's help and erected by him. The wings and machines should last ever so much longer and save the government thousands of pounds. They have been officially approved as a standard design and are to be adopted by the whole corps.

The major being away sick, Marsh doing O.C. Squadron and Tennant on some job with the wing, I find myself temporarily O.C. 'B' Flight; Marsh very glad to get another pilot as 'A' Flight is on detachment at Poperinghe and 'C' Flight is now wireless only, so Marsh and Adamson have been the only two pilots for the daily reconnaissance, and as Adamson has been sick for the last week, this left only Marsh for the job.

This might be all very fine but Archie has been busy and perforated the Liverpool* every time she went out. So I was put on reconnaissance at once, starting 7 a.m. the following morning."

Lanoe was struck by the contrast of the life at the front and that which he had led in England, and also by the patience and fortitude of the dear ones at home, who bore their losses and gnawing anxieties without complaint. He was constantly thinking of Beatrice.

" 17.2.15.

It is such a new existence out here that I almost feel as if I were another person—'sufficient unto the day'—I rarely think of the future but carry on cheerfully the work of the moment, and this was brought home to me on my brief spell of leave, when I seemed to step back into my old self.

When the war is over—and God grant that may be soon— what then? I do not seek to answer the question.

Towards you, dearest one, I remain the same; you are ever in my thoughts and prayers. Your courage is splendid.

Knowing the extent of my own grief, my heart aches for you poor dear ones, who have suffered so much. It seems so pitiless and cruel, and yet when I think of my poor England, the whole of Europe, bereaved and devastated by boundless suffering and sorrow, I cannot but believe that God in His

---

* The Liverpool was a B.E.2c, similar to Lanoe's 1780, but subscribed for by Australian citizens, and presented to the R.F.C. by the Mayor of Liverpool on their behalf

great mercy will in time comfort us on this earth. And I hope and expect that a truer Christianity will rise from the ashes of our imperfect civilisation.

May God bless and protect you till we all meet again."

Back at work Lanoe was delighted with his new B.E.2c. The engine had 20 h.p. more than that of the B.E.2, and the performance of this latest machine was appreciably better. Owing to its inherent stability it was nicknamed "Stability Jane".

"18.2.15.

The machine is a beauty and flies along gaily with my hands off the controls!

It was allotted to our squadron so has now become my own machine!"

Between photographic flights, ranging and reconnaissances, on which Lanoe was out with Marks, Vachell or Clarke on every fine day, he fitted in instructional flights for observers and joy-rides for enthusiasts. On wet days he walked many miles to see his friends.

Diary :—

"Wednesday the 17th, rolled up just before 7 a.m., strong wind blowing. Because I wish to see how the machine behaves, try the air, with Marks as rather unwilling passenger. Wind quite 60 m.p.h. as we travelled backwards while climbing. Clouds at 4,000 so decided not good enough and returned to terra firma. The B.E.2c behaved very well."

"Thursday, 18th, out on reconnaissance with Vachell."

"Friday, 19th, was hopeless, raining all day, nothing doing except a great conference of the nuts of the Flying Corps— General Henderson, Colonel Sykes, Lieut. Colonel Burke, Lieut. Colonel Trenchard and a major from the War Office, secret conference in my bedroom of all places. They wouldn't have lunch, but consumed most of my monthly cake and 3 or 4 bottles of wine, and left a stink of smoke in the room. Wonder what 'divilment' they were hatching!

"Saturday, 20th. Out with Marks."

"Sunday, 21st. Foggy in the morning but, as it often does, cleared later. Reconnaissance at 2.30 with Vachell."

"Monday, 22nd. Fog all day; two new observers reported, so gave them lunch and then took them to have a look at the Liverpool with all her shot-holes nicely marked with red circles."

"Tuesday, 23rd. Rotten day not good enough for reconnaissance but took Haywood round to have a look at the country. Wind up at Corps headquarters about some agent's report, so out we go on an 'important reconnaissance'.

"24th and again on Thursday, 25th, it snowed and rained alternately, "les grèles de Mars," as the inhabitants call it.

What a blessing our sheds are. If it blows or snows there is no need to worry."

"Friday, 26th. I took Clarke up to photo trenches round Wytschaete."

"Saturday, 27th. Strong S.W. wind. Up with Vachell and climbed to 6,500 then over Wervic. Suddenly got it 'proper' from an Archie at Becelaere. BANG—crash, deafening noise, burst just off the left wing-tip, pushed nose down and edged north, but took a long time working against the wind, one of the most unpleasant quarter hours I've spent 'waiting for the next'.

It is most unpleasant being shelled when beating home against the wind, as if the engine stopped you know it is all U.P. and I don't relish a trip to Germany under those circs. Liverpool is always unlucky."

"Sunday, 28th, started dud, but cleared later, with a stronger wind than ever, about 55 m.p.h. N.W.

Frantic messages that Neuve Eglise is being shelled, so to up and spot the flashes. Probably they will stop when they see us. Combine this with photography, taking up Clarke. As expected Germans stopped their shelling and we took photos, Archied by all three forces, I think, tho' none came near enough to worry. Yellow H.E. are German; pairs of white, surely that is us; and small white are soixante-quinze.

Getting off and landing was somewhat exciting with westerly wind. Found getting off across a 55 m.p.h. wind rather a struggle."

"Monday, 1st March, starts like a lion so hope it will go out like a lamb.

In spite of wind we got some photos in Messines before clouds came up.

Strange arrived to take over 'B' Flight."

The arrival from No. 5 Squadron of Capt. L. A. Strange of the Special Reserve, started a great friendship and sporting rivalry between Lanoe and himself.

"Tuesday, 2nd. Day starts dud, but clouds thin later so up with Cherry in 1780 for the usual reconnaissance. Wind N.W. about 40. Got height towards Poperinghe saw Archies south of Hazebrouck, English shelling a German, so off we go.

About 7,000 now and find an Aviatic 1 to 2,000 feet above us beating up wind towards Hazebrouck. Get under him and give him 4 from my revolver, no good, observer cannot use rifle because of top plane so take it from him, leave machine to look after itself, good old 'Stability Jane', and pot 3 at it myself. This puts the wind up them. Know we are going down wind over enemy's country and think he'll make for his aerodrome at Douai, but we just have the legs of the wind and can risk it.

Deutscher puts his nose down and forges ahead, so pass rifle back to Cherry, two of them now, both making for home, they're no sportsmen. No. 1 shuts off and glides down, so Cherry puts in some steady firing, and then we turn to No. 2 and do likewise. Daren't lose height on account of our fight back against the wind.

Well, we didn't down the beggars, but put the wind up them, spoilt their reconnaissance, saved H.Q. at Hazebrouck from bombs, and drove them ingloriously to earth.

Had a long fight back against the wind and continued our reconnaissance. Over La Bassée a shell burst low-left-front and we saw the case extraordinarily plainly. This battle and Archie took place just over T. so wonder if he saw it. Two hours and a half, not bad for these days."

The German airmen regarded war in a different light to the sporting spirit of the British. To them it was a serious business, and they avoided risks if they possibly could, but they were not lacking in courage. On the other hand, Lanoe, like many British pilots, could not resist the challenge of an enemy machine in the air, It was this contrast in the outlook of the British and German pilots which was to have such an important influence on the amount of help which each service was to give its own troops on the ground. This early sign of the greater boldness and fighting spirit of our pilots was very welcome to our generals, and Sir John French mentioned this fight in his bi-weekly report of the 4th of March.

12

Looping

Diary :—

" Wednesday, 3rd. Rain so no flying. Colonel came to see Todd. First thing led him down to THE pond. Result :— that evening I'm told by my squadron commander :—

' Hawker, you're a sapper. FILL IN THAT POND and start tomorrow ' ! Oh lor ! "

" Thursday, 4th. Shephard arrived and took over the squadron from Todd ! No. 6 has been through some awful convulsions and now is no longer the same unit that set out from England 5 months ago. This week we have had no less than 6 officers in command of the squadron.

Investigate pond, roughly requires 1,000 tons of earth, drains run in one end and out the other, these would have to be joined and even then the surface would never be firm. Hit on the ingenious plan of roofing it in, less labour, less expense, always dry, a good surface and no trouble with drains. Roughly 10,000 feet of timber required, draw out rough scheme, submit to C.R.E., get his approval and consent for R.E.s to carry out the job. Consider that's a good bit of work."

" Vendredi, 5th. Dud but sent out with Mosley on a wild scheme flying low over our own lines to spot gun flashes. Clouds were 800 to 1,000 so crashed up and down between 500 and 800 just our side of the line. Occasionally we got rather near the Huns and were potted at but our people were very good and left us alone so we were all right. Quite the most amusing joy-ride I've had, flung about all over the place in a gale, low clouds and bumpy, and results quite successful, in fact it has established a precedent."

" Saturday, 6.3.15.

I saw Ian Gourlay last Monday. I'm going to try and get off another night and he'll take me up to his listening post in *front* of our lines, which would be very exciting indeed."

My gramophone arrived at last, hurray ! Had it out and started the band at once. Really is delightful getting good music again, one does miss music quite badly."

64

" 11.3.15. In the field.

I've got Ave Maria and Mums darling, it just takes me back to the hall at Broxwood with Dad sitting tired from shooting listening to it! And my other favourite is 'Destiny' —it is playing now, which somehow recalls the happiest times I've had specially associated with Gordon and Beatrice, but it makes me sad now when it used—I loved it in Ireland—to make me happy and contented."

Diary :—

" March 13th. There was awful consternation when we received our orders to quit and proceed next day to Poperinghe! No sheds, no good billets, rotten aerodrome; and we had put such a lot of work in the Bailleul ground and had made it really habitable. Also the Voisins, who took over from us, can't get into our sheds, so there they stood looking at them in their silly manner. They are a sort of night-mare in which the staid old four-poster canopy-bed takes to flying— while we imagined our nice machines picketed out in the rain!

However, we got room in the French sheds, so that was all right. But the move is annoying as it is another 15 miles from T. and I was just considering ways and means of getting a day off to see him."

Lanoe was soon reconciled to the change of aerodrome, especially as he had already made friends with Commandant Bordage and the pilots of Escadrille M.F.33, who received No. 6 Squadron with great hospitality. He set about improving the aerodrome, and supervising the erection of sheds of his own design to house the machines and workshops. His next activity was to uphold the prestige of the R.F.C. in the eyes of the French pilots.

" 17.3.15.

By the time we moved here I was really at home on my new machine and since Marsh left, was the only one that knew her little tricks, so was requested to exhibit, chiefly for the benefit of the French who share this ground. Apart from spirals which every machine can do equally well, its chief parlour trick is ' tail sliding'. When you pull the elevator back and point the machine's nose at the sky and she starts to slip back the tail seems to stay where it is while the whole front of the machine falls like a stone—most alarming—till she points nose down and then as she gathers speed again up comes the nose. This is a harmless stunt but I did a much worse thing which is strictly forbidden but the temptation was irresistible.

There was one French pilot who was always talking about looping—they're Maurice Farmans which can't loop—and why didn't we loop. ' Angly! it wasy zo nice ze looooping ! ' And having long wanted to, just to say I had, I did.

Being inexperienced I didn't pull her over quick enough and so stuck on the top of the loop hanging upside down ! All sorts of funny things fell out, signal lights, cartridges, mud, paper, oil and petrol, and I was watching anxiously to see if my passenger would follow."

These early machines were not suited to looping the loop, nor was the correct technique known then as to how to do such stunts without subjecting the machine to excessive strain and several accidents were attributed to this cause. Later some pilots, including Captain Ball, as mentioned by Kiernan, were obliged to sign an undertaking not to stunt their machines.

Lanoe wrote a more detailed account of this experience, which he posted home headed in large capitals.—

" NOT FOR PUBLICATION

Extract from diary of a young aviator :

Mar. 25/15.

Am now chief exhibitor of the BE.2c so, by request, showed how she tail slides—incidentally my first attempt at same. Shut off, pull elevator back till she gets her nose up in the air. She stops ; hold it hard back and pivoting round the tail-plane. The nose of the machine falls rapidly till she is nose down when machine slips forward again and comes back to normal angle as she regains her flying speed.

The automatic, or rather inherent stability seems to be composed of two items : Fore and Aft by the non-lifting tail-plane, and sideways . . . with correctly adjusted C.G. No. 1 in normal circumstances prevents her nose diving or stalling and No. 2 from side slipping. My first attempt a little cautious —sensation of falling I find distinctly unpleasant, but it seemed all right, so repeated a little more boldly.

Forgot to switch off at first, so got very much tail down and began actually slipping backwards (true tail slipping). She fell though as before, but slightly sideways and got absolutely vertical, before getting up enough speed to answer the controls. Alarming, but apparently all right, and decidedly spectacular. Latter should rightly be barred, especially now, but was wanted to show off our B.E.'s to the French, whose aerodrome we share.

Next day took Kinnear up (ostensibly to test the Liverpool) for a tail slide at his own request. Day was misty as usual so no other flying. Now I've always wanted to loop, largely to say I've done it and for some time I've been working up to the point. Its rather a responsibility and if anything should happen . . . no excuse. But this time I definitely decided before asking Kinnear to come up, that I would do so, if I had the courage when it came to the point. This resolution was in no ways impaired by a Frenchman, who was a nut, civilian pilot and had looped, talking about it. However I didn't tell Kinnear. I knew he would not object, he being up for stunt flying, anyway, and it was very doubtful if I should do it. After all one can never tell. Well, I gave him a couple of tail slides and then climbed to 3,500—he said afterwards that he knew I was up to some devilment when I started climbing again, and he might well have read my thoughts, they were strung to such a pitch of apprehension.

Well, we are now high enough, shall I, dare I? . . . Snap . . . my mind was made up suddenly, all excitement, apprehension and fear vanished and I started. Down with the nose till she showed 90°, then back with the stick gradually but firmly. How I hate that intense centrifugal force, pushing me through the seat. Hallo! its gone, impression we're vertical, not sharp enough, we'll stick—hard back with the lever—suddenly feel my belt pulling hard—rather sideways— engine pops and misses, things start falling out of the front seat—mud, oil, petrol, paper. Is Kinnear going to follow? We are hanging upside down—that belt will twist my body in half—round we come—nose vertically down. Slightly bewildered by now, so rather slow in pulling her out—notice pilot " all red " but that may be due to our position. Throttle down and pull her out to normal gliding position. Kinnear turns round and smiles and we do spiral and land. . . . Well, I've done it, but I don't know what it feels like all the same. Some day, a long time hence, I may try again, this time with complete confidence, but don't feel as if I shall want to for ages. Pleased, but a trifle apprehensive as its almost a Court Martial offence, but I have never seen any order against it. Congrats. of onlookers, who condole with Kinnear."

From now on Lanoe threw his machine about with great ease and confidence, and became one of the most skilled pilots in the R.F.C. He never lost his respect and affection for the B.E.2c.

He was particularly fortunate at this time in his squadron commander, Major Gordon Shephard, who gave every help and encouragement to his pilots.

On the 14th of March Lanoe took 1780 up by himself for a test, but landed too fast without a passenger, and turned the machine over on its back. The machine was not damaged and Lanoe, undeterred, was up again that same afternoon with Vachell, taking photographs.

> " 17.3.15.
> A German dropped 6 bombs on our town last Saturday and killed 10 unfortunates. The move has disturbed everything and in addition I've been busy improving the aerodrome which is very bad. Being a sapper those sort of jobs always come my way."

Lanoe wrote home and to T. giving his new location, which was strictly forbidden, by means of a somewhat transparent code :—

> " My favourite sweet of crispey halves
> Filled with luscious cream,
> Put in Pop for the leading M
> And then I think you have him.

> Not a very good rhyme, but the best I could do."

It gave the French pronunciation of Poperinghe, was easily deciphered, but passed the censor.

13

Archie

" 18.3.15.
  I did my trip early this morning with Haywood, much to
everyone's surprise, as it was a rotten day and I had to go low
to do it, but I calculated on catching Archie asleep, and I
did too ; I hope he gets into dreadful trouble with his general ;
I feel as if I'd got a little of my own back on him. However
there was nothing doing so relieved their minds at G.H.Q.
as our men were all standing to arms."

Lanoe's frequent references to Archie were largely due to the
fact that No. 6 Squadron worked in the Ypres Salient, and their
machines came under fire from three sides long before the lines
were crossed, and the German anti-aircraft gunners had, by
constant practice, attained a disconcerting degree of accuracy.
Col. Burke, the wing commander, reported that it would be
" difficult to visit any one squadron without finding a machine
being repaired owing to the damage caused by the enemy's fire."
Unfortunately casualties from Archie were only too frequent.

Sir John French reported :—

" Artillery observation and photography are two of the most
trying tasks the Royal Flying Corps is called upon to perform,
as our airmen must remain for long periods within easy range
of the enemy's anti-aircraft guns."

Lanoe's classification of Archie's shooting was as follows :—

"No. 1. Visible but inaudible ; harmless and laughable.
  No. 2. Visible and audible ; still harmless but apprehensive.
  No. 3. Noisy cough ; very nasty and dangerous.
  No. 4. Galvanised iron hit by sledge hammer ; shakes the
          whole machine. The limit ! "

Activity in the air increased as the weather improved, and
during the last week in March, Lanoe was out almost every day
on reconnaissance or ranging our guns, dodging Archie and

chasing away occasional hostile machines. He flew solo over the lines dropping propaganda pamphlets, for which the penalty, if caught, was a spell of solitary confinement, also dropped packets on streamers containing small balloons for the use of our agents, the penalty for which was still more severe, but he ignored these German threats. A sample pamphlet and a balloon, which Lanoe sent home, can be seen at the Imperial War Museum.

Diary :—
" Sunday, 28th.
I got a box of arrows ready to drop over Houthem, a dreadful hot-bed, when Haywood spotted a German machine, great excitement. He was somewhere underneath, uncomfortable for us, and I circled to let Haywood get in some shooting. Mister Boch made off home and finding that we had been blown back over our own lines, again set off down the Menin road. Looked for arrows and found them gone! Question, did they drop out over our lines or the German's? "

" Monday, 29th.
Injudiciously I switched off while still over their lines and discussed our ranging, when a shell burst somewhere very close, just above and behind my right ear! Nasty jar, bits whizzing by and shadow over machine, put wind up me properly, switched on and fled at 100 m.p.h.
This shell shook me up, as I was more or less deaf in my right ear, both were very sore, and my head ached a good deal, slight concussion I suppose, as the effects lasted."

The concussion that Lanoe mentioned left him with a headache for some weeks to come, " a tight ache at the back of the head ". It was possibly responsible for two extraordinary incidents that occurred in 1916, when on each occasion he fell into a kind of trance after a blow on the head.

In these early days of the war, our anti-aircraft guns, also alluded to as " Archies ", were not always good at identifying our planes and all too often opened fire on them in mistake for Huns.

Lanoe, very annoyed on one such occasion, sent the offending gunners a message by motor cycle orderly saying that, if they needed practice, he would be pleased to fly over them for half an hour the next day. Their reply is not on record !

Diary :—
" Tuesday, 30th.
Out with Vachell photoing. I changed tactics steadily and
so defeated Archie.
Suddenly saw and engaged a German coming from our lines
over Ypres. This time had my own rifle and put in some good
shooting. German as usual above, put his nose down and
forged ahead.
Before going up on this flight, while arguing about a hop-
field, a German suddenly appeared and dropped a couple of
bombs close by. A most unpleasant sensation, and frightened
me dreadfully."

Alas! This is the end of Lanoe's diary. Pressure of work,
during the greater activity and longer hours of summer weather,
obliged him to give it up. Only a few extracts have been given
here for fear of wearying the reader with full descriptions of
each of his activities continually repeated. During this period
Lanoe put in many hours of steady hard work. He was constantly under fire, but never complained. His observers were
grateful for the consideration and attention he always gave them.
He did much " looking " himself, but was ready for their hand
signals should they wish to examine some particular place with
special care. Their only complaint was that he was " too
damned brave ", and when he planned a fight to the finish, if
forced to land through engine trouble in Hunland, his observers
did not agree that this would be " a great party ".

One of his outstanding characteristics was his cheerful and
optimistic talk at all times, especially in the mess when some
pilots occasionally dwelt on the dangers and discomforts of their
work. Lanoe believed strongly in morale, and that good morale
could be induced or destroyed by certain behaviour. He
explained that an angry man wore an angry expression, and
that by deliberately wearing an angry expression he could make
himself feel angry. Similarly he held that an optimistic and
cheerful opinion not only improved his own spirits, but the
morale of all those around him. His demonstration of putting
on an angry expression to make himself feel angry never failed
to cheer up his companions.

His good spirits became a by-word in the squadron, and his
infectious laugh, rippling up to end on a high note, was

frequently taken up by his comrades, who had grown very fond of him and called him ' Jolly Old Hawker '.

Behind this cheerfulness was a longing for peace, for the companionship of those he loved, for home. When high up in the sky on clear days, his task accomplished, he would turn to the west where he could see across the channel sometimes a clear line of cliffs, sometimes a blurred shadow in the distance. Then it was that his longing became almost painful in its intensity. Quickly he sought refuge in other activities.

> " Our reconnaissance finished, we turn home and gaze lovingly at the white cliffs of Albion, showing up clearly on the horizon, before we spiral down—to breakfast AND the gramophone."

Lanoe was soon to see those beloved cliffs again, for he was given seven days leave from the 1st of April. When the day came most pilots would have been glad enough to pack their bags and go on leave without tempting providence or Archie, but Lanoe took Hawkins up on reconnaissance in the morning before departing.

This time he arranged his leave to coincide with T's, and both arrived at Pinhoe at the beginning of April. It was a tremendous joy for them to see each other again, and to be able to compare experiences. Lanoe's were the more thrilling and filled T. with envy and a determination to make a fresh effort to join the R.F.C., which however, met with the same fate as all his others.

Lanoe returned to France by rail and boat, and on the latter found Strange. These two friends had much in common, both full of the joy of life and ready for any enterprise.

During Lanoe's absence the weather had been stormy, but he returned to the squadron at the beginning of a period of intense activity due to the longer days and a sudden fine spell. He carried out a number of reconnaissances, some of them " solo ", that is without an observer, including flash spotting. He was now recognised as one of the most experienced and reliable observers in the R.F.C., and he was detailed for tasks of special importance. Due to his aggressiveness he was also selected to learn to fly a scout (as single-seater fighter aeroplanes were called), more difficult to fly than the larger two-seater, but faster and therefore more effective in attacking the German machines.

" Sunday, 18.4.15.

Stood the journey here quite comfortably—very tired but a healthy tiredness, without the dull ache at the back of my head. Been quite busy and look like breaking my record for a week's flying.

On the 11th I did 6 hours in two spells, No. 1 2 h.40 starting at 5 a.m. unsuccessful owing to weather but succeeded that evening 3 h.20 landing just before dark. Very tired after this but took a morning in bed the next day—13th, retired to G.H.Q. for a rest and change learning to manipulate a young scout. Had a peaceful time Wednesday, two trips on this new machine and rest of time—weather rotten—looking up old friends.

I always carry a rifle just to the right of my legs, which is lucky as a shrapnel bullet came through the side of the fuselage, leaving an interesting dent in the stock. It would have gone through my leg if the rifle hadn't deflected it."

14

Zeppelin Shed

ENGLAND was suffering from Zeppelin raids, and so that these airships might be within range of our country the Germans had erected sheds for them in Belgium. If we could drive them out of these sheds they would be forced to abandon the raids.

An agent reported that a Zeppelin was using a well defended shed at Gontrode near Ghent. The task of bombing this shed was allotted to No. 6 Squadron, and Major Shephard selected Lance as the most likely pilot to succeed. On the 18th of April he was told to find this shed and test its defences.

Here is his account of this exploit :—

" 22.4.15.

Last Sunday—most of my excitements seem to be on Sundays —I went out to look for a Zep. shed reported S.W. of some-where or other and took 3 bombs on spec. not expecting to find much.

But it was there, and I dropped a couple from about 4,000 feet. It was a huge mark and I thought no one could miss it, but different bombs vary so and I let fly too soon. The first went off about 200 yards short; the second I did not see. There was a silly captive sausage balloon there that annoyed me so I spiralled at it dropping hand grenades, he had a machine gun on board, the brute, so deserves no sympathy, but it must have been horrid to see a mad aeroplane circling down at it, however, it was impossible to aim going round at that speed and finding I had got below it I shut off and dived down at the shed, the anti-aircraft battery had no chance as I must have been moving over 120 m.p.h. but the machine-guns were unpleasant Zip-zip-zip-zip-zip-thud as they struck some-thing. I think I got down to about 200 feet and flew across the shed (I was away to one side or I might have flown along it) and let fly with No. 3, again just too soon, as I looked back when circling away and saw the smoke up alongside the shed.

I suppose I hit 6 or 10 feet short. Awful bad luck, but I ought to have reserved them all for the dive, but then I had not got definite orders to go low tho' it seemed such a pity to miss the opportunity once there, so I tried high first and when that failed came low.

However, I expect it did some damage.

They shelled me going away but I kept low and Archie didn't make good shooting at such an unaccustomed angle.

It was a ticklish moment when I switched on again, wondering if the engine would come on or not, but it was quite different from a cold-blooded affair such as sitting still being shelled, my blood was up and nothing mattered. In fact I enjoyed it if anything, but wish I'd seen flames shooting about.

They hit me 6 or 7 times with bullets but luckily not through anything that mattered so the machine was in commission again the next day. In fact I went out twice, but the engine was running very badly and suspecting an air-leak I told my man to carefully examine all the joints on the induction pipe, and he found a bullet imbedded in one of the rubber joints! It had gone through my shield, chipped the back cylinder, through the shield again, cut one rubber pipe, badly dented the copper one underneath and lodged in the third!

A fraction further forward would have broken the cylinder, a fraction further back it would not have got checked by the gills of the cylinder and would have pierced the induction pipe, and a little further back still it would have pierced the petrol tank. It came in from slightly above, so must have come from the sausage. Hope I frightened him some, probably he thought he'd hit me when I dived and must have been angry when I stopped, dropped a bomb and then flew away unscathed, it will make them think a bit even if it did no damage. . . .

Gordon is still very much in my thoughts, and I am just beginning to be able to think of him without suffering agonies of grief, especially in my prayers when one naturally contemplates the beyond."

In this bombing exploit, as in his fights in the air, Lanoe showed a courage which had been characteristic of him since childhood. He saw his enemy, sized up the position in an instant, and attacked directly without wasting time in manoeuvring or contemplating the danger. His " blood was up ", as he put it, and by his determination he conquered all fear.

In his report of bombing this shed, he was careful not to claim a hit, since he had failed to see " flames shooting about ", which he would have expected if a Zeppelin were set on fire, but the agent appears to have reported the raid successful. In fact Lanoe's last bomb, carried by its forward velocity, struck the side of the shed, and the one he failed to observe hit it also. A translation from the log-book of the shed, supplied by the courtesy of the Reichsarchiv, reads as follows :—

> " 18.4.15.
> 3 bombs thrown, of which 2 bombs on the empty shed which only caused small damage."

The shed was empty because Zeppelin LZ-35, which used it, had crashed five days earlier. (V. III, p. 97 and A. II.)

Though Lanoe was disappointed at having failed to destroy a Zeppelin, the result of his raid demonstrated to the enemy that the shed was at the mercy of our boldest airmen, and that an airship could only shelter in it at great risk. Eventually German military airships were forced to abandon the sheds in Belgium, and so moved out of effective range of England.

In his report Major Shephard pointed out that Lanoe had seen immediately how he could turn the defensive balloon to his own advantage and had attacked the shed from very low down without hesitation. For this exploit Lanoe was appointed a Companion of the Distinguished Service Order.

> "Yesterday I was promoted flight commander with temporary rank of Captain, and best of all I'm not leaving this squadron, but have got 'A' flight, its late captain having hurt himself badly in an accident, but as usual the poor observer, Clarke, got the worst and I regret to say died from his injuries ; he was a very popular and efficient officer."

Lanoe was sad at losing this friend who had shared the perils of Archie with him. The war provided a succession of such tragedies, friendships made on the firmest foundations of courage under constant danger, only to be broken one after the other by the relentless hand of death. One dared not ask a soldier from the front how his friends were for fear that they had gone.

In the first instance Gordon Bayly had been reported missing, and Lanoe had cherished a hope, ever growing fainter with the lapse of time and the lack of news, that he might have been taken prisoner.

> "As I looked up through the clouds at a patch of blue sky just before my attack on the Zep. shed, I wondered if Gordon was watching, and somehow I felt as if he was very close. I think it was then that I definitely realised that there was no hope left."

15

Gas Attack

AT the end of March the Tenth French Army, on the right of the B.E.F. in the Ypres salient, received warning from a German prisoner of the installation of gas cylinders in the nightbourhood of Zillebeke. Further precise warnings were received on the 15th of April. It now seems amazing that our staff made no attempt to verify this startling information when, on the 17th of April, our troops captured Hill 60, a mile south of Zillebeke, in the trenches of which the Germans had already installed their gas cylinders. Probably the truth was that neither British nor French G.H.Q. could believe, as Sir John French wrote in his despatches:—" that an army which hitherto has claimed to be the chief exponent of the chivalry of war should stoop to employ such devices against brave and gallant foes." A final warning came in the Wolff communiqué of the 17th, which accused the British of using gas, a sure indication of a guilty intention.

No. 6 Squadron was ordered to discover any signs of preparation for an attack, and on the 15th Lanoe did a solo reconnaissance of $2\frac{1}{4}$ hours beneath low clouds, giving a long and detailed report of all movements behind the German lines. On the 16th he went out with Clarke, and on the 17th took him up twice, making a detailed reconnaissance and taking photographs. Apart from minor movements, there was nothing to indicate an impending attack, because the Germans were making a small trial of this new device, and with customary military obtuseness, they threw away the advantage of surprise, just as we did with the tanks in 1916. It was not possible from the air to see anything of the gas cylinders; they were dug into the parapet, or hidden in the support trenches.

The attack had first been planned against the southern shoulder of the salient, but had been delayed by unfavourable winds, and in consequence the Germans installed further cylinders of gas opposite the northern shoulder. This sector should have been taken over by our troops, but the 29th Division had been diverted to Gallipoli, a " side-show " not favoured by the French Commander-in-Chief, who had expected us to relieve his troops at Ypres for the battle he was preparing in Artois. He left in the line on our flank two weak divisions, one of colonial troops and the other of aged territorials. By pure chance this weak sector of vital importance to the defence of Ypres, and contingently of the channel ports, was the one selected by the Germans for their experimental attack with chlorine gas.

The attack came as a complete surprise. On the 22nd of April, during an early morning reconnaissance with Brown as observer, Lanoe noticed unusual activity in the Langemarck area, and landed immediately at the 1st Canadian Brigade H.Q. at Vlamertinghe to report this verbally, but it was not considered sufficient to justify alarm.

At 5 p.m. the Germans opened a heavy bombardment on Ypres, and released a cloud of 18,000 kilograms of chlorine gas from cylinders on the French front of $3\frac{3}{4}$ miles under ideal conditions of wind and weather. This new weapon terrified the colonial troops who disappeared, and the territorials did not do much better. It is doubtful whether seasoned troops, blinded and choked as they would have been by this heavy concentration of poisonous gas, could have arrested the German attack.

Strange was in the air at the time, saw the gas advancing, marked its flanks on his map and returned to the aerodrome to give the alarm. Little could be done in the first confusion; nothing was known as to the fate of the French troops, and it was only after dark that it was realized that their line had ceased to exist, that there was a gap of several miles on the British left flank, and that the way was open to the Germans to occupy Ypres, to turn left and right and cut off the British and Belgian defenders in that part of the line. Such small reserves as were available were rushed up during the night to form a defensive flank, but it was imperative to know how far the enemy had advanced.

Lanoe went up solo on the morning of the 23rd to clear up the situation. The weather was fine, and hastening to the front without pausing to gain height, he came under heavy machine-gun and rifle fire from the German advanced positions. Realizing that the enemy held a continuous line of trenches, which his troops had dug during the night, he proceeded to plot it carefully on his map and draw up a reconnaissance report, which gave the first full intimation to the H.Q. Staff of the extent of the German advance. This report was remarkable in that it covered with absolute accuracy the whole of the new German positions opposite both the British and French fronts.

From a moving aeroplane much skill and practice were needed to identify on the map each position seen on the ground. It was vital that the observer should not make the mistake of reporting a German position in our hands or vice versa. Lanoe never made a mistake of this kind in spite of the French and German troops wearing uniforms of similar colour, but the accuracy of his reports was largely due to the risks he was prepared to take in flying exceptionally low over the enemy's positions.

Whilst he was on leave in England and free from censorship Lanoe wrote a detailed account of the part he took in the battle from which extracts are given below.

" 4.5.15. Pinhoe, Exeter.

Now I am home and have a little time free from worry I will give you an account of what I know of the Second Battle of Ypres, also I can put in names and say what I like.

We have been stationed at Poperinghe, the headquarters of the Vth Corps—27th, 28th and Canadian Divisions—out of shell fire. We had very nice wooden hangars—built to my design—and nice sheds, etc.

The show started on Thursday, the 22nd of April. The evening reconnaissance reported gas blowing over the French trenches. Friday morning I was told to hurry out single seated and verify the number of bridges over the canal and the new line of German trenches. I didn't waste time climbing but went straight over Ypres, which was being shelled heavily and turned north up the canal against the wind, arriving at the bit of canal between Steenstraat and Het Sas at the low height of 3,000 feet and was greeted by a salvo of rifle and machine-gun fire, so sheered off and climbed higher. This firing came from a clearly defined trench facing west. The bridge at Het Sas was open and there were about six footbridges and the swing bridge at Steenstraat had jammed.

I followed the new line all the way round to where it joined the Canadians. The French troops, demoralised by the gasses, broke and ran, and parties had to be sent out from Poperinghe with rifles to prevent them rushing through the town. The Germans dug themselves in and hung on to the ground they held. They do dig remarkably well and I had no difficulty in placing this beautiful trench.

Things were quiet as I flew over at 8 a.m. No great movement behind the German lines. They were surprised by the extent of their success and quite unprepared. If troops had been to hand Friday morning they would have captured Ypres.

That evening there was an extraordinary panic in Poperinghe started by the stories of the terrified refugees; all the civvies were in a wild state of agitation, many packed up and fled, and it was only with considerable trouble that we soothed the shattered nerves of our billet hosts and sundry others who asked if all was up. We cheerfully assured them that all was well and there was no danger—" Mais ils bombardent Ypres! " as if they had never done that before. Asphyxiating gasses? What of them? Two can play that game. There was not this panic in November when there was a very thin line, and if the Germans failed to get through then how could they possibly expect to succeed now, when we had so many troops behind our line?

So off to bed early as I had to rise before dawn and repeat my reconnaissance. This said reconnaissance was apparently satisfactory. 'A very useful report,' I heard the general say and I was told off to the particular job of placing the line till further notice."

The gas had drifted with the wind, and was distinctly smelt in Poperinghe, though not in dangerous strength. It was a startling, even a terrifying weapon at that time, for no one had the least protection or defence against it, and at any moment the Germans might make a fresh discharge. With our present knowledge and experience of gas, and our effective masks and other means of defence, it is not easy to realize the feeling of helpless fear which overtook the French troops and the civilians at that time. Lanoe's calming of the panic-stricken inhabitants, and his placid retirement to sleep at the height of such a crisis, was a masterly piece of " sangfroid ".

The next day the town of Poperinghe and the aerodrome came under shell-fire from an armoured train near Langemarck, and most of No. 6 Squadron retired to Abeele, leaving Lanoe's flight at Poperinghe.

With the few reserves that could be scraped together an

attempt was made to drive the Germans back. On the other hand the enemy was making a belated effort to exploit his unexpected success. The result was a confused and changing line with many gaps in it. Great difficulty was experienced by the staff in determining, not only the positions held by the enemy, but those held by our own troops, for all communications had broken down, the restricted and pronounced salient was under constant shell fire from three sides, the position of our troops on the broken flank was unknown, reserves were scanty, a further attack by the Germans was expected, and if successful would lead to a disaster. At all costs the line must be re-established. In consequence Lanoe's clear reports were of great value.

His next reconnaissance starting at dawn on the 24th was more difficult, but he reported with unfailing accuracy the positions held by our troops and those held by the enemy.

"I ordered the car for 3 a.m. Saturday morning so arrived on the aerodrome when it was still too dark to start. I left the ground at 4.20 a.m. and returned just after half past six. I knew we had attacked Friday evening so expected to find we had driven the Germans back. There was a strong north wind blowing and I arrived over Steenstraat just under 3,000 feet, and as I was again greeted by a fusilade of bullets I retired south and crossed the canal near Boesinghe. I could see a line of trenches covering Pilckem. 'Oh ho!' thought I, 'we drove the Germans back quite a lot last night'.

Ignoring the old line I sailed gaily on and examined this new line carefully from a respectful distance as we* crabbed sideways across the wind. I was disturbed by the sound of heavy rifle fire and looking down found I was vertically over a farm crowded with men in blue greatcoats who were firing at me! Looking at my planes I saw the marks of several bullets so retired and flew over yesterday's line. Again rifle fire was audible and I could see that the trench was crammed full of soldiers in blue uniform facing south. They were Germans, our attacks must have failed, they still held their ground to the St. Julien Wood and the trenches round Pilckem were their second line. I then noticed a series of fortified points behind their first line. I flew along the railway from the canal to Langemarck, carefully noting their second line and various gun positions and parks of vehicles and then back towards St. Julien.

The British line from St. Julien northwards was very hard

_____
* Himself and his aeroplane; he was flying solo.

to place even though I came down again to under 3,000 feet and I could only roughly place the general position.* Finally I climbed again, had a good look at the ground behind the German lines and returned home, indulging in a scrap with an Aviatic whom I met coming from Poperinghe. I gave him 15 rounds from my rifle, but did not give chase as I had important information that was urgently required.

Walking through the main square after lunch we were startled by the arrival of the first shell—a peculiar shrill noise followed by the dull crash of the explosion—at first everyone looked for the aeroplane, as bombs were by no means uncommon, but there was nothing to be seen, and these explosions still continued. Then the truth burst on the agitated populace who had been soothed with so much difficulty last night; Poperinghe was being shelled. Help! and everyone started running about in all directions each to his house or a friendly cellar.

Bricks and mortar are unpleasant when shells are about so I walked up to the aerodrome, my first walk under shell-fire, and most unpleasant too."

---

* There were gaps in our defences in this part of the line, which were causing great anxiety at H.Q.

16

Courage Unsurpassed

A CRITICAL situation had developed in the St. Julien area. Our generals wished to know at once which farms and other strong points were held by our troops, and which held by the enemy. It was known that German reinforcements were on the way, and information was urgently needed as to when and where their attack was likely to fall.

Lanoe went up again soon after 5 p.m. on the 24th, but owing to the low clouds, mist and poor light it was extremely difficult to distinguish friend from foe, except from very low down. His method of obtaining reliable information was to fly so low that he offered an irresistible target to the enemy troops, and at the same time could actually see them raise their rifles to fire at him. He could also see the colour of their uniforms and the direction they faced when standing in their trenches. This close view gives some indication of how low he flew over the German positions. It was only a matter of time when he must inevitably be hit. Bullets constantly ripped their way through his machine, but he stuck stolidly to the work, patiently marking on his map where he saw the Germans firing at him, and where he saw our troops looking upwards without firing.

The inevitable came at last. A bullet passed through the floor of the fuselage and entered his heel at the Achilles tendon; piercing his puttees, his boot and his sock, it tore up the heel and struck the bone without breaking it. Lanoe made light of the wound, but the pain at first was such that he felt sick and giddy for a few minutes. Instinctively he turned back over our lines, but as soon as he regained control of his senses he returned to complete his work.

Not only did this reconnaissance give valuable information as to the situation near St. Julien, the critical sector, but it gave timely warning of the German reinforcements arriving at this point. " These observations left no doubt that the enemy was making rapid movements to develop the break-through which he had made at St. Julien earlier in the day, and the Second Army commander was enabled to make his dispositions to counter this move." (V. II, p. 104.)

Copy of reconnaissance report.

Date	Aeroplane	Pilot	Observer	Duty	Time
24.4.15.	B.E.2c, 1780.	Capt. Hawker.	Nil.	Recon.	5.30 p.m. to 7.15 p.m.

Germans hold farms at C 16a and C 16b, C 17a and C 17c d. British hold farms C 22b across to stream C 18b, C 18a and C 12b. Thence line of trenches from stream at C 12b 1.8, East through centre of C 12, North to cross-roads C 6d 4.0, North of road to D 1c 0.0, along South of road D 7a to old line in D 2.

Germans hold farm D 1d.*

British reserves estimated about one brigade D 8c.

About 6 or 7 trains observed running to and from LANGE-MARCK.

A column of transport about 30 vehicles advancing S.E. along road from LANGEMARCK to KEERSELARE.

Two columns of infantry each about 1,500 yards halted line LANGEMARCK—POELCAPPELLE and KEERSELARE. Observation difficult.

(signed) L. G. Hawker,
Capt. R.F.C.

" That evening about 5 p.m. I set out again on the same reconnaissance, a job for which I had now been reserved. This one was far more difficult than the morning reconnaissance owing to the poor light, low clouds and hazy mist. Urged to be cautious, I tried at first to work above the clouds, but found that impossible. I came back over Ypres and drove off a German who appeared to be reconnoitring.

I had orders to specially note the ground from St. Julien wood eastwards as the French had now taken over the line to the west. The Germans must have made an attack and broken through between St. Julien and the Wood† as they had made a considerable advance just there. The firing was particularly heavy that afternoon. Above 4,000 feet all noise from the ground is drowned by the roar of the engine. At the height I was working rifle fire was audible and the noise made by

---

* " Stroppe Farm." Lanoe was wounded by a bullet fired from this farm.
† They broke through at mid-day. (V. II, p. 103.)

the guns firing and the bursting of the bigger shells was very marked, nearly as loud as the smaller variety of anti-aircraft shells.

We still clung on to that part of St. Julien S.E. of the stream which seemed to be forming our line of resistance at the moment. From here the line went N.E. again and I had a very careful look at that bit of ground, circling and going over it again and again till I could make sure of the exact positions we held. It was while flying low over a big farm to the north of this bit that I received a bullet just above my left ankle that solved the problem as to who held the farm! It was remarkably painful at first and I headed for home but as I could use my foot I turned back to deny the Germans the satisfaction of having driven me off, placed the farm carefully on the map and then turned and went home.

Walking was not easy but I could hobble along. The bullet had gone through my leather and puttees and vanished somewhere inside, though I could not find the end of the hole with my finger, there was no blood about, so the damage was not serious, which was fortunate.

I went to headquarters and delivered my report and then went off to my billet to investigate the damage. The doctor put on iodine and bound it up and I hobbled across to the mess and had supper.

Most of the squadron had retired to Abeele with the motor transport for fear they should bombard the aerodrome, but 'A' Flight's mess stayed behind and fed the stragglers."

Lanoe was commanding 'A' Flight.

The next day, the 25th, did not see the situation cleared up. Ground reports were lacking from the St. Julien front, where a gap in our line was feared, and there was a strong north-east wind with low clouds which prevented observation from the air till the evening.

Lanoe refused to go on sick leave, and asked to be allowed to continue his perilous work. Headquarters were aware of the difficulty of finding another pilot as skilled and as reliable in his observations. A misleading report from the air was made by a less experienced observer that very morning. (See " Military Operations," 1915, p. 248.) Some idea of the difficulty of distinguishing friend from foe may be gathered from the reports of our infantry that the Germans were wearing khaki. (See idem. p. 250, note.) To obtain an accurate report there was no alternative to taking the heavy risk of flying low over the German positions for considerable periods of time. There was something very grim in the way Lanoe offered himself as a bait to the enemy. It was not as if he could strike back, as airmen did when " ground-strafing ", the name given by our airmen to the low-flying attacks they made later in the war, with machine-gun fire on enemy troops, transport and other targets on the ground, nor was it a quick or passing danger, such as flashing over the lines and back, nor had he the companionship of an observer with whom to share the danger. His reconnaissances averaged over two hours each, and for most of this time he was hovering against the wind, a most tempting target. This was the test of courage which he himself had just rated higher than any other. " It was quite different from a cold-blooded affair such as sitting still being shelled," he had written concerning his bombing exploit. He could both see and hear the Germans shooting at him, and noticed the marks of their bullets as they perforated his planes. He knew that it was only a matter of time when he must be hit again, and he could hardly hope to escape so lightly a second time. He had Gordon's fate as an example of what he might expect. It required an inflexible will-power to continue this perilous work after he had been wounded.

Thus in the evening, when the clouds lifted a little, he set out again. On account of his wound, which was still stiff and painful, though not serious, he had to be lifted into his aeroplane. His report stated :—

"Drove off German machine flying at 3,000 feet over our lines."

One wonders what the German pilot and observer would think if they knew that they had been driven off by a tired and wounded pilot who, single-handed, had to control his aeroplane and manipulate his rifle. Lanoe made a long and careful reconnaissance lasting two hours, his report ending :—

"Observation very difficult."

On one of his flights after he had been wounded Lanoe again landed at Vlamertinghe, this time to ask for some information from the Canadian Brigade H.Q. Hearing the sound of the machine taxiing towards the billet a young Canadian officer came out, and seeing Lanoe's difficulty in walking, had him carried indoors. The situation was precarious on the Canadian flank, and these staff officers had every reason for feeling anxious, but their courage was magnificent. They gathered round this wounded and tired pilot, who smiled at them with large confident eyes, and in his quiet steady voice explained the situation to them. Despite his wound, despite his fatigue, despite the strain on his nerves of these low reconnaissances which he was still to continue, Lanoe brought into the harassed headquarters a breath of cheery optimism and confidence which was most infectious. He was surprised and indignant when he found that this brigade, which was vitally interested in the situation, had not received copies of the previous reconnaissances, which he had made at such risk. He marked at once on their map the information he had collected. They told him that they were particularly anxious to know whether certain points were held by friend or foe. Without further delay Lanoe was carried back to his aeroplane, and he headed straight for the lines. At the Canadian Brigade H.Q. he left a feeling that their troops were being looked after from the air, and that the Commander-in-Chief was kept well informed of the situation. Lanoe's plucky disregard for his wound and his cheerful confidence left a vivid impression on the mind of at least one of the Canadian staff officers.

Within twenty minutes of landing he was back in the air again, and to the rattle of musketry and machine-guns, was circling low over the positions about which news was required, carefully marking them on his map. Thus his report was of singular value, since it included just that information which was most urgently needed.

" 24.4.15.
It's rather a difficult proposition—placing the position of the ' line ' which is always shifting just now, but I think I've solved the problem by a simple and ingenious method—fly low and draw their fire—then mark it down on the map. The result seems worth the obvious risk."

In spite of all his trials Lanoe could still indulge in an atrocious pun.

" 26.4.15.
I have been doing a series of special reconnaissances solo —so low in fact that Saturday I picked up 50 bullet holes thro' my planes in two trips, one chipped the propeller, one a strut,

one thro' my exhaust pipe, one thro' my tail skid and one into my leg. . . .

I hobble about with the aid of a stick and fortunately it does not stop my flying.

Everyone has been very nice to me, all ' A ' Flight said how glad they were to have me as captain, and yesterday the colonel rang up to ask how I was and congratulated me on what he called my ' splendid work '. The generals* seem very pleased with the result so I hope it was useful.

The Canadians are splendid and have undoubtedly saved Wipers.

It seems ages since this fierce battle started. I shall be glad when it is over, as the rush is tiring. The last two days— Sat. and Sund.—they managed to put about ten 6-inch shells each into the town and aerodrome—most unpleasant.

We decamped further back, but returned today as things seemed quiet, and the beasts started putting huge crumps into the town from an armoured train—so off we went again— they might do so much damage to material with one lucky shot. It's the moving to and fro that worries."

Poperinghe was shelled at intervals, both during the day and the night of the 26th, the largest shells coming from a German 15 inch gun with a range of 36 miles, but only 15 miles away. The very first of these huge shells demolished one of No. 6 Squadron's billets, but fortunately no one was in at the time.

" 26.4.15.

Some excitement today, as doing our reconnaissance—my usual one with a passenger (Wyllie) this time—we met and chased away two Germans. So far so good. A third appeared and we gaily approached it and found it had a machine-gun aboard—the first German I've met who showed fight. I only had my 10 rounds and had to turn and fly—a strategic retreat we call it in the best society—but each time I loaded my rifle I turned and let him have it. He hit us, but having a machine-gun he soon finished his ammunition and then we had the pleasure of chasing him away as we hadn't finished ours. One of his bullets went thro' the cushion on which sat my observer."

On the 27th there were low clouds all day and air reconnaissance was impossible, but Lanoe went up from 4 to 4.30 p.m. and again from 7.30 to 8.20 p.m. with the object of giving confidence to our troops.

* General Smith-Dorien, commanding the Second Army and General Plumer, commanding the Vth Corps were both at Poperinghe.

" Wednesday, 28th.

Horrid day yesterday—low clouds cleared at sunset and so I went out for a trip over the lines and landed by flares and moonlight, not that I saw much but chiefly the moral effect.

I'm back at Wing H.Q. for the moment. Colonel sent me in for a hot bath and good night's rest; I'm feeling much rested in consequence, not disturbed by terrific ' crash' and flying debris—which shakes the whole town, some huge shell; the brutes have managed to reach our quiet little town."

By the 30th it was realized that the crisis was past, No. 8 Squadron arrived to share the work of the Second Wing, and Lanoe was given seven days sick leave, which had to be extended to three weeks owing to his wound being more serious than was thought at first.

In one week he appeared in the casualty lists as wounded, in the honours list as receiving the D.S.O. for bombing the Zeppelin shed, and in the Gazette as being promoted Flight Commander and temporary Captain.

His Wing Commander, the " utterly brave and determined " Col. Burke, wrote the following report on Lanoe's work during the Second Battle of Ypres :—

" During the critical period after April 22nd, he often flew low over the enemy rather than fail to get the required information. His machine was hit by a variety of missiles and it was only a question of time until he himself was at least wounded. While things were still critical he was hit in the leg but remained on flying duty until matters settled down. He then went sick.

He is now back flying as daringly as ever and has inflicted damage on German aircraft by combats in the air."

For his services during the Second Battle of Ypres he was mentioned in Sir John French's despatch of the 31st of May. Later in 1915 some of those, who knew of Lanoe's extraordinary courage during this battle, connected it with his award of the Victoria Cross, until they learnt from the Gazette of his further exploits in the air.

Lanoe's continuous devotion to duty and his unfailing courage, even under the most exacting conditions, undoubtedly were taken into account when he was recommended later for this highest of all awards.

17

Bristol Scout

THE strain on Lanoe's health and on his nerves had been severe, and his sick leave was granted only just in time. For the first few days in May he had the companionship of his brother, who was eager to hear every detail of his exploits.

The work of reconnaissance, artillery ranging and photography over the enemy's lines, all under constant shell-fire, was alone sufficient to wear out the staunchest pilot in a short time, and Lanoe had been entrusted with still more difficult and dangerous duties. He made light of his bombing attack on the Zeppelin shed, and tried to make little of his low reconnaissances during the Second Battle of Ypres, but those long hours spent under machine-gun and rifle, as well as shell-fire, had been more trying than he liked to admit.

Looking down from his aeroplane, watching some hundreds of German soldiers raise their rifles, and hearing the crackle of their fire above the roar of his engine might sorely try the stoutest nerves. Lanoe was highly sensitive and constantly aware of his danger. The fatigue and strain of his low flying each day was increased by the added disturbance and danger of the shelling of the aerodrome and billets. Little wonder if on his arrival at Pinhoe he appeared completely exhausted.

Gone were the soft boyish curves of his mouth never to return. His lips were set in a firm line from the constant habit of drilling his spirit to face danger unflinchingly. His large bright eyes had lost their gay laughter for the moment, and had sunk back in their dark surrounds. Instead of gazing out smilingly they seemed to ask some pained question, whilst they pierced through and beyond the person upon whom they were turned in a disconcertingly direct look, that became familiar in those who faced death day by day.

Lanoe now possessed the calm dignity of full manhood, and though he was to recover his jolly spirits and fresh laughter, the care-free boyishness had left him for ever. ' Jolly Old Hawker ' he would always be, ragging and romping with full zest, but life had taken on a new and more serious shade, and in every sense of the word Lanoe was now a man. He had been a manly child, a manly boy, a manly youth, at all times showing more forethought and consideration than might be expected from one so young. He now had the training, the experience and the capacity for a more responsible post, but lacked alone that number of years in his age which service tradition required for promotion.

The quiet of the country, the rich flora of Devon in May, which he loved, the soft warm air, the good food and above all the peace and serenity of the family life at Pinhoe, combined to effect a rapid cure. Lanoe's wound healed steadily as he rested his leg, lying out in the garden in a long chair, drinking in the soft balmy air, and forgetting as quickly as possible the harassing hours he had passed in battle. There was great jubilation on hearing the news of his award of the D.S.O. for his exploit in bombing the Zeppelin shed, but he made the announcement to Beatrice with characteristic modesty.

" 8.5.13.

My leg is getting on slowly but steadily ; the bullet had gone down to the bone ; and I've got 14 days extra leave. Also a D.S.O. ! "

He had left France exhausted. He returned on the 20th full of vitality, keen to be back at work, gay and jolly as before, though his wound was not yet completely healed.

" 23.5.15.

I have arrived safely after a tiresome journey. My leg is very tired, but in spite of this it is healing rapidly and has lost its raw meat appearance. Everything is very quiet with us. My old machine has gone, but I expect one of the new ones any day now."

Pilots who returned to the front after recovering from a wound often had a feeling of apprehension, not so much of the danger of being hit again, but of their own behaviour under fire, and some of them never flew again with their former boldness.

A month almost to an hour after Lanoe had been wounded, he took up again his low reconnaissances over the German lines under identical conditions. No sooner was he back in No. 6

Squadron than the quietness was broken by the enemy launching another gas attack on the Ypres Salient, and making a fresh breach in the line. Lanoe was up for $2\frac{1}{4}$ hours on the evening of the 24th of May, flying solo in B.E.2c 1781 over the hostile lines " as daringly as ever ". He made a detailed reconnaissance of the whole area immediately behind the enemy's trenches east of Ypres on a seven mile front, gathering valuable information. But this time the Germans had to deal with British troops, against whom they made little progress in spite of their poisonous gasses, and their attack soon died down.

With the longer days, clearer weather, further practice and better ranging instruments, Archie's shooting had improved considerably during the three weeks of Lanoe's absence.

" 29.5.15.
I have been up about four times and have had two very hot receptions. In one case Archie removed two inches completely from one of my longerons, i.e. cut right through one of the four pieces of wood that are braced together to form the fuselage which supports the tail. This if you please at 8,500! So I retired to 10,000 and then did the recon. at about 10,500, and even then they got uncomfortably close at times.
I knew the machine had been hit but not the extent of the damage till I landed. Ignorance is bliss."

Lanoe did not allow Archie to have his own way all the time. The Germans produced a new type of anti-aircraft shell with a double burst, and this led him on several occasions to practice a piece of fooling to the great entertainment of our troops, who watched his antics. Flying his B.E. solo, he circled over Archie till he saw a shell with the double burst, then he did a tail slide, a half loop or a pronounced side-slip, recovering and limping away only to return for more. His intention was to make Archie think he had scored a hit, only to disappoint him. After half an hour of this stunting, in which he induced the enemy to waste a prodigious amount of ammunition, and which greatly entertained our troops below, Lanoe returned to our lines, derisively wagging the tail of his machine.

He also teased a German 37 m/m automatic repeating gun, which fired bursts of tracer shells. Seen from the target aeroplane the distances between these burning shells were foreshortened, so that they appeared strung together, hence the name given to them of "flaming onions". Lanoe discovered that he could foretell the direction these shells would take from the angle of the "string" of onions, and he easily avoided them.

He fitted in these jaunts with tactical reconnaissances, trench photography, artillery ranging and flash spotting. He also took great interest in the organization and administration of his flight. His men regarded him as a strict disciplinarian, but he was popular with them on account of his scrupulous fairness, and the constant interest he took in their welfare and comfort. For example, he initiated bathing parades in a nearby stream which were very popular with the men, and he made improvements in their billets and in their cooking arrangements.

At the beginning of June, No. 6 Squadron received its first F.E.2 aeroplanes which were to replace the B.E.2cs. The new machines were pushers of the Farman type, but much improved.

On the 3rd of June Lanoe started a new phase in his career. He was sent to St. Omer to fetch Bristol Scout No. 1609. It will be seen from the following table that its performance was markedly superior to any other machine he had flown.

Aeroplane type and engine.	Speed.	Climb.	Service ceiling.
Henry Farman (pusher) 80 h.p. Gnome (rotary)	60 m.p.h. at ground level	3,000 ft. in 18½ mins.	(doubtful)
B.E. 2c (tractor) 90 h.p. R.A.F. (stationary).	72 m.p.h. at 6,500 ft. 69 m.p.h. at 10,000 ft.	6,500 ft. in 20 mins. 10,000 ft. in 45 mins.	10,000 ft.
F.E. 2b (pusher) 120 h.p. Beardmore (stationary).	73 m.p.h. at 6,500 ft. 72 m.p.h. at 10,000 ft.	6,500 ft. in 19½ mins. 10,000 ft. in 45½ mins.	9,000 ft.
Bristol Scout (tractor) 80 h.p. Gnome (rotary)	89 m.p.h. at 6,500 ft. 86½ m.p.h. at 10,000 ft.	6,500 ft. in 10.8 mins. 10,000 ft. in 21.3 mins. 15,000 ft. in 50 mins.	15,500 ft.

The "service ceiling" is the greatest height at which the aeroplane can climb at least 100 feet in one minute. The figures in this table are taken from "WAR IN THE AIR", Appendix XXVII.

The figures for the Bristol Scout are probably rather high for the machine produced in 1915, but correct for the better made machine of 1916. Lanoe appears to confirm this in January, 1916, when comparing the performance of the 1915 Bristol Scout with that of the more modern D.H.2.

The Bristol Scout was a handy little machine, and Lanoe was entranced with its performance, and retained for it a respect and affection when others considered it obsolete. He created a sensation when he arrived at Abéele, stunting the machine over the aerodrome, and showing off its outstanding capacity for zooming, climbing and turning. It was clear to all present that he handled the machine with remarkable skill and confidence.

" 7.6.15.
I have a beautiful little toy, a new Bristol Scout that goes at 80 and climbs 5 or 600 feet a minute! I'm having a machine-gun fitted to see how they like it."

In his methodical and mechanical way Lanoe studied the machine carefully, saw that the best way of fitting the Lewis gun would be for it to shoot obliquely forwards, slightly downwards and to the left of the propeller. He made neat drawings of the necessary brackets and sights, and these were made and fitted by Aircraft Mechanic E. J. Elton, who later became a noted air fighter. Lanoe then carefully sighted the gun.

The arrangement by which the gun had to be fired to one side past the propeller required of the pilot an abnormal amount of skill, for he had to fly in one direction whilst aiming and shooting in another. Later aeroplanes were fitted with synchronizing gears enabling the machine-gun to be fired straight ahead through the sweep of the propeller. This made aiming a simpler matter, and with this gear pilots could dive at their opponents or zoom up beneath them, much easier methods of attack than the crab-like manoeuvring required of the earlier pilots.

Whilst waiting for his Bristol Scout to be fitted with its Lewis gun, Lanoe continued his routine flights in B.E.2cs and Fe.2bs. He also found time to visit Gourlay again, but missing the way came under shell-fire. This did not seem to worry him much.

" 8.6.15.
I took the wrong turning on the way there and had to retreat hastily—whir-rr-rr-rr—BANG—the gunners from whom I asked the way were all in a dug-out."

Early in June, a new arrival in Lanoe's flight was Lieut. Noel Clifton who, as an Infantry officer, had been badly wounded at La Bassee in January, 1915. On recovery, he took a three-weeks' course at Brooklands, as an observer, and was posted to Lanoe's ' A ' Flight in No. 6 Squadron.

Lanoe, knowing well the importance of very close co-operation between the pilot and the observer, who also manned the machine-guns in a two-seater aeroplane, welcomed this zealous new arrival and took him in to share his tent. Clifton soon found that Lanoe had a sweet tooth and no scruples about helping himself to his observer's chocolates. Had not the generals helped themselves to Lanoe's cake? However, Clifton saw much to like and admire in his new mentor, noticed his springy walk and his good humour, and soon came to realise that though he was obviously working under nervous tension, he was very thorough when in the air. Lanoe took Clifton up in the Fe.2b, a pusher aeroplane with two Lewis guns linked together and fitted to a pivoted mounting at the front end of the nacelle, giving the observer a wonderful view and a wide and unobstructed field of fire. Clifton noted, " If there was any doubt as to whether proper observation had been carried out, we hung above, greatly to my dislike, until every detail had been visible for the preparation of the usual report."

Clifton found another of Lanoe's habits somewhat trying. As pilot, he sat behind Clifton, and could not bear to see a German without having a go at him. In Clifton's words he " had a foul habit of carrying an ordinary rifle which he used to loose off if he didn't think I was doing too well. The noise just over my head was most alarming and annoying."

The Germans were not the only ones to suffer from Lanoe's aggressive spirit. He took an active part in the Squadron's staple sport of catapult shooting. The " instruments " were cut from the hedge, shock absorbers split up for elastic and shot procured from the ballast bags used when the F.E.s were flown without a passenger. There were great competitions in exterminating the frogs in the ponds near the aerodrome, which made an awful noise at night time. On one occasion Lanoe and Clifton stalked an unpopular officer when washing in his rubber bath and made quite fair shooting at the running target.

Another of their light-hearted activities took place when bad

weather made flying impossible. During a "dud" day they
went off together in a tender and penetrated behind the Belgian
lines, using quite illegal passes, with the object of buying a cask
of beer in Roosbrugge. They were much gratified when their
request was answered by the publican, "Oui, mon Capitaine,
voulez-vous le Bass stout ou le Bass Burton?" Needless to say
they purchased both casks and returned to the Mess in triumph.

The Bristol Scout was ready on the 7th and Lanoe took it up
for a 'test', and test it he did by diving on a German aeroplane
flying low over its own lines in self-supposed security. The
enemy spun down out of sight.

> "8.6.15.
> My little beast is a beauty and no mistake. Was up twice
> this morning and worried a German each time but they don't
> wait as a rule.
> However, it is an art that requires practice and I hope to get
> proficient soon."

At noon a thunderstorm flooded the aerodrome and flying
was not possible till the 12th when Lanoe met and attacked an
Aviatic, but without decisive results.

> "13.6.15.
> I have badly frightened one or two Boches but have not yet
> had the luck to knock them out I'm afraid. It's quite exciting
> diving at 120 m.p.h. firing a machine-gun! She is a little
> beauty and climbs like anything, it's like going up in a lift for
> the first thousand—a process which hardly takes a minute!—
> and makes the spectators gape.
> I hope T. may get a battery up this part of the world, in
> which case I think I could easily manage to let him get the
> 21 days gunner's course. Even if he doesn't stick to observing
> it would be a very useful experience and of course a pleasant
> holiday."

But Lanoe was again disappointed; T.'s major approved
neither of holidays in the air, nor of losing the only regular
officer in his command.

> "21.6.15.
> I've frightened several Huns very badly, and the last one
> vanished leaving a huge trail of smoke so perhaps he came to a
> bad end, anyway I expect the bullets buzzed all round him
> as I 'hosed' the machine-gun on him pretty steadily."

Lanoe undertook another activity at this time, which he classified as ' frightfulness '. A persistent north-east wind with ground mist or haze made observation difficult and there was a shortage of hostile machines to attack, but the same wind favoured a quick return from a visit to the German flying school at St. Denis, only five miles from Gontrode. Here Lanoe circled round in his Bristol Scout waiting for a young German pilot to climb above the mist, and he then pounced on him and sent him diving for home with bullets streaking past him. " So good for the morale of the young pilots," Lanoe explained.

In 1915 pilots who flew scouts, and attacked the German machines alternated this work with other duties. Lanoe continued to do the routine work of the squadron, and sometimes did reconnaissances solo in a B.E.2c, sometimes in his Bristol Scout, though he found the latter a difficult machine from which to observe. It was only later in the war that certain pilots were chosen to specialize in fighting, and were relieved of all other duties.

At this time the Second Army issued a circular impressing on our pilots the importance of keeping the German aviators " in a thoroughly well hunted condition ".

Lanoe, as well as other pilots, set about this task, but, to get within effective range, the enemy had to be carefully stalked, for he did not stay and fight, but dived home at the first alarm. In 1915 the Germans had superiority both in the number and quality of their machines and engines, but their airmen lacked enterprise, and lost the opportunity of imposing their superiority upon us. The British scout pilots, of whom Lanoe was the most combative, seized the initiative, and gained a moral ascendency which was retained by our flying service throughout the war.

18

V.C.

In air fighting Lanoe's successes were limited by the equipment at his disposal. No other pilot achieved such success with the machine-gun mounted in this awkward manner. The side-shooting required of Lanoe from his Bristol Scout was too difficult to give him more than a small proportion of confirmed victories in his many combats. Most of his fighting took place over the enemy's lines where confirmation was difficult, especially when the prevailing west wind carried the damaged hostile machines far behind their lines.

There were many very gallant pilots doing excellent work at this time, but it was not till over a year later that we produced efficient aeroplanes, with two machine-guns firing straight ahead, which enabled our more outstanding fighters to achieve their fame.

Lanoe's offensive patrols in the Bristol Scout were fitted in between reconnaissances and other routine work of the squadron. Yet with these limitations of equipment and opportunity he set a standard of aggressiveness that endured for all time. His example was followed by British, French and German scout pilots, who later, with better equipment, much more reliable engines and greater opportunities, scored a larger number of victories. With much experience they became more skilled and cunning, and some of them more cautious, choosing their victims so as to reduce their own risks, but none ever exceeded Lanoe in courage and dash. He attacked every hostile aircraft he saw regardless of how it was armed or where it was flying, and by his boldness did much to establish in the enemy's flying service a wholesome respect and fear for our fighting pilots.

Although Lanoe was the outstanding fighter pilot of any nationality in the summer of 1915, he had no liking for war, and longed for it to end. He shot down his opponents because it was his duty to do so, but he was sorry for his victims, and would far rather have seen them fall unharmed in our lines. It was a strange paradox that one so loving and gentle to every creature, as Lanoe always had been, should become, in the hour of his country's need, the most redoubtable air fighter. Yet in his hour of success he still longed for peace.

" 21.6.15.

It's taken England about a year to realize that there is a war on, so I suppose it will take us longer to get tired of it than the others.

I think the chief hope of an early peace is that the Germans will see nothing to be gained by continuing the war and will be all for getting peace soon."

On the 22nd of June he had further encounters which ended in a forced landing south of the Dixmude flooded area, the only occasion in the whole of his flying career when he seriously damaged an aeroplane.

" 23.6.15.

I had bad luck with my new beast yesterday returning from a patrol.

I left the ground and chased two who had the cheek to come right over us! but they turned and made for home at once and I never got near them, so I did a little patrol their side.

One Hun must have got a ' norful ' fright, if nothing worse, climbing peacefully well his side ; I dived at him from in front and opened fire at about 50 yards!

But we passed so quickly that aiming was very difficult and time so short. He vanished in a spiral nose-dive, but then they all do that when frightened and I could not see if he flattened out safely or not.

Another of them saw a couple of shells burst just close to me and shut off his engine and went down at once when about two miles away.

Time being up I started home, and then saw a third on our side again. I thought I had him beautifully, but just as I approached my petrol gave out! and I had to make a forced landing. He saw me being archied and turned back home at once, but I could have intercepted him if I had had my engine.

Hopeless country to land in, just S. of the floods and I took a barbed wire fence and turned upside down! Total damage to me—breeches torn and slight bruise on right leg. Machine hors de combat but damage not vital."

Lanoe telephoned for the tender to bring mechanics to dismantle the machine, whilst he looked on gloomily. He was afraid there might be trouble over this; Bristol Scouts were scarce and were only given to careful pilots. He was sent for by his stern wing commander. He did not know what reception to expect from Col. Burke's rough tongue. Arriving on the aerodrome at Wing H.Q. his punctilious salute was received in silence. Col. Burke led the way to a hangar inside which was a new Bristol Scout, and he was evidently well pleased at the delight Lanoe showed at seeing another of his " beautiful beasts ".

The new scout, No. 1611, was fitted with its Lewis gun and special sights, whilst Lanoe was given four days leave in England. The forced landing had been unavoidable, and neither his squadron nor his wing commanders were inclined to be hard on so keen a pilot. His leave passed like a flash, but even the shortest visit was a joy to those who loved Lanoe, and owing to his temperate habits he had a wonderful power of recuperation.

" 7.7.15.
   I haven't wasted much time since I'm back, having put in over four hours already! All on my new little beast, patrol work.
   Yesterday, starting at 11 a.m. filling a gap and testing my new fittings, as the other squadron had some bad luck with its machines, and today guarding K. of K. though the weather was such—a 60 m.p.h. gale—that I doubt any German coming over and I had a worse chucking about than crossing the Channel in a small boat and what with that and the castor oil felt quite poorly, though by sticking my head in the draught I got enough good air to keep me going for two hours."

The Gnome engine was lubricated with castor oil, which it threw back continuously in an evil-smelling, half-burnt and wholly nauseating spray.

Lord Kitchener inspected the squadron in company with Mr. Asquith, and in consequence of his patrol, Lanoe missed seeing these two contrasting personalities.

On the 8th Lanoe did a strategic reconnaissance north-east of Lille in his Bristol Scout, and, despite the difficulty of observing from this machine, his report is an example of the wealth of detail which he put into this work.

COPY

"RECONNAISSANCE.

| No. 6 Squadron | Bristol Scout 1611. | Capt. Hawker. |
| 8.7.15. | 3.25 to 4.40 p.m. | Map 1/100,000. |

3.50	Commines	2 trains rolling stock N. station.
		1 train rolling stock S. station.
	Houthem	15 transport parked N.W. of village.
	Wervicq	2 trains rolling stock. 3 vehicles approaching from N.E.
3.55	Menin	6 trains rolling stock in N. station.
		4 trains rolling stock in S. station.
		9 barges E. of town.
		20 vehicles M.T. parked.
	Wevelghem	Clear.
	Moorselle	30 small black vehicles* parked, 15 each side of road leading S.
4 p.m.	Courtrai	8 barges.
		30 small black vehicles parked S. of canal.
		Sidings very crowded with rolling stock estimated at 40 trains.
4.10	Ledeghem	Enough for one train rolling stock in station.
		1 train approaching from North.
		8 vehicles moving W. across railway, very similar to small black vehicles reported above, either small M.T. (size of light tender) or more probably two-horsed vehicles.
4.15	Moorslede	Observation interrupted by clouds, but no unusual movement observed in surrounding area.

1 copy 5th Corps.
1 copy II Army.   (signed) L. G. Hawker, observer.
2 copies II Wing.   Capt. R.F.C."

On his return from leave Lanoe had found a "usurper" commanding his flight, and it seemed as if he would have to take over one of the other flights. Very sensibly he had learnt not to allow these minor annoyances to upset him.

"15.7.15.
I have been handing my flight over to a newcomer and taking over 'B' Flight so everything has been unsettled and now we have had the misfortune to lose one of our flight commanders.† so I may go back to my old flight again.

* G.H.Q. suspected these small carts of carrying gas cylinders.

† Captain James, pioneer and chief exponent of wireless telegraphy from aeroplanes, was shot down by Archie.

However, nowadays nothing disturbs me, and I refuse to have any preferences, for I'm sure to be disappointed and get the one I didn't want."

Capt. Strange, Lanoe's especial friend, and an expert in bombing, was posted to England after 11 months service in France, so far a record time at the front for any pilot. As a result Lanoe had to command both ' A ' and ' B ' Flights.

For a few days rain, clouds and strong winds restricted flying, and he took the opportunity of having a new engine fitted to his Bristol Scout. It was ready for action by the 25th, a Sunday. With the new engine Lanoe's scout now climbed well enough to reach the German reconnaissance machines. He spotted two enemy biplanes just behind their own lines, but each time Archie warned them of his approach and though he dived after them with wires screaming and fired a drum at each, he could not get close enough to make sure of hitting them. They fired back at him, and he heard one or two bullets strike his machine close to his head. Half an hour later, with a sudden thrill, he saw a German two-seater behind our own lines, the rare chance which every scout pilot longed for. This time he took every precaution to approach his enemy unseen, so that he should not escape by diving home. Manoeuvring into the sun, his favourite ruse, he dived on his unsuspecting enemy, and held his fire till he was so close that he could not miss. He saw his stream of bullets hitting the German machine which dived down out of control, burst into flames, and turned over throwing out the observer. Lanoe's first feelings were not exultation at his victory, but pity for the fellow aviators who were hurled to this terrible death.

His success was more important than he imagined at the time, for the German observer carried valuable information on him, and this led to our pilots being warned against a similar mistake.

COPY
" COMBAT REPORT No. 93.

No. 6 Squadron.   Bristol Scout 1611.   Lewis Gun.   Capt. Hawker
25.7.15   7 p.m.   Ypres.   10,000   Patrol.

The Bristol attacked two machines behind the lines, one at Passchendaele about 6 p.m. and one over Houthulst Forest about 6.20 p.m. Both machines dived and the Bristol loosed a drum at each at about 400 yards before returning.

The Bristol climbed to 11,000 and about 7 p.m. saw a hostile machine being fired at by anti-aircraft guns at about 10,000 over Hooge. The Bristol approached down-sun and opened fire at about 100 yards range. The hostile machine burst into flames, turned upside down, and crashed E. of Zillebeke.

(Signed) L. G. Hawker, Capt."

" On the body of the dead observer was found a map in which had been pencilled the exact location of one of our batteries that had been firing at the time. On the map, also, were marked the positions of four German batteries. One of these was recognised as a battery (identified by our own artillery as ' Percy ') which had been persistently troublesome and had been searched for in vain by the Flying Corps for some weeks. All three German aeroplanes which Hawker had attacked were armed with machine-guns." (V. II, p. 142.)

No. 20 Anti-Aircraft Section reported that the second machine Lanoe attacked was forced to land behind its own lines. The machine that he set on fire was seen by thousands of our troops to fall 1,000 yards East of Zillebeke.

Copy of telegram to 2nd. Wing R.F.C.
" 25.7.15.
The Army Commander (General Plumer) is very glad to hear of your success this evening and wishes his congratulations to be conveyed to the officer concerned.

2nd Army
9.40 p.m."

The following is quoted from the Air Ministry Short History of No. 6 Squadron :—

" The first hostile machine to be brought down in flames fell fittingly to Capt. Hawker. . . .

As a recognition of his determined attacks on enemy machines culminating in the above mentioned exploit, Captain Hawker was awarded the Victoria Cross, the second to be gained by the Royal Flying Corps and the first for success in Air Combat."

" He had at the time of his award, much distinguished service behind him. On the 19th of April he had made a daring bombing attack on the Zeppelin shed at Gontrode near Ghent, and during the critical days of the Ypres battle he had been responsible for some brilliant reconnaissance work." (V. II, p. 143.)

Lanoe wrote :—

" 1.8.15.
I strafed a Hun, last Sunday, over Ypres on the Bristol.

Opened fire at about 100 yards—I had come on him from behind unawares—and he burst into flames and crashed in our lines.

I felt very sorry for him when he fell in flames, but war is war and they have been *very troublesome of late.*

They go so high now, two miles up, that it is very difficult to get at them, and they've taken to attacking our long reconnaissances, they have a large supply of new and faster machines that, for the moment, beat most of ours in speed and climb."

The new German aeroplanes were all equipped with machine-guns. In this fight Lanoe " collected " several holes in the centre section, near his head and in the top plane.

His form of attack remained ever the same. He saw the enemy, sized up the position quickly, and went straight at him from the most favourable direction, disregarding the bullets that zipped past his head and struck his machine.

The next day Lanoe set out with Clifton and his mechanics to inspect the wreck of the German aeroplane and he recovered the dead pilot's Iron Cross, cracked by the heat. The party had a lively time under rifle fire, and a noisy return passage through Ypres, which was being heavily shelled. For Lanoe the battle line had a strange fascination, and he seemed to delight in going up there, whereas most people were only too glad to keep well away from it, if they could.

He did not know of his award of the V.C. till later, since it took time to settle these matters. This combat was the culmination of much courageous work. In every department of flying he had been outstandingly successful. He had initiated both low flash spotting and low solo reconnaissances, and in each case his fearless example had established a precedent. In air combats he devised the approach down sun, and by his resolute attacks set an example that fitted well the sporting and gallant spirit of the British airmen.

Neither French nor German fighting pilots had come into prominence at this time. Their turn was to come later, each with an equipment superior to the British.

First in many things, Lanoe was the first pilot who, for fighting in the air, was awarded the Victoria Cross.

A list of the airmen who were awarded the V.C. in the 1914/18 War is given in Appendix I.

19

White Feather

IN June, 1915, Antony Fokker, the Dutchman, invented the first synchronizing gear enabling a fixed machine-gun to be fired straight ahead between the revolving blades of the propeller. He fitted this gear to a monoplane with good diving capacity, and in the uniform of a German aviator he flew the machine at the front, but lacking the nerve for fighting he handed it over to Boelcke towards the end of June. Further Fokkers were sent to the front, one of which was flown by Immelmann. The Germans also brought out large fighting machines with movable machine-guns. With this improved equipment they attacked our reconnaissance and bombing machines with considerable success.

On the 31st of July Col. Brook-Popham wrote :—

> " The German aeroplanes are becoming far more active and are making a regular habit of attacking our machines when on reconnaissance and we are having to fight for all our information."

There was a risk that the German airmen might establish an ascendency over our pilots, and this could only be countered by hard fighting. Lanoe's unhesitating attacks on every hostile machine he saw went far to preventing the enemy from gaining confidence in the superiority of his equipment, and was an ideal example to our pilots.

In consequence of the German attacks we were compelled to escort our reconnaissance machines, which reduced the effective work of the R.F.C. Lanoe solved the problem for his flights (he was commanding both ' A ' and ' B ') by carrying out the strategic reconnaissances in his Bristol Scout, which could out-manoeuvre the hostile machines. He also handled the F.E. so well that it was able to hold its own with any German aeroplane, and he had several successful combats in this machine. The observer was armed with two Lewis guns linked together, and Lanoe supplemented his fire with a rifle. The weakness of this machine, like all pushers, lay in its defencelessness against attack from behind.

The performance of the Bristol Scout was limited by the unreliability of the Gnome engine, and, in a combat on the 31st of July, Lanoe could not get above 11,500 feet, though the tanks were nearly empty. In 1915 it was seldom if ever that the machine attained the performance given in the statistical table, but Lanoe urged his mechanics to give the engine the greatest attention, and by his keenness got the utmost out of the Bristol Scout.

One of the disadvantages from which our pilots suffered was the frequent jamming of the Lewis gun at the critical moment, and Lanoe was to endure several exasperating experiences of this kind.

"6.8.15.   Friday.

They have huge machines now, and they do give us trouble —they are certainly far more upish these days, and have been actually known to *attack* us more than once!

I think they made a determined attempt to obtain the mastery, and in consequence we have had several casualties but we've come up to scratch all right. We hear they have 'wind up' and my last letter shows they haven't had it all their own way.

On the 31st I got beautifully over one, but my gun jammed and though I frightened him I didn't get him.

Last Monday in an F.E. on our way home we came up behind a couple ranging. Left No. 1 diving steeply after 140 rounds, attacked and chased No. 2 well home till we got too low over their lines—5,000—and later attacked a third, who made off at once into clouds.

We since heard No. 1 landed just behind their trenches (confirmed by the King's Own Regiment) so evidently we at least did in his engine—unluckily there was a strong wind in his favour.

They are all armed with machine-guns now, of course, and don't hesitate to use them.

Further south I believe they are giving the French an awful lot of trouble."

Another activity which Lanoe initiated at this time was the co-operation with our artillery in rendering their battery positions inconspicuous from the air. He started this work on the battery position built by T. near Bois Grenier, took a photograph of it, and made some useful suggestions. When these had been carried out Lanoe pronounced the position successfully camouflaged. In October the Germans undertook a destructive shoot for two hours on the battery with aeroplane observation, but not one shell fell on the real position.

On the 9th of August the 6th Division made an attack at Hooge during which, to reduce hostile shelling, No. 6 Squadron kept a wireless machine over the lines to range our guns on to active German batteries. Lanoe was given the task of protecting this wireless machine, and managed to get into position close behind a German scout, which was about to attack it, but again his machine-gun jammed, and to his exasperation and disappointment his enemy escaped.

On the 11th of August T., without knowing that he was watching Lanoe, had the good fortune to witness one of his combats in an F.E. From his observation post, with the aid of a powerful Voigtlander telescope—a valuable gift to the army from some patriotic sportsman—he saw an F.E. over Lille being heavily shelled by salvoes of eight Archies. Suddenly from amongst the stale smoke of these shells a small monoplane dived to attack the F.E. from behind. Would our pilot see the enemy in time? It was an anxious moment, but the answer came at once. The F.E. seemed to tilt right up and pivot round on one wing-tip till it faced the Fokker, for such the hostile aircraft turned out to be, and then flew straight at it.

To avoid a collision the Fokker turned aside, and passed close in front of the F.E. Then its dive became vertical, and down it went with a queer flicking motion, down, down, down, out of sight. Up came the telescope to watch the F.E. returning to our lines, cleverly anticipating Archie's fire, which it avoided.

T. reported the enemy aeroplane shot down, and sent a description of the fight to Lanoe, who recognized it as one of his many combats that day. It was his first encounter with a Fokker, possibly the first Fokker shot down, and he owed his escape from almost certain destruction to his unfailing vigilance.

COPY

"COMBAT REPORT No. 13.

No. 6 Squadron.   F.E. 4227.   Double Lewis Gun and rifle.
Pilot : Capt. Hawker.   Observer : Lt. Clifton.

11.8.15.

6 to 6.45, then 7.15 p.m.   Reconnaissance.   Houthem-Zonnebeke at 8 to 7,000.   Later Lille-Roubaix at 9,000.

I.   The F.E. met, attacked and drove off an Albatros over Houthem.

II.   It was then attacked by two Halberstadt Scouts and an Albatros over Polygon Wood.   Luckily they did not all come within range at the same moment.   After a fight lasting about 20 mins. they all retired.

III.   The F.E. then attacked an Aviatic over Houthem and left it in a nose-dive.

IV.   This left only one and a quarter drums of ammunition. Between Lille and Roubaix at 9,000 feet the F.E. was attacked by a very fast scout monoplane which tried to get behind the F.E.   I turned the F.E. very sharp and succeeded in facing it. The scout crossed about 50 yards in front, firing at us.   The F.E. kept head on to the scout, which suddenly nose dived absolutely vertically for about 4,000 feet and then seemed to flatten out a bit.

Note Ammunition used :—Lewis guns 360 rounds.
                    Rifle   20 rounds.

(Signed) L. G. Hawker,
         Capt. No. 6 Squadron."

Twenty minutes is a long time to carry on a fight in the air, and it says much for Lanoe's handling of the aeroplane and his rifle, and Clifton's use of the Lewis guns that they were able to prevent the Germans from carrying out a concerted attack which must have succeeded.

The 12th Division reported the fall east of St. Yves of the Aviatic figuring in Lanoe's third combat and the 8th Division reported the fall of the Fokker in its Intelligence Summary, popularly referred to as " Comic Cuts ".

A few days later the 8th Division was holding its annual horse show when Lanoe and Clifton arrived by car to claim the Fokker.   T. was delighted at seeing Lanoe and meeting his observer, and learning that it was they who had shot down this machine.   Lanoe rode T.'s charger with complete confidence,

but Clifton declined the loan of a horse in spite of its armchair
qualities on the plea that he was unwilling to trust himself to
something " not under proper control " !

" 16.8.15.
    I enclose a letter from T. giving an interesting description
of my last fight which he luckily witnessed.
    It was our 4th scrap that flight. We ran into a host of them
just as we crossed the lines and driving one off, had a scrap
with three of them for twenty minutes, and then a few
minutes later attacked a fifth, an Aviatic which we hear came
down.
    T.'s was much later down south. We had little ammunition
left, but he came close and both guns shot well. It was a very
fast little monoplane scout—one man up—and it tried to get
behind us, but I got the old beast round very quickly, nose
at him, and my observer got in some steady shooting at fifty
yards only.
    He suddenly turned nose straight down and fell away at a
terrific speed. So we hope he is done for. We got a statement
from T. to send to Hqrs.; we've claimed him as sunk, this
making my 5th !
    What bad weather we have been having lately.
    P.S. I went and saw T. and chased him to a horse-show.
Saw him jump, later he took 3rd prize for officer's chargers,
much to his own surprise I think. Very nice little outing for
us."

Here is Clifton's description of this " nice little outing ".

    " We were rather lucky to get it (the Fokker) as we had not
seen any Hun monoplanes, and when it appeared about 1,000
feet above us, we both thought it was one of No. 1's Moranes
from Bailleul, until he started shooting, [when] Lanoe kept
us in as steep a turn as the F.E. could manage with the other
going round on the outside. He got fed up and straightened
out, by luck right in front of us and even I couldn't miss him.
    The earlier one that day I think must have been very close
to getting us, as it was the only time I have actually heard the
bullets go past, they sounded just in front of my face."
    " I well remember the abuse we had to stomach following
the confirmation of the Fokker we got over Lille, when it
transpired that this came from T., obviously a family ramp."

Lanoe drew up a table of his combats covering his last three
weeks flying.

" 3 weeks.

Sunday, July 25th to Saturday, August 14th.

July 25th Bristol Scout solo	1 attacked and brought down at Passchendaele. 1 attacked and put to flight over Houthulst. 1 attacked and crashed in flames at Ypres.	1 1
July 31 Bristol Scout solo	1 attacked but gun jammed completely.	1 defeat
Aug. 2 F.E. Plane Lt. Payne	2 attacked and brought down at Wulingham.	1
Aug. 9 Bristol Scout solo	1 attacked and put to flight over Langemarck. 1 attacked gun jammed temporary defeat but eventually kept off.	
Aug. 11 F.E. Plane Lt. Clifton	1 attacked and put to flight over Houthem. 3 attacked *us* but successfully driven off. 1 attacked and brought down at Houthem. 1 attacked *us* and crashed over Lille.	 1 1

In 12 flights out of 15 reconnaissances or patrols	German machines were encountered	In 12 fights that resulted	15 hostile machines were engaged of which 5 brought down and 9 put to flight.

L.G.H."

At this time Lanoe was completely overworked. It will be remembered that ' C ' Flight was employed on ranging our guns by wireless, so that all reconnaissance work was allotted to ' A ' and ' B ' Flights, both of which he commanded till about this time, carrying out himself the more distant reconnaissances. His patrols included some at dawn in an attempt to intercept raiding Zeppelins. He experimented with the dropping of

Major Lanoe George Hawker, V.C., D.S.O.
Royal Engineers and Royal Flying Corps.

Lanoe's father, Lieut. H.C. Hawker, R.N.

Lanoe and his younger brother.

Happy times at Cricklewood.

Their sister, Sally, joined them at Geneva.

At Geneva.
Lanoe, aged 10.

Hawkins, Hargreaves and Jolly Old
Hawker at "Pop".

Homecroft, Longparish.

Naval Cadet,
L.G. Hawker.

Corporal L.G. Hawker,
Gentleman Cadet.

2nd Lieut. L.G. Hawker,
Royal Engineers.

He held himself very straight on parade.
Lanoe: Front, centre.

With McDonald at St. Omer.

Mr Barber's "Valkyries" at Hendon.

Leaning a hard clean life. From left to right:
Ian Gourlay, Gordon Bayly, Lanoe.

Lieut. Gordon Bayly, Royal Engineers
and Royal Flying Corps.

"D" Flight, Central Flying School,
September 1914. From left to right: R.C.G.
Carpenter (K), L.G. Hawker (K), J.B.B.
Leighton (K), A.R. Arnold, E.P. Graves (K),
Gresley R.N.R., J.E. Tennant, Landon.

Lanoe's Henry Farman on the Ostende
race-course.

"'B' stands for Bomb in
which hawker delights."

"All that was left of my first machine – the
Henry I flew the Channel in."

"He found a bullet embedded in one of the rubber joints."

"I'm having a horrid dull time."

"The precautions we take against cold."

Over the Ypres salient his Be2c was under constant shell fire.

Escadrille Maurice Farman 33 and some officers of No. 6 Squadron R.F.C. at Poperinghe. From left to right. Back Row: (3rd) Awcock, (5th) Clarke, (7th) Hawker, (8th) Kinnear, (11th) Hawkins, (12th) Hargreaves. Second Row: (2nd) Bovill, (3rd) Capt. Bordage, (4th) James. In Front: Vachell.

Hawker, Kinnear and Adamson at Bailleul.

He was afraid there might be trouble over this.

No. 6 Squadron at Abeele.
(*Imperial War Museum*)

Tidmarsh, wearing "The Fug Boots" had a narrow escape when a shell passed through the nacelle of his DH2.

He designed a simple and practical gun mounting.

Hawker's Squadron at Bertangles in 1916. Note the circle in front of the centre shed and "The Boche" well away from the sheds. (*Imperial War Museum*)

De Havilland 2 Scout single seater fighter, pusher biplane. 100 h.p. Gnome Monosoupape, rotary engine. (*Imperial War Museum*)

No. 24 Squadron Mess at Bertangles aerodrome. A fine example of Middle B.E.F. (1916) architecture – plain but practical.

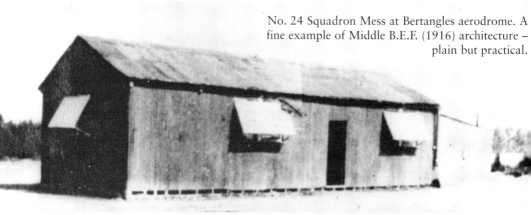

Lerwill's aileron control snapped and, with engine off, he spun slowly into the ground. From left to right: Ker, Sibley, Hughes-Chamberlain, Lerwill, Manfield, Cowan.

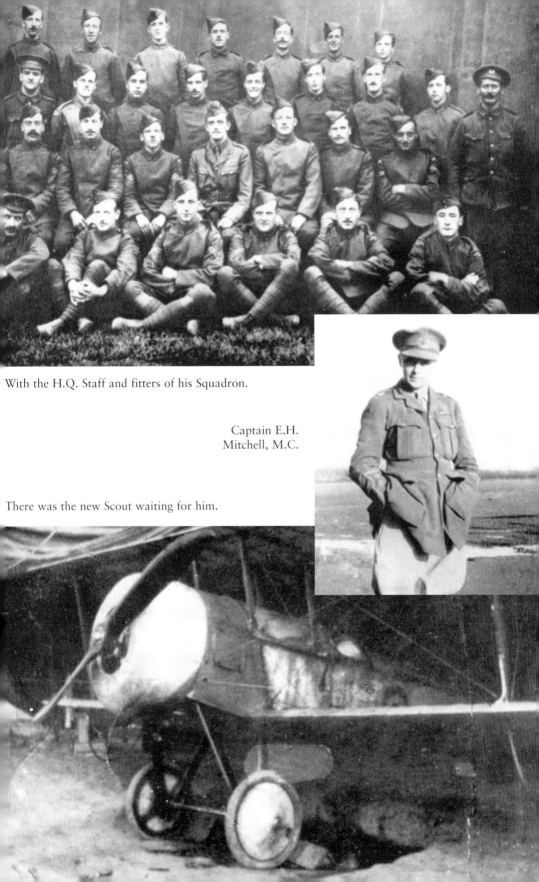

With the H.Q. Staff and fitters of his Squadron.

Captain E.H.
Mitchell, M.C.

There was the new Scout waiting for him.

Fokker E III Scout single seater, tractor monoplane. 160 h.p.
Oberursel engine. (*Imperial War Museum*)

Hawker's Squadron ready for the Battle of the Somme.

The "Rocking Fuselage". Ker watching
Hughes-Chamberlain at practice.

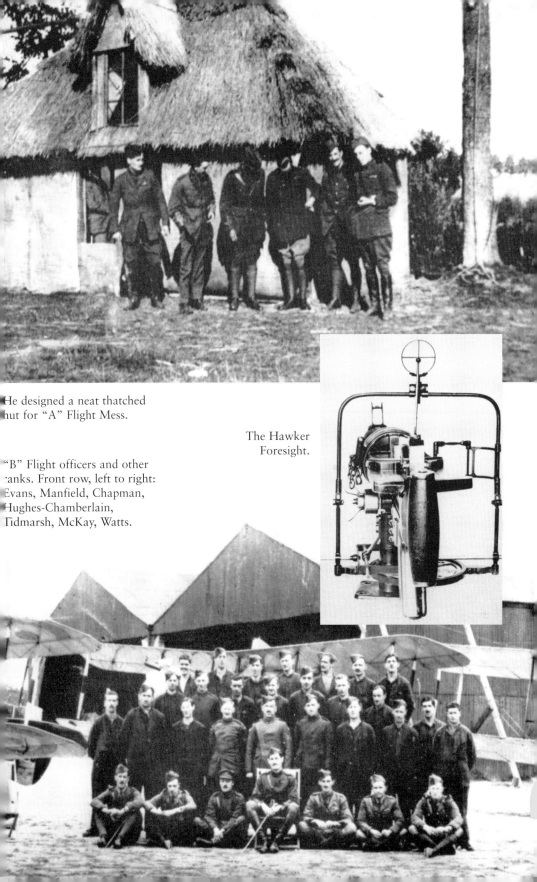

He designed a neat thatched
hut for "A" Flight Mess.

The Hawker
Foresight.

"B" Flight officers and other
ranks. Front row, left to right:
Evans, Manfield, Chapman,
Hughes-Chamberlain,
Tidmarsh, McKay, Watts.

The B.E. 12's
destroyed by a gale.

The Albatross D.II.

Resting between patrols.
Left to right, Back Row: Cowan.
Hughes-Chamberlain, Morgan.
Front Row: Ker, Andrews, Manfield.

Lieut. D. Wilson, M.C.

The Last Man Home. Bertangles
Aerodrome in 1916, with the village in
the background. (*Reproduced by kind
permission of Sir Robert Saundby*)

He was buried beside his fallen machine.
(The cross over his grave can be seen behind the wreck.)

HE whom this scroll commemorates was numbered among those who, at the call of King and Country, left all that was dear to them, endured hardness, faced danger, and finally passed out of the sight of men by the path of duty and self-sacrifice, giving up their own lives that others might live in freedom. Let those who come after see to it that his name be not forgotten.

Mjr. Lanoe George Hawker 'V.C.', 'D.S.'
Royal Engineers & Royal Flying Corps

The Air Services Memorial at Arras.

The waterlogged shell-holes near Luisenhof Farm, where Lanoe fell. (*Imperial War Museum*)

They shall not grow old, as we that are left grow old; Age shall not weary them, nor the years condemn. At the going down of the sun and in the morning, We will remember them. We will remember them.

Capt. J.O. Andrews, D.S.O., M.C.

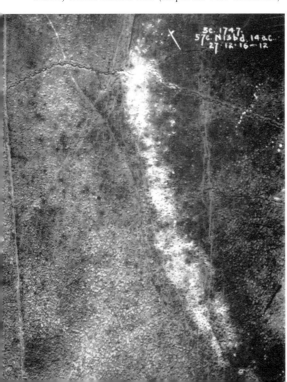

incendiary darts and bombs on the enemy's observation balloons.

When James was killed the squadron's private scheme for co-operation with the artillery was ordered to be withdrawn as irregular, and Lanoe worked out a fresh scheme for the use of all squadrons. The gunnery he had learnt at Woolwich was essential for this purpose. As usual he was responsible for the improvements to the aerodrome, and in this connection designed and had built a thatched hut for 'A' Flight's mess. He was constantly working on improvements to the equipment, gun mountings and sights. He was occupied with the intricate calculations of an important invention. He was called upon to give his considered opinion on questions of air fighting, aiming allowances and similar matters.

Lanoe was showing signs of the strain; he looked thin and tired with dark rings round his eyes. It was impossible for anyone to work at such high pressure for any lengthy period. He was saved from collapse by a timely spell of leave.

He had arranged for Mrs. Bayly and Beatrice, who were on a walking tour, to spend a few days with his sister, Sally, at Pinhoe. They foregathered there and went down to Exmouth for a picnic on the sands. It was a very happy time, and after supper they sat on the beach whilst Lanoe, who had found an old spade, dug sand castles. It was a beautiful, peaceful evening of the kind when the sea and the sky merge together. Protected by the channel, it was no wonder that England could not conceive the brutality of the fighting now raging on the continent, and to Lanoe it seemed worth any sacrifice to keep the war away from the country and the dear ones he loved so deeply.

The following morning he was sharing the newspaper with Beatrice when she saw his name in print. It took her some minutes to understand that it was the announcement of his award of the V.C. It was news to Lanoe.

On the occasion of his receiving the D.S.O. the newspapers had discovered copy of interest in Lanoe's antecedents, and now came out in huge headlines of " The Fighting Hawkers ", with his portrait filling a whole page. Some of the correspondents detected a Nelson touch in the directness of Lanoe's attacks. However flattering these articles might be, he was in no doubt that such publicity was prejudicial to the career of a junior officer, but he was powerless to prevent it.

A few days later, when Lanoe was shopping in Exeter, an incident occurred which appealed particularly to his sense of humour; he was wearing mufti when a foolish woman presented him with a white feather. He accepted it politely, kept it to show his friends as a treasured trophy, and refrained from informing the poor creature who presented it of the ludicrous mistake she had made.

One of the penalties of his fame was a flood of letters from well-wishers and autograph hunters. Lanoe was tired enough without having this extra work thrust upon him, but he courteously answered them all.

A much more agreeable incident occurred when Lanoe was invited, as guest of honour, to a party given by a home stationed Squadron. To entertain the guests, this Squadron also invited some celebrated singers who were accompanied by a distinguished pianist. After they had performed to loud applause, one of the hosts asked Lanoe if he could sing. " I know one song," he said modestly. The accompanist offered his services and was obviously put out when Lanoe said, " Thank you, but I prefer to accompany myself ". He then sang his own parody of " Gaily the Troubadour " which he changed to " Gaily the Aviator ". Not only was he, as usual, well off the note, but his accompaniment was discordant and his performance could hardly be classed as musical. Nevertheless it was a smashing success and brought the house down. The accompanist, who laughed till he nearly fell off his chair, was heard to say that Lanoe was quite right to accompany himself as no professional pianist could ever hope to do it as well.

Unfortunately the strain of nearly a year's active service on the western front could not be repaired in a few days of rest at home. On the 28th of August he flew back to France in a new machine. His leave had been a very happy one and though he said little he felt he was winning a place in Beatrice's heart.

" 3.9.15.

Many thanks for all your letters, they have been of the greatest help.

It is almost impossible to write about the ' deep things ' as no words can adequately express emotions we don't quite understand. They belong to the sub-conscious mind, the soul, and are best transmitted by telepathy, and this we do unconsciously. If you want to help that way, don't try and write, it is so easily done by prayer.

I was tired that day in the train and perhaps exaggerated, but I had noticed a tendency to selfishness in small things and had decided to put a check on it.

I am not quite as well as I should like, and if I don't get better soon I shall apply for a home job. Only I am very keen on completing a full year out here, a thing no one else has done.

This weather is very trying, rain and cold, everyone is going sick through chills.

This must be a short letter as I am tired of writing, I have had so many to answer."

To those, who knew Lanoe, this suggestion of selfishness, even in small things, appeared to be fantastic. At this moment of his triumph he made light of his own achievements, and extolled the modest deeds of others.

When asked how he won the V.C. he would give an amusing and probably coloured account of an actual experience that had occurred about this time. He was about to take off in his aeroplane, when he discovered that he had left his map in the office and, leaving the engine ticking over, he ran back to fetch it. The telephone was buzzing, and as no one else was there to answer it, he picked up the receiver and found, to his surprise, that he had been put through to the General, who was complaining that his headquarters were being shelled and that he wished an aeroplane to go up at once and spot the offending German battery. In a great hurry, as he had left the engine running, Lanoe said, " Yes, Sir," put the receiver down without ringing off, raced to his aeroplane, took off and flew low over our lines, spotted the battery firing, which was one he had previously marked down, landed at once, ran to the office with the idea of reporting its position to our counter-batteries for immediate treatment.

When he picked up the telephone, he found to his surprise that the General was still complaining and he was able to reply with the exact locality of the offender, which pleased the General so much that he recommended him for the V.C.

Although this tale may have been somewhat exaggerated, it went down well with pilots who, too frequently for their liking, had been requested by the General Staff to go up at once and stop enemy shelling which disturbed their quiet routine.

" 7.7.15.

I find I am very busy as usual; two F.E. pilots on leave, one sick and one missing, which leaves me as the only pilot for these machines. Quite a lot of work, and yesterday I was out three times. First taking photos, then fetching a new machine from headquarters and then a patrol. However, the weather is reasonable and that has made me feel ever so much better.

I've been at it again strafed a boche this morning in my scout, caught him napping at 9,000 feet, got up to 50 yards without his knowing I was there, and opened with the machine-gun.

He was seen by an aeroplane, our Archie gunner and a whole division to crash in their lines just opposite our trenches, much jubilation and more congratulations.

A swift revenge as they got one of our machines day before yesterday, brought down by shell-fire in their lines, ' B ' Flight Commander and his best observer [Capt. Adamson and Lieut. Bradyll] both excellent fellows and a great loss to the squadron.

I'm feeling more chirpy today, I suppose the strafed Hun has bucked me up, poor beggar, but I think I shot him dead on the spot as the machine went down like a stone, a single-seater scout, so no unfortunate observer to throw out like the Ypres one.

However, such is war. I will try and get the telegram of congratulations sent to the squadron. [Instead of to himself personally.]

Our new flight commander turned up today, so they have not kept us waiting like before. He has just been up in the F.E. plane for the first time and damaged it landing. Fortunately not seriously."

Copy of message

" Army Telegraphs ECO. 7.9.15. 2.0 p.m.

To 6th Squadron R.F.C.

Congratulations and thanks from units of the 18th Infantry Brigade for your prompt and most successful action against the German aeroplanes this morning.

18th Infantry Brigade."

" To O.C. 2nd Wing.

I should very much like to keep this message if you have no objection; could you please return?

(signed) L. G. Hawker."

"To Captain Hawker.
Herewith.
My best congratulations.
(signed) J. M. Salmond, Lt. Col.
7.9.15."

Lanoe valued highly the congratulations of the infantry. They were doing the heavy fighting, and to help them in any way, or to cheer them up gave him great satisfaction. He frequently expressed his admiration for their courage and fortitude. He kept and treasured their generous message.

" 18.9.15.
I have been feeling ever so much happier and more cheerful lately. I have been very busy—apart from flying and looking after my flight—on a scheme for reorganising our co-operation with artillery—so time has slipped by and it will be my turn for leave again soon! "

On account of the expansion of the R.F.C. Lanoe was due for promotion to command a squadron. Well aware of his capability for such a post, and hoping that it would give him a complete rest, Major Shephard recommended him for the command of a squadron in England. We shall see later what rest Lanoe was given. He was posted to home establishment on the 20th of September.

He was the last of the original pilots of No. 6 Squadron, who crossed the channel in October, 1914. He had completed a year all but 17 days of active service, a record for a pilot. Though he left No. 6 Squadron and his Bristol Scout with regret, he realized that he had reached the limit of his strength and endurance. No other pilot had put in such continuous, strenuous and nerve-wracking work.

No. 6 Squadron had been fortunate in its officers. James, the wireless expert, Strange the bombing enthusiast, Lanoe the fighter, a gay and keen lot of pilots and observers, commanded and encouraged by Gordon Shephard who inspired their enthusiasm, they made up a happy and notably efficient squadron.

Fortune had smiled on Lanoe this first year of the war, for, without her favour, when taking such risks, none could expect to survive for long; but if to be brave is to earn that favour, he had certainly deserved it.

Into that year he had crowded a variety of duties, enterprises, exploits, schemes and adventures, including piloting several types of aircraft, observing, ranging, photographing, trick flying, flash-spotting, bombing, reconnaissances—many of them solo—fighting, improving the aerodromes, working out schemes for co-operation with the artillery, designing hangars, sheds, gun brackets and sights.

With all these capabilities he was modest, kind and cheerful, loved and looked up to by his men and his brother officers. All were sorry to see the departure of Jolly Old Hawker.

PART III

HAWKER'S SQUADRON

20

Early Days at Hounslow

ON arrival in England, Lanoe spent seven days leave in Weymouth, where the family had now moved, but his active and ingenious brain was never at rest. His dentist, Mr. Prideaux, showed him a patent clip for quickly reloading a revolver. Lanoe suggested that a machine-gun belt would be more up to date, and this remarkably ingenious little man set about making a metal belt. On several occasions Lanoe gave him help and encouragement till finally, in spite of official difficulties, he produced the " Prideaux Disintegrating Belt ", hundreds of thousands of which were used by the allies. Alas! he was unable to obtain payment for his invention, and died a ruined and disillusioned man.

On the 28th of September, 1915, Lanoe was ordered to take over the command of No. 24 Squadron of the 5th Wing, stationed at Hounslow. This squadron had been formed on the 1st of September from the supernumeraries of No. 17 Squadron, and consisted of one officer, four N.C.O.s and eighty men. It expanded rapidly as both personnel and machines of various types were posted to it.

The duties of the squadron commander were numerous and varied, and at the beginning Lanoe had not a single officer in the squadron to whom he could delegate a task and feel confident that it would be carried out without his personal supervision.

" Sat. 2.10.15. R.F.C. Hounslow.

There is a lot to do here, not so much continuous work, as small points to be decided.

I have no flight commanders, so have to arrange everything myself. So I could not get away till late this afternoon and have to put in an appearance tomorrow morning.

I have now got *six* machines, but only one of them is in flying order and *it is* scarcely fit to fly, I am told.

However, three of them are on the point of being ready so I ought to be going well by Monday."

The following is a list of some of the work Lanoe was called upon to undertake : —

(1) Organise the personnel into flights with proper routine and administration.

(2) Receive and test a miscellany of aeroplanes, see to their repair and overhaul and allot them to their most suitable tasks.

(3) Test and train a number of young officers (pupils) on Curtiss and Henry Farman machines to re-inforce squadrons overseas or to complete the establishment of squadrons about to proceed overseas.

(4) Improve the aerodrome, especially as regards roads and erect quarters for officers and men.

(5) Train instructors for night flying on Avro and B.E.2c machines so that they could in turn train other pilots for action against raiding Zeppelins.

In this connection No. 24 Squadron maintained and manned the earliest night flying stations at Wimbledon, Sutton's Farm, and Hainault Farm, all of which had to be visited frequently, especially at night time.

After spending a few days at Gosport advising on the training of pilots there, Lanoe returned to Hounslow and set about his tasks with great energy and thoroughness. Unfortunately he was still tired from a year's strenuous service at the front, as can be seen from a photograph taken of him when he attended an investiture on the 5th of October.

His Majesty was pleased to congratulate him, and noticed that he was due to be invested with both the V.C. and the D.S.O., which were not pinned on at the same time, but successively. The ceremony had no terrors for Lanoe, who appreciated especially the knowledgable interest which His Majesty took in him.

" 7.10.15.

A rather amusing experience as I had to trot round twice.

Many people say they would rather face shell fire than an ordeal like that, but personally I think an investiture far more safe and pleasant."

Home on a week's leave, T. called at Hounslow, and was duly given his first joy-ride. The sensation of being free from the heavy clutch of this earth filled his soul with delirious joy, but the experience turned out to be a bitter one, for, though the son of a naval officer, he turned out to be the world's worst sailor, and only escaped sickness by a hasty landing.

"I took him up for a joy-ride which he liked immensely though his 'little Mary' did not."

Besides the tasks allotted to him, Lanoe was working on his inventions, and on the 19th of October was asked by the War Office to undertake the supervision of the manufacture of one of them. He was still occupied with this when, in February, 1916, he was posted to France and handed it over to another officer, who completed its tests and put it into production.

As soon as he had settled down at Hounslow, Lanoe arranged a visit to the aerodrome for Beatrice and her mother, followed by a dinner and theatre party to bring together several of his friends and relatives, who happened to be available.

" 14.10.15.
You all take the district railway to Hounslow Barracks where I hope to meet you and show you round the aerodrome.
Then we'll all go back to town and be bombed in a theatre. Do come if the prospect pleases you!"

In a Zeppelin raid on the previous night two bombs had fallen outside the Lyceum and Strand theatres, killing 21 people and injuring 36.

Lanoe was in great form. He took up a machine and put it through its paces, and he showed his guests round the hangars and workshops. Outside on the tarmac stood a small steam roller, having completed its day's task, proudly wearing a notice hung on it by some wag :—

"NOT TO BE FLOWN"

a satirical commentary on some of the lumbering aeroplanes with which the squadron was trying to train its pilots at that time.

Lanoe was asked to show his medals, and produced them with a grin of delight, the beautiful gilt and enamel D.S.O. in a silk-lined case, contrasting with the plain bronze V.C. rattling about in its cardboard box, the latter the most modest in appearance and yet the most coveted of all decorations, since it was the only one of them that could be won solely

" FOR VALOUR ".

In the box, around the V.C., he had tucked his white feather.

" All the same," Lanoe said later with a sigh, " I would have liked an M.C. It has such a pretty ribbon." This remark was perhaps intended to give added value to his brother's modest decoration.

The dinner and theatre party were a great success, and they all enjoyed every minute of it, but there was to be only one more of these parties before Lanoe left for France. In addition to the pressure of work in forming No. 24 Squadron, a newly issued order obliged him to be on duty all night as well as all day, no matter what the weather, on account of the air raids on London.

> " 15.10.15.
>
> It's hard work, as I am forming it [the squadron] from the beginning and running a school at the same time. Orderly dog does keep me trotting about.
>
> Zepps are rather a nuisance as they are remarkably hard to collar, chiefly a matter of seeing them, as they go pretty high, the sky is a wide area to search and they don't advertise their exact locality by headlights, etc."

The execution of Nurse Cavell was announced at this time, and caused widespread horror and indignation. Lanoe never became excited over these acts of " frightfulness ", as he called them. He considered that the Germans were acting according to their idea of right, and it was everyone's duty to do his utmost to see that we did not fall under the domination of a race which showed such deplorable ideas of justice, humanity and chivalry. If possible, he concentrated a little more energy on his task.

One of the difficulties in the R.F.C. was to keep the pilots physically fit. There was no satisfactory means of obtaining enough exercise during the winter. Lanoe went far to solve this problem by running his pilots round the areodrome before breakfast. As he led the pack, none could lag behind for very shame, but though acknowledging the beneficial results, the officers considered that "those early runs were sweats and no mistake."

The officers, now arriving in No. 24 Squadron, had passed a rudimentary pilot's course at a training squadron or the Central Flying School, but few of them had seen service in France. Lanoe's first task was to test their flying ability, and to do this he made each one take him up in a dual control Avro. On one occasion he took up a pupil, who started a turn as soon as he had left the ground, and not approving of this, Lanoe gave the controls a light touch, and put the machine level again. Almost at once the young pilot repeated the turn, and annoyed at this unsafe procedure Lanoe took over the controls, and landed at once so that he could explain the matter clearly. " Don't start turning till you have got height, at least 400 feet. Goodness knows who taught you, but I don't like your style." The pilot gaped at him with astonishment, then pulling himself together said :—" I didn't touch the controls, Sir; I thought you were doing the flying." It was Lanoe's turn to gape; the docile Avro had taken off by itself.

By the middle of October the squadron " possessed " the following machines for training purposes :—

3 Curtiss, 1 Caudron, 3 Avros, 1 Bristol Scout, some Martinsydes, Maurice and Henry Farmans.

There was a shortage of pilots qualified to instruct in flying, and Lanoe had to do most of this work himself. He was very insistent upon his young pilots taking no unnecessary risks. The unique absence of any casualties in the squadron during four months of hard training at Hounslow was the reward for his trouble and care.

21

Strenuous Training

AFTER dark Lanoe visited the night flying stations, which were spread round London.

He flew at night as instructor, also when he thought there might be some chance of meeting a Zeppelin. On account of his reputation as an exceptionally safe pilot there was keen competition to go up as observer with him. The landing lights were primitive, consisting of a few petrol tins filled with cotton waste soaked in kerosene, yet there was no occasion on which Lanoe damaged a machine, and his example and insistence upon extreme care resulted in an exceptional freedom from accidents.

The work was continuously heavy, and no one man could stand the constant strain day and night. On one of the rare occasions on which Lanoe managed to snatch a few hours leave from his endless duties he acted as best man on the 6th of November to his friend of No. 6 Squadron, Captain L. A. Strange, then commanding No. 23 Squadron at Gosport. The photograph taken of Lanoe after the ceremony shows how desperately tired he was, but there seemed no chance of a respite. He had no competent officer at that time to take his place, and as soon as he trained one or two pilots as instructors they were posted to France. The shortage of trained pilots was acute.

Lanoe was always out on the aerodrome to see his machines in, and never failed to encourage his pilots when they did well, sometimes rewarding their better efforts with a few days' leave.

Their duties included fetching and delivering machines, and whilst so employed Sibley,* delivering a Vickers to Thetford in Norfolk, was obliged by fog to land at Hendon, and stay there for several days with the Royal Naval Air Service. The feeling

* For a full list of the officers and other ranks who served in France in No. 24 Squadron, also the Roll of Honour, list of decorations and Summary of combats, see *A History of 24 Squadron,* by Illingworth and Robeson.

between the R.F.C. and the R.N.A.S. at this time left much to
be desired, and Sibley's reception was not what it should have
been. As he was taking off to continue his journey his propeller
broke in half, and he was forced to land at the far end of Hendon
Aerodrome. This time his reception at the R.N.A.S. sheds was
cooler than ever, as they had to send mechanics to wheel the
aeroplane back to the sheds, and there was some doubt as to
whether they would put it inside or not.

This behaviour was quite exceptional, as it was a point of
honour in both services for the officers to show hospitality and
courtesy to each other, and this was all the more so when an
officer of the other service was in difficulties.

Fortunately at the same time as Sibley took off another 24
Squadron pilot had left on his way to Hounslow, and he reported
to Lanoe that he had seen Sibley forced to land. Lanoe flew
at once to Hendon, and after a few words with the naval gentlemen they accorded Sibley a very different reception, and he
" was treated like a lord ". The fact that Lanoe was the son
of a naval officer, and had himself served in the Britannia was
useful to him in establishing good relations with the R.N.A.S.

This is only one example of the personal interest Lanoe took
in his pilots, and they found it hard to imagine any other
commanding officer taking the trouble to fly to another
aerodrome to enquire how a junior pilot was getting on. His
constant concern for their welfare soon gained their complete
confidence, and they quickly came to regard him, not so much
as a C.O., but as their best friend. Nevertheless he could be
strict at the right moment.

In November the work piled on to the unfortunate commander
of No. 24 Squadron became almost unbearable, and he nearly
broke down under the strain. Early in the month the squadron
threw off a supernumerary flight to form No. 27 Squadron. On
the 10th Lanoe was called to the War Office to advise on
straight-ahead fire. Various types of synchronizing gears to
enable the machine-gun to be fired through the propeller were
in the experimental stage, and it was clear that if one could be
made reliable and effective the inefficient pusher-type aeroplane
would be outclassed and superseded by a tractor machine with a
fixed machine-gun firing through the propeller.

" 27.11.15. R.F.C. Hounslow.

I have never been so busy in my life before, heaps and heaps of it. The most annoying thing is that I have been cheated out of my week-ends by now having definite orders to stay here every night after dusk. However, they will have to give me leave soon or I shall collapse.

I am training my one and only flight-commander to do the work while I am away. I am busily fighting a squadron into form, I think fairly successfully. I expect they will want me to throw off a second young squadron soon."

The one and only flight commander saved the situation. He was Captain E. H. Mitchell, M.C., who " took his wings " in February, 1915, and had done excellent work in France in No. 4 Squadron. He was not only a reliable, hard-working and efficient pilot, but a good-looking, jolly and most likeable young fellow. He saw at once that Lanoe was almost dead with over-work, and quickly took over a great deal of the tiresome routine. In consequence Lanoe was able to get away to spend a Sunday afternoon with Beatrice and her mother, but he was too tired to do anything except sleep in an armchair by the fire, completely exhausted. He had now trained several pilots sufficiently for them to teach the others, and so the work in this direction was also lightened, but only just in time.

" 4.12.15.

My flight commander has greatly reduced the pressure of office work, and I am feeling much better in consequence.

But for the month, when I was all by myself, it was really too much and I nearly had to take a week's sick leave. Pleasant as that would be, I cannot afford it as so much happens nowa-days in so short a time.

However, the more the squadron progresses, the better it is, as I am training my people to fend for themselves.

I am very bored with having to stay here every night but now we are training more night pilots I hope to get relieved next week.

I have a fine motor these days, with a special permit to use full headlights, what oh ! "

Lanoe could not get away for a week-end, and even his Sunday afternoon off had to be paid for.

" 14.12.15.

Something always seems to turn up on a week-end. Rather a trying one last time, as my nice arrangements for organizing a certain job were not properly carried out by my officers.

I didn't have time to inspect it myself, and the colonel did. Bit of a rumpus in consequence. However, nothing very serious and I think it has passed off already."

Lanoe gathered his young pilots in the office, and in his quiet, serious way explained to them the magnitude of their crime. They fidgeted uncomfortably; they felt they could have stood more easily a " blasted ticking off ", but Lanoe had no difficulty in excusing them for this lapse, as they were nearly all under twenty years of age, and at the end of his lecture, his bright smile drew them towards him. It was characteristic of him that even when he scolded his officers they ended by liking him the better for it, and they never let the squadron down again.

More officers began to arrive now, including another flight commander, Capt. R. E. A. W. Hughes-Chamberlain, who had been promoted from No. 11 Squadron (Vickers Fighters), for his excellent work in France, and he soon settled down to teaching the other pilots, including night flying. Two other officers who showed great promise at this time were 2nd Lieut. E. A. C. Archer and 2nd Lieut. S. E. Cowan, both of whom were gifted with natural flying ability.

Noel Clifton, who had been Lanoe's observer and gunner in No. 6 Squadron, returned to England at the end of 1915 to " get his wings " (qualify as a pilot) and had been posted to the Royal Naval Air Service Station at Chingford to fly B.E.2c's in an attempt to intercept the raiding Zeppelins. This was considered a tiresome and almost hopeless assignment.

He appealed to Lanoe, who rescued him from this unpopular task, and he became an efficient pilot in No. 24 Squadron, but unfortunately, soon after arrival in France, he was invalided home with severe asthma.

22

The D.H.2

Up to this time no decision had been made on the type of war machine with which to equip No. 24 Squadron. So far all squadrons in France, allied or German, had two-seater general purpose aircraft and, in addition, one or two scouts for fighting. But a crisis had arisen owing to the arrival on the German side of the lines of a large number of single seater Fokker monoplanes, fitted with machine-guns synchronised to fire between the propeller blades, which attacked and too often shot down our reconnaissance and bombing machines. To counter this Fokker scourge it was decided to form scout (single-seater fighter) squadrons, whose task would be to seek out and fight the enemy scouts.

It was natural that Lanoe should be given the command of the first of these scout squadrons; the choice was a happy one and he was happy at having been chosen for the task. It required of him great initiative, inventiveness, forethought and leadership; everything had to be created from the ground upwards; there was no precedent to follow. It was his task to found the traditions of a new tactical unit and he possessed the qualities needed to fulfil this work.

On the 10th of January, 1916, there was great excitement when No. 24 Squadron received its first de Havilland Scout, the D.H.2. This machine was one of a series of pushers, and had its prototype in an aeroplane designed by Captain Geoffrey de Havilland in 1910. It was evolved from the D.H.1 two-seater, and followed the well known lines of the usual pusher type, open fuselage biplane with nacelle thrust well forward giving the pilot a splendid view. It was designed specially to take the 100 h.p. Gnome Monosoupape engine of French design and manufacture. This large engine rotated behind the pilot, carrying the propeller with it. It had a higher power-for-weight ratio than any other engine of that period, but there had not been time to test it properly before putting it into production, and it was unreliable and extravagant in fuel. Instead of a normal induction system, petrol was fed to the engine via a hand-controlled needle-valve. There was thus no throttle to control the speed, and reducing the petrol supply made the mixture too weak to fire. This was a great disadvantage, as the engine had either to run at full revolutions, or be fully cut out by turning off the petrol, or cutting off the ignition by means of a switch, fitted later to the top of the joystick or control lever. In consequence the D.H.2 had three " speeds " only, full speed, " dud " and stop. Owing to primitive design and hasty manufacture, and the fact that No. 24 Squadron was allotted a number of old reconditioned engines, " dud " appeared with monotonous frequency in the log books of the pilots of these machines.

" The first D.H.2 was tested in July, 1915, and was ordered in quantity the following month. The first aeroplane of this contract arrived in France in December, 1915." (V. III, p. 266.)

The D.H.2 gained an evil reputation when it made its first appearance at the front, and was nicknamed the " Spinning Incinerator ". (V. I, p. 427.) The reader will be able to judge for himself whether it deserved such a name. Lanoe imbued his pilots with more respect for it, perhaps more than it deserved, for it was vital that they should have confidence in the machine they had to fly.

Some of the early accidents arose from a failure to appreciate the combined effects of the torque of the propeller and the gyroscopic action of the large rotary engine in a small aeroplane. The machine was liable to get into a spin at the moment when the engine was switched off, and if the pilot instinctively attempted to raise the nose by pulling the joy-stick he accentuated the spin with disastrous results. Lanoe understood the problem perfectly, and impressed upon his pilots the method of getting out of a spin, and how to avoid one when close to the ground. The unhappy fact remained that the spin had been the cause of many fatal accidents in the R.F.C., and was the chief bogey of aviators, who mostly believed that there was little chance of recovering from a bad spin.

The D.H.2 could not be thrown about with the same confidence as later scouts, such as the S.E.5, nor could it be dived steeply with the engine on, and almost any German aeroplane could dive away from it. It was a cold machine to fly in winter owing to the large exposed cockpit, and every pilot remembers this discomfort.

The following figures give for comparison the performances of the D.H.2, the Bristol Scout and the Fokker E.2, which the D.H.2 was later to meet in battle. By the time No. 24 Squadron reached France, the Fokker monoplane was fitted with a 160 h.p. engine and two fixed machine-guns firing through the propeller.

Aeroplane and engine.	Armament	Speed in miles per hour.	Rate of climb and ceiling.
Bristol Scout.* 80 h.p. Gnome (rotary).	1 Lewis gun firing obliquely past the propeller.	89 at 6,500 ft. 86½ at 10,000 ft.	6,500 ft. in 11 mins. 10,000 ft. in 21 mins. 15,000 ft. in 50 mins. Ceiling 15,500 ft.
D.H.2.* 100 h.p. mono-soupape Gnome (rotary).	1 Lewis gun firing forwards.	86 at 6,500 ft. 77 at 10,000 ft.	6,500 ft. in 12 mins. 10,000 ft. in 25 mins. Ceiling 14,000 ft.
Fokker E.2.† 160 h.p. Oberursul 2 rotary engines linked together.	2 machine-guns firing through the propeller.	98 to 105 m.p.h.	10,000 ft. in 15 mins.

* See *War in the Air,* Appendix XXVII.
† See *Max Immelmann—Eagle of Lille,* pp. 128 and 160.

It will be seen that the D.H.2 was inferior in some respects to contemporary machines. It had, however, the great advantages of a splendid view, a clear field of fire for the pilot, who was perched right out in front of the planes, and it was highly manoeuvrable, that is to say it could be made to turn very sharply without losing height. This latter point was a most valuable feature, and later it will be seen that Lanoe attached great importance to his pilots extracting the utmost from it. The inherent aerodynamic inferiority of the pusher, as compared with the tractor aeroplane, was a serious handicap to the performance of the D.H.2.

The armament consisted of one Lewis gun, with five to seven ammunition drums holding 47 rounds each, later increased to 97 rounds each. All going well it took about five seconds to change an empty drum for a full one, during which time the pilot had both hands off the controls and his attention off the fight. The gun was mounted on a universal joint, known to the pilots as the " wobbly mounting ". Apparently the pilot was expected to manoeuvre his aeroplane with one hand, whilst he aimed and fired the gun with the other, an operation which was clearly impracticable.

The D.H.2 was not a machine in which any individual pilot could run up a big score of victories, no matter what his skill or determination, since any German aeroplane could escape by diving, most German machines were faster and could climb quicker and higher, and the single Lewis gun, which gave constant trouble in the early days, was not conducive to reliable, continuous or accurate shooting from its wobbly mounting.

As an example, one of our most successful pilots, Major McCudden,* flew a D.H.2 from the 3rd of August, 1916, to the 23rd of February, 1917, in which time he scored one hostile machine crashed and three forced to land. Practically all of his 58 victories were scored in the S.E.5, a machine greatly superior to the D.H.2.

On the whole the D.H.2 was a good machine for the spring and summer of 1916, and on account of its excellent manoeuvrability was particularly suitable for escort work, where its shortcomings in speed, climb and dive were of less importance.

The navy, which had precedence in all supplies at this time, and exacted it in the supply of aeroplanes, monopolized the output of our best factory, the Sopwith, and almost the whole of the supply of scouts that could be spared by the French from their Nieuport factory, so that the D.H.2 was all that was available to the R.F.C. (V. III, C. IV.) Lanoe, though realizing the defects of his machines, optimistically dwelt on their virtues, and extracted the utmost from them.

---

* Author of *Five Years in the Royal Flying Corps.*

23

The First Scout Squadron

" 15.1.16.

Great day today, I've handed over my out-stations to another man (poor unsuspecting major of a newly-formed squadron near here) and can now turn my full attention on to this squadron. About time too; as I'm supposed to be ready to move by the end of this month.

First new machine arrived t'other day, a beauty, beats my Bristol on speed and climb, but has one or two faults I don't like."

Lanoe, always enthusiastic, undoubtedly over-estimated the speed and climb of the D.H.2. The new machines only arrived slowly, and realizing the inevitable engine trouble, which was their normal lot, the home authorities forbade them to be flown more than just enough (about two hours) for the pilots to be able to take them across the channel on the appointed date. The army staff expected squadrons to arrive according to a promised programme, and the only way of accomplishing this was to reserve the inevitable engine trouble till the aeroplanes reached France. Lanoe and his pilots were no less keen to cross the channel than the home authorities were to get them safely across.

More pilots arrived to make up the establishment to 12, for most of those who had joined in 1915, had either left as reinforcements to other squadrons, or remained to man the night-flying stations. Apart from the flight commanders and one or two officers who had been specially recommended for scout work, the pilots had no previous war service, and were not in any way specially picked, as was done in the French and enemy air services and later in our own. Far from having any grounds for complaint, Lanoe always spoke and wrote of his pilots in the highest terms of praise. The whole squadron, headed by Lanoe, was now all eagerness to reach the front.

" 15.1.16.
I should certainly be in France by March, and glad I'll be to get back again, but remember shell-dodging isn't my job now. I'm strictly forbidden to cross the lines, squadron commanders being (I suppose) too valuable."*

The last few words were intended to be of comfort to his mother. He carefully concealed from her the extent of his risks as far as possible, and made the most of any safeguards.

Lanoe realized that his work as a squadron commander was very different to that of a pilot. Gone were the days when he could light-heartedly fly alone stalking German machines and shooting them down. Far more important was the task set him of producing an efficient fighting unit of 12 well trained pilots, whose duty it would be to maintain a continuous offensive all day against the German air service. His squadron must accomplish far more than could possibly be done by a single pilot, no matter how successful he might be.

At this period of the war many squadron commanders did not fly at all, but this would have been a severe privation to Lanoe. As it was, his flying activities in France were to be limited by the responsibilities of his command, but he could not reconcile himself to staying on the ground, nor could he be restrained from crossing the lines to supervise and join his patrols. He no longer flew as an individual, but as a part of his squadron and solely for its greater efficiency. In this way he participated in the risks of his pilots, and by his fearless example went far to build up the morale of his squadron.

At last the date for crossing the channel was fixed for February the 6th, but owing to a storm was postponed till the 7th, the only snag for Lanoe being that he himself was ordered to cross by boat on the 2nd, for he would far rather have crossed with his pilots and kept an eye on them.

Before leaving, he had one final supper and theatre party on the night of the 31st, to which Beatrice and her mother were invited. He was in the best of form, and the apex of his joy was provided by an air-raid, and the feeling that some other poor devil had taken over from him the onerous responsibilities of the night flying stations.

* The original order had forbidden squadron commanders to fly at all. See *Memoirs of Gordon Shephard* ", p. 204.

"2.2.16.   Southampton.

Just a short line to say I'm off, by boat I regret to say, my aeroplanes follow next Sunday.

I have had such a lot to do, handing over my job to my unfortunate successor, that I've had no time to think of anything else.

I spent the Zep. raid* comfortably in the Gaiety Theatre, "Tonight's the Night". Zeps were no job of mine, as I had been relieved, and it was much too bad a night for aeroplanes to do any good.

I was told to put up my crowns today, but my gazette has not yet appeared."

His promotion to major and squadron commander was published in the daily papers the next day with suitable comments. He had actually been in command of his squadron for over four strenuous months with the pay and rank of a flight commander.

The squadron left Hounslow on the 7th, a wild and blustering morning. Several machines were slightly damaged, but rejoined the squadron within a few days.

The following is a list of the 12 original pilots of No. 24 Squadron who flew across the channel to France :—

" A " Flight.

  Capt. E. H. Mitchell, M.C. (commanding) (specially promoted from No. 4 Squadron).

  2 Lieut. J. O. Andrews (specially recommended for his splendid service in No. 5 Squadron).

  Lieut. E. N. Clifton (who flew as Lanoe's observer in No. 6 Squadron on several occasions).

  2 Lieut. S. E. Cowan (one of the first pilots to join the squadron).

" B " Flight.

  Capt. R. E. A. W. Hughes-Chamberlain (commanding) (specially promoted from No. 11 Squadron).

  2 Lieut. D. M. Tidmarsh.

  2 Lieut. R. H. B. Ker.

  2 Lieut. E. A. Cave.

* This raid was made by nine airships on the Midlands on the night of the 31st of January. The London defence aeroplanes went up on patrol, but failed to locate the airships owing to the thick weather.

" C " Flight.
>2 Lieut. E. A. C. Archer (commanding) (one of the first officers to join the squadron).
>2 Lieut. S. J. Sibley.
>2 Lieut. A. M. Wilkinson.
>2 Lieut. O. Lerwill.

As far as is known the above pilots had no previous war service in the Royal Flying Corps except where mentioned. It would have been difficult to have found a more optimistic and happy lot of young fellows.

Lanoe's good humour was infectious, his friendliness, even intimacy with his pilots off parade gained their affection. His efficiency and capability gained their respect and confidence, and that rare quality called leadership gained their passionate loyalty and enthusiastic *esprit de corps*.

In the whole of the Royal Flying Corps, noted for its jolly messes, there was no keener nor happier unit than Hawker's Squadron.

24

The Fokker Scourge

SINCE Lanoe left France in September, 1915, the position had grown serious. The German airmen were no longer content to allow our machines to fly freely over their lines and bomb their back areas. Mounted in the Fokker monoplane, with a machine-gun synchronized to fire through the sweep of the propeller, two exceptionally enterprising German pilots had taken to attacking our almost defenceless machines when well over the German lines.

Diving steeply on his foe, a manoevre at which the Fokker was particularly fast and steady, Immelmann would hose the British aeroplane with bullets from an angle which precluded retaliation. If the first attempt failed, he zoomed up again, made that quick turn-about which bears his name, and repeated the attack. Boelcke would carefully manoeuvre under the tail of a Farman or B.E.2c and, with unerring aim, shoot it down while himself in perfect safety. These German pilots took the minimum risks, for they easily kept out of the arc of fire of our more cumbersome machines, and only attacked them when well over the German lines. We were soon obliged to send an escort of at least three machines with each reconnaissance, bombing or photographic aeroplane. This checked the losses for the moment, as the German pilots were reluctant to attack under fire, but it led to a serious shrinkage in the effective work of our squadrons. (V. II, p. 156.)

The English Army was expanding rapidly so that it could take over from the hard pressed French Army a fair share of the line. A definite proportion of squadrons to each new army was indissable to the efficient employment of our artillery and the protection of our half-trained troops from the German artillery, which possessed heavier guns and howitzers with a much greater supply of ammunition. During the first half of the war there was no time to give new pilots a complete training, nor could our factories produce an adequate supply of new and efficient aeroplanes. As a result half-trained pilots on obsolete machines fell easy victims to the Fokker Scouts, and swelled the score of the more enterprising German pilots.

The Fokkers created a sensation, and their pilots, encouraged by the success of Boelcke and Immelmann and the rewards showered on these German aces, emulated their tactics, and attacked our slow and heavy reconnaissance and bombing machines whenever they could find them behind the lines and in inferior numbers; to meet the grouping of our aeroplanes the Fokkers attacked in ever increasing strength.

We lost in the winter of 1915 the superior position we had won by hard fighting in the summer. The Fokker predominance became the subject of agitation in England and questions in Parliament. Public opinion favoured the creation of an Air Ministry, but Mr. Asquith's " remedy " was to appoint a new committee which had no power to put an end to the damaging competition between the Royal Flying Corps and the Royal Naval Air Service. (V. III, p. 268.)

Thus the Fokker became a veritable bogey, and though its moral effect outstripped the material damage it inflicted on the R.F.C., the situation was serious. By doubling the power of the Fokker's engine and adding a second machine-gun to its armament the Germans were in possession of the most efficient fighting aeroplane at the beginning of 1916. By grouping the Fokkers in formations they made the work of the R.F.C. more difficult and dangerous, and our casualties grew apace. This alarming position called for an effective counter-measure, which logically was the formation of squadrons of scouts to seek out and fight the Fokkers. So it came about that Lanoe, the leading British fighter pilot at that time, was appointed to command the first of our scout squadrons. He and his pilots were well aware of the paramount importance of putting an end to the Fokker scourge. The more enthusiastic of them felt that this was the most important mission in the war.

Lanoe preached and taught the policy of attack; attack at all times and at all costs. Only by attack could the Fokker be defeated. A scout could not fight except by attacking. He infused the spirit of the offensive into his squadron, and by the time the pilots had crossed the channel they were all eagerness to come to grips with the dreaded Fokkers, and show what Hawker's Squadron could do. But most of them were inexperienced as yet, and all were lacking practice in the D.H.2. Furthermore they were due to pass through a period of major engine trouble and other difficulties, particularly with the Lewis gun and its 'wobbly' mounting. Heartbreaking accidents robbed Lanoe of some of his most promising pilots.

That the squadron never faltered nor lost courage was due to Lanoe's leadership, the spirit which he inspired, and the magnificent response and loyalty of his pilots. They were as " keen as mustard " to make the first fighter squadron of the R.F.C. an outstanding success. In spite of every discouragement and difficulty they were happy and proud to be in Hawker's Squadron.

25

Arrival in France

ALL eyes were on No. 24 Squadron, and its arrival in France was hailed as a great event by the H.Q. Staff, for the machines were erroneously credited with a speed of 100 miles per hour. Their excellent performance in crossing the channel and landing ten machines at St. Omer, followed shortly by the other two, gave a false impression of their reliability, since it was not realized in France that the engines had been deliberately husbanded for the crossing. There was no doubt at all that the engines were a dud lot, and every account of the activities of a D.H.2 squadron is punctuated by constant reference to engine trouble.

As soon as the squadron arrived at St. Omer orders were issued for daily protective patrols between 8 a.m. and 3 p.m. at a height of 14,000 feet, plus two machines ready to take off at three minutes' notice to repel any possible attack on General Headquarters. This gave the pilots time to practice and get used to their new aeroplanes, and the mechanics to get to grips with the troublesome engines.

The weather was bitter, and the pilots suffered severely from cold in the exposed cockpit of the D.H.2. The day after arriving at St. Omer, Archer, returning from a patrol, spun into the ground and was killed. It was thought that his legs were so cold that he could not control the machine. Archer's death was a sad blow to Lanoe and a great loss to his squadron, for he was a bold and skilful pilot, and very popular in the mess. Wilkinson took over command of " C " Flight, and Morgan arrived the next day to fill the vacancy.

Lanoe had realized that the exposed cockpit of the D.H.2 would be cold, and he had designed and ordered special thigh boots, known in the R.F.C. as " fug boots ", but as yet there was only one pair in the squadron. They were one of Lanoe's many successful inventions; the vital need for them was so

139

apparent, and they were so favourably reported on that the War Office took up their manufacture, and they became a standard issue in the R.F.C.

At this time the artillery and reconnaissance squadrons were re-grouped into corps wings, and the fighter squadrons into army wings, a wing of each kind forming a brigade. A special wing was under the direct orders of headquarters, and a brigade was allotted to each army. On the 10th of February No. 24 Squadron came into the 12th Wing which, to Lanoe's joy, was commanded by his erstwhile squadron commander Colonel Shephard, and it flew to Bertangles near Amiens, where it was to spend the rest of the year.

" 13.2.16.
      Funny little village this, so many of the houses have got mud and straw walls, not very permanent."

On the other side of the railway was No. 11 Squadron, B.E.2c's, commanded by Major Hubbard, who had been Lanoe's instructor at the Central Flying School in 1914.

The squadron's activities were, for the time, limited to patrolling behind our lines and practice flights, which were badly needed. The engines gave constant trouble, and from this moment onwards the mechanics worked ceaselessly at all times of the day and night to keep the machines in flying order. They soon found that they had a considerate and sympathetic squadron commander. Lanoe frequently visited them at work, making suggestions and encouraging them in their efforts. He never spoke harshly, and it seemed to them impossible for him to be unkind to anyone. He had meals ready for them when they finished work, or sent to the sheds if they were kept there, and a mechanic who worked into the night could be sure of a good rest in the morning, for Lanoe had him excused early parades. Under such conditions the mechanics worked with a will, and very soon developed an affection for and devotion to Lanoe and a pride in the squadron which contributed greatly to its efficiency. With an engine that was dishearteningly unreliable, only the most devoted and constant hard work could keep the machines airworthy.

As an example of the engine trouble met with, a flight commander's log book shows that in 38 flights made between crossing the channel on the 7th February and the end of March, no less than 17 were attended with engine trouble. Plugs, piston rings, valves, tappets, guides, magnetos, in fact the whole contraption was flimsily designed and hastily made, and most of the engines were already half worn out before they were handed over by the French factory. The fortitude, patience and constant good humour of the mechanics, pilots and above all their commander, who was responsible to H.Q., were remarkable under such trials. In April the engines gave trouble once in every three flights; in May once in four; in June once in three and a half; in July once in four and a half; in August once in seven; in September once in eight; in October once in five; in November once in four. Lanoe sent both officers and mechanics to the French factory at Pontelarge on courses of instruction on the maintenance of the engines.

He kept a keen eye on his pilots and selected for these courses those who were suffering from the intense effort of constant fighting. In this way he combined their training with a most opportune rest without making them feel that their nerves were showing any sign of the strain. As the engines were more skilfully cared for and more frequently overhauled the breakdowns became fewer, but sometimes much more serious. Many of the cylinders had been re-bored. This made the walls thin and weak, especially near the base where they were already pierced with a ring of holes for inlet ports. As a result the cylinders would crack off and fly out, sometimes cutting through the tail booms with fatal results. This trouble was known as " cylindritis ".

" A soldier who has no confidence in his weapons is already half-way to defeat. A pilot who knows that he must mistrust his engine is in equally bad plight because he is aware that when the engine fails, all his qualities, no matter how brilliant, will avail him little." (V. VI, p. 36.)

The courage and fortitude of the pilots was almost incredible in cheerfully flying these machines that threatened to destroy them at any instant through defects in their construction. Added to these troubles the machine-guns, of which each aeroplane only carried one, constantly jammed or jumped out of their mountings at the critical moment, robbing the pilot of his victory, and leaving him at the mercy of his opponent, often far over the lines.

The 13th of February turned out to be a critical day for the squadron. Cave on his way back from a patrol got into a spin, crashed and was killed on the neighbouring aerodrome occupied by No. 11 Squadron. Two of his best pilots, for to Lanoe all his pilots were his best, were killed before a shot had been fired at the enemy. Lanoe, with his ready sympathy, felt their loss acutely. The D.H.2 was living up to its evil reputation.

Major Hubbard sent Lanoe a polite message requesting that, if his pilots wanted to kill themselves, would he please arrange for them to do it on their own aerodrome. Lanoe decided to take the message seriously, and solemnly walked across to No. 11 Squadron mess to apologize, but apologies were drowned in laughter and " vin ordinaire ". It sounds callous, but to dwell on these tragedies in war-time would have seriously affected the morale of the squadron. These were the occasions when courage, cheerfulness and leadership were required. Lanoe never needed them more than at this moment, for his squadron had reached a crisis. When he returned to his own mess, he found a discussion being carried on by some of his pilots as to whether it was really possible to get the D.H.2 out of a spin when once it started. So far it was considered fatal to get the D.H.2 into a spin, and the pilots had taken great pains to avoid it. Some were of opinion that it was not possible to recover, and that the fault lay in the weight of the engine being too near the centre of gravity of the aeroplane; others that the tail surfaces were inadequate and that the machine was a death trap. Listening quietly, Lanoe realised that the fighting value of his squadron was in peril. His was the first squadron of D.H.2s, and there was a possibility of his pilots losing confidence in their machines, in which case the morale of the squadron was gone. " Nothing is so calculated to sap a pilot's morale as a lack of confidence in the flying capabilities of his aeroplane." (V. III, p. 352.)

Without a word Lanoe left the mess and ordered out a machine, climbed to 8,000 feet and deliberately threw it into a spin. If he failed to get it out of the spin . . . but Lanoe never thought of failure. Putting his theories into practice he recovered from the spin without difficulty. He tried again and again, with engine on, with engine off, left spin, right spin. Each time the spin could be cured providing that there was sufficient height in which to recover, and that the pilot kept his head and used the controls correctly. Down Lanoe came to the aerodrome and radiating confidence he walked briskly into the mess. " It's all right, you fellows," he said, " You can get the D.H.2 out of any spin. I have just tried it out."

The pilots gathered eagerly around him, and he carefully explained the correct manoeuvres until they all understood them clearly, but he warned them above everything not to get into a spin near the ground. Out they all went to follow his example It was an anxious moment, for another crash might have shaken irreparably the confidence of his pilots, but all went well. Led by Cowan, the pilots were soon putting the D.H.2 through its paces, and they gained a complete mastery of its tendency to spin.

Cave was buried quietly and, though Lanoe showed a brave face to his squadron, he carried a heavy heart.

" 13.2.16.
After four months of school work at Hounslow without an injury to anyone, we have struck some dreadfully bad luck—one of my lads was killed on Wednesday, and another again to-day, two in a week is really too terrible, and both flying accidents. Two so close together is dreadfully hard—and I am feeling very depressed in consequence. I have such nice keen lads, and it does seem such a pity and it is such a waste, and I have to write to their people as their commanding officer."

These letters conjured up in Lanoe's mind all the agony of those at home when they received the sad news. He, who could never bear to hurt anyone, who was never harsh nor unkind to his men, shrank from the task of causing so much pain.

" It wouldn't be so bad if it was a war casualty, i.e. by shot or shell, but it does seem so hard to lose good fellows by flying accidents.
I am making everyone be very cautious now, so hope to God we will not have any more, so remember me in your prayers and give me your moral support."

The prayers were answered, at least for the time being, the squadron kept its morale high, and the pilots remembered the lessons which Lanoe had taught them. Whilst he was in command of the squadron there was not another casualty from spinning into the ground.

The weather continued to be vile, with three inches of snow

on the ground, and most of the pilots had colds of some sort. To Lanoe's great regret Clifton fell ill and left the squadron. It was nearly a month before he was replaced by Breen. Lanoe first had an internal chill and then a raging cold in the head, which he found depressing.

> " I wonder when the war will stop, if it ever does, and what it will be like when it does."

This was a speculation which troubled us all at one time or another, but Lanoe's depression was always shortlived.

On the 24th of February the squadron provided a protective patrol of four machines during a bombing raid on Cambrai Aerodrome, and this cheered them all up. The patrol was successful and no machines were lost although far over the enemy's lines. Lanoe was soon in good form again.

> " 1.3.16.
> The weather today was a delightful change, sunny and warm . . . and I am now enjoying perfect health again.
> We are having an awful run of bad luck, incessant engine failure, forced landings and broken machines, very uphill work for the squadron, but I hope we will get over all our bad luck in one bunch, and then get a run of really good luck as the weather improves."

The bad weather had made a quagmire of the aerodrome, and the surface outside the sheds had been spread with cinders. Several propellers were split at the tip by sucking up with their draught and striking pieces of cinder. The split spread and soon ruined the propeller, an expensive item. To get over this difficulty, Lanoe had the propeller tips tightly covered with fabric and then doped; the dope caused the fabric to shrink and lie flush with the wood of the propeller. This protection was so successful that it became universally adopted, and even twenty years later wooden propellers were seen strengthened and protected in this manner.

On the 1st of March the squadron left the 12th Wing with the re-grouping due to the arrival of the Fourth Army, preparatory to the battle of the Somme.

> " 1.3.16.
> My colonel out here was my major in No. 6, very pleasant

indeed, unfortunately this has failed to last and today we've changed.

I am not quite so hard worked now, thank you, my job chiefly being to drive others and make them work, not very satisfactory, but I suppose it is the change from executive to command.

I am much amused at the respect I inspire in strange officers, specially subalterns. When I pause to ask the way even captains touch their caps and say " Sir " and some of them look old enough to be my father.

Really a squadron commander in the Flying Corps can be called a " soft job " as far as this war is concerned, jolly good pay and no risk (except from over-eating). But I suppose I can claim to have earned it, and it certainly carries its worries and responsibilities with it. It is rather hard, sometimes, to order people off on what is obviously a very risky job, but I have a great moral advantage in my little bit of ribbon, it comes better from me than from a squadron commander who was never a good flier and perhaps has never seen active service conditions. Actually, nowadays however, I am glad to say most squadron commanders are expert fliers and have seen quite their share of the mill, even colonels know what they are talking about, it is only those higher up still, who unfortunately are chiefly responsible for sending machines out, who have in any way lost touch—or have never been in touch—with modern conditions, and they are influenced considerably by their wing and squadron commanders and so I think the R.F.C. is about to enter on a far more advantageous stage as far as the morale of pilots is concerned."

Senior officers found themselves in a perplexing position. For example, the army staff demanded regular distant reconnaissances, which the R.F.C. considered it a point of honour to carry out, and yet their machines were hardly able to make headway on the return journey against the prevailing westerly winds when these happened to be very strong. The casualties caused by the rigidity of this system seemed unnecessary to the junior officers, who if allowed more freedom, would have chosen days when the weather was less unfavourable, with better results and fewer losses.

Another difficulty lay in the impossibility of senior officers taking part in the flying duties of the squadrons. However, the change which Lanoe saw taking place, where they took into consideration the practical experience of their juniors, gave promise of improvement in a difficult situation.

As to himself, Lanoe determined not to lose touch with the rapidly changing conditions, cost what it might, and alas, in the end, it cost him his life. In the autumn when the German machines improved, and their numbers increased so that the fighting became heavy and our casualties grew, then despite orders not to cross the lines, Lanoe took a more and more active part in his offensive patrols; no squadron commander had a clearer idea than he of the difficulties and dangers under which his pilots flew and fought. This they knew and appreciated; the risks he took through exceptional zeal, they accepted willingly.

It might be supposed from the early part of Lanoe's letter that at this period he did no flying and took no risks. This was not the case. He tested new machines, often joined his own patrols, and boldly threw the D.H.2's about to give his pilots confidence in the strength and manoeuvrability of their machines. One of his experiences shows that this was very far from being without risk, and that he owed his life to his presence of mind and flying skill.

" 6.3.16.
I had rather a nasty experience yesterday : I went out and did a patrol with a little reconnaissance, quite interesting for a change, but on the way back a wire came adrift and went into the propeller.

There was an awful wrench (with a bang like an Archie) which very nearly pulled the machine to pieces in mid-air, and then the propeller broke.

The engine going round all out of balance vibrated the machine so badly that poor me was just like a pea on a drum.

I managed to knock off the petrol enough to make the engine misfire, but till the engine slowed down I was quite helpless and really for a moment things were critical. I didn't know whether the machine was going to collapse or not, but it got better as the engine slowed down, and I managed to make a perfect landing in a convenient field.

But the machine has to go back to the base to be thoroughly overhauled, carefully examined and absolutely rebuilt, and all the damage was done 3,000 feet above Mother Earth.

I am thinking of changing my nickname of Jolly H. to Lucky H.

But I must be careful not to start a habit of boasting about my luck or I will kill it and come to grief. I wish I could pass it on to the squadron as a whole."

26

Many Inventions

MENTION has already been made of two of Lanoe's civil inventions, one of which he patented prematurely, and the other, on which he was working more cautiously and thoroughly before applying for a patent, when the war put an end to this work.

In 1915 he had called several times at the War Office on the subject of one of his inventions which was to revolutionise our defence against raiding aircraft, both in this country and in France, which was to cause the enemy the most serious losses amongst his bombers, and which almost put an end to his raids both by day and by night in clear weather.

It may interest the reader to know firstly, why Lanoe was such a prolific inventor and secondly how he set about his work on this subject.

Firstly, he realised that there were many problems capable of solution if he gave his mind to them, but the difficulty was to recognise them clearly. He was, therefore, constantly on the look-out for the need of an improvement of something which interested him or affected his work and which might be achieved by some practical device.

Secondly, having recognised the need, he would define clearly the desired result.

Thirdly, he would analyse the problem into separate parts and study carefully the known facts affecting each part. Lastly, he would concentrate his thoughts on the subject to such an extent that he became completely oblivious to all around him. He seemed sometimes to go into a trance, occasionally even in the middle of a meal, with his mouth full and his jaw stilled, whilst his eyes took on a glassy stare. He resented fiercely being interrupted or brought out of this state as, no doubt, it interrupted a train of thought which he believed might lead him to a successful solution of some problem on which he was concentrating.

He had a mathematical and mechanical background and a knowledge of physics and chemistry well above the average. As a cadet at Woolwich he had studied Infantry and Cavalry tactics and weapons, as well as the science of gunnery, including the curves of trajectories and, lastly, he had specialised still more in the intricate art of the Royal Engineers. Added to this he had the accumulated knowledge of a most enquiring mind, exercised in many and sometimes odd directions since early childhood.

As a fighter pilot in France, Lanoe had frequently seen German aeroplanes a few thousand feet above his own, and had been frustrated by his inability to climb quickly enough to attack them at a range likely to be successful, say 50 to 25 yards, before they spotted him and dived for their own lines.

It was useless to fire at them 2,000 feet or even 1,000 feet above him; a bullet fired upwards would be swept back by the pressure of the air due to the speed of the aeroplane; moreover it was impossible to judge the correct distance or range between the aeroplanes and, without this, the sights could not be set to allow for the trajectory of the bullet; and then allowance had to be made if there were any difference in the speeds and directions of the two machines. There was an urgent need to get over this difficulty, a need for some means by which the lower fighter pilot could aim his machine-gun accurately at his enemy as much as 1,000 feet or even 2,000 feet above him. Here then were Lanoe's first two steps, the recognition of the need and a clear definition of it.

He set his mind methodically to work and he solved the problem. Those who know this simple and highly satisfactory invention, may be interested in following the likely train of Lanoe's thoughts in finding the solution; others may wish to pause here, and see if they can think out the answer for themselves, before obtaining it by reading further.

At the beginning of 1916, Lanoe was required to tackle an entirely different problem; owing to the " Fokker Scourge ", which had become very serious, he was assigned the task of forming and training the first British Squadron of Scouts, sometimes called " chaser squadrons ", with the sole object of seeking out and fighting the enemy aeroplanes, not from below, but by attacking them, preferably from above by diving on them, but in any case at close quarters, the closer the better.

Lanoe's fertile brain was constantly at work devising new methods and inventing new apparatus for the greater efficiency of his squadron; no sooner did he discover or devise something which he recognised to be of real value than he passed on the idea to H.Q., and it was promptly adopted as standard through the R.F.C.

His first invention in No. 24 Squadron was the design of the " fug boots ", made whilst he was at Hounslow; his second was the protective covering of the propeller tips. But now Lanoe was faced with the urgent and essential problem of equipping his aeroplanes with an efficient machine-gun or guns, fitted with improved sights, and training his pilots to shoot straight and make the correct allowance for the speed and direction of the hostile aircraft.

The official gun mounting, as already mentioned, was quite impracticable; the pilot could not fly in one direction with one hand, and aim and fire his gun in another direction with the other hand; when elevated, the gun got in the way of the joy-stick. Lanoe first tried firmly clamping down the muzzle of the gun in the straightforward position; this was at once forbidden by higher authority; the gun on a Nieuport Scout could be fired upwards successfully; so it must be with the D.H.2, regardless of the fact that the relative positions of the pilot and of the gun were quite different. Orders were orders, and even though the pilot of a D.H.2 could not aim his gun upwards, and obviously he could not put his head upside down between his knees to do so, the gun must be free to fire upwards. Lanoe partly got over the difficulty by making a spring clip with a catch to hold the muzzle down, but enabling it to be released if required; it did not hold the gun as rigidly nor as securely as when clamped, but it was the best compromise possible with red tape.

A single Lewis gun proved unsatisfactory; it was liable to jam owing to weakness in design, faulty manufacture both of the gun and the ammunition, or the freezing of the lubricating oil; in any case the drum only held 47 rounds, after which a fresh drum had to be put on, usually at the critical moment of a fight. Wilkinson and Tidmarsh each mounted two guns; Lanoe encouraged these experiments, and soon several pilots had two guns fitted; this gave them a feeling of confidence and security in action; their fire power was doubled, and it was unlikely that both guns would jam at the same time; pleased with the improvement, Lanoe showed it to his brigade commander, and was ordered to take the extra gun off at once as being a non-standard fitment, thus contrary to regulation; again there was no alternative but to comply. Such interference with the details of the equipment of a squadron commanded by the greatest fighting expert of the day was unfortunately normal to the military mind; regulations were static and efficiency dynamic; they were not easily reconcilable.

Lanoe could not accept defeat by red tape; somehow the difficulty of running out of ammunition at the critical moment must be overcome; he thought of doubling the size of the ammunition drum, and under the supervision of an exceptionally capable engineer, W. L. French, who had enlisted as an air mechanic, he set about joining two drums together. He asked the War Office to take up their manufacture when he called there during his leave in May, 1916; the double drums were made in England, and the first samples were received in the squadron for trial in July; Lanoe tested them carefully, detected the weaknesses and defects, wrote suggesting the necessary alterations, and accompanied his letters with neat sketches; the double drum came into universal use for aeroplanes.

It was clear to Lanoe from his pilots' reports of their first engagements with the enemy, that they were not making the correct allowance for the speed and direction of the hostile aircraft, and for this reason they had, in many cases, failed to achieve a definite victory at once. Careful discussion with Wilkinson, amongst others, convinced him that the existing sights and methods of training the pilots to shoot were inadequate. Obviously the Fokker with two efficient fixed machine-guns firing through the propeller 500 rounds each without change of drum, or the machine-gunner of a German two-seater firing 250 rounds from an efficient parabellum gun mounted on a steady platform, would get the best of it in any fight against the D.H.2 armed with one unreliable Lewis gun firing 47 rounds with luck from a wobbly mounting, unless Lanoe could give his pilots some outstanding advantage.

The spirit of attack, with which he had imbued them, made up for many deficiencies in their mechanical equipment, but more than this was required to produce a series of victories. The additional advantage which Lanoe determined to give them was more accurate shooting; if his pilots could aim better than the Germans they might make up for the handicap they suffered from inadequate and unreliable gun power.

The first step was to make a sight which predicted the distance the H.A. (Hostile aircraft) would fly during the short space of time the bullet was travelling towards it; on the back sight Lanoe fitted a miniature aeroplane, shortly afterwards replaced by an arrow; when this was turned in the same direction as the H.A. was flying, it carried the back sight into the correct position to make the required forward deflection; Lanoe had the calculations at his finger-tips. There remained the obvious disadvantage that the pilot would hardly have time to adjust his sight to each fresh position of the H.A. To get over this difficulty Lanoe invented the ring-sight, later in universal use; by manoeuvring the fighter so that the target aircraft appeared in the proper position relative to the ring, the correct aiming deflection was obtained, but careful judgment and much practice were required to use the sight accurately, especially when the H.A. was moving obliquely across the sights or diving.

The next step, therefore, was to train the pilots to make the correct use of the ring sight; for this purpose Lanoe invented the " Forward Aiming Model ", a simple, but effective apparatus with which the pilot, by practice on the ground, corrected and improved his aim; this training model was adopted throughout the R.F.C.

Lanoe decided that the next step was to train his pilots to steer the aeroplane on to the target, and practice firing; for this purpose he invented the " rocking fuselage " which was adopted in the R.F.C. for training scout pilots; by means of dummy controls the rough wooden model of a fuselage, with machine-gun attached, could be manoeuvred, much like an aeroplane, so as to bring the sights on to a target running along a wire against the railway embankment.

The pilots now needed practice in air firing, and for this purpose Lanoe made on the aerodrome, well away from the sheds, a full sized silhouette of a German aeroplane in chalk; this was known as the " Boche ", and can be seen in the photograph of the aerodrome; pilots practised diving and firing at the "Boche", and often emptied the remainder of a drum at it on their return from a patrol over the lines; soon every squadron had its "Boche" to fire at.

There was yet one more step to success, which was to bring the pilots into contact with the H.A. so that they could carry out the teachings of all the previous steps; this was not as simple as it may seem, for after the first encounters, the German airmen kept almost entirely to their own side of the lines, dived home on the approach of our scouts, rarely came over on reconnaissance, and then usually very high up and for a short time only. Lanoe instituted a system of report or intelligence with the anti-aircraft-artillery sections, with whom he was connected by telephone; by a careful study of these reports he was able to anticipate the German movements to some extent, and sent up his offensive patrols at the most likely moments, as far as routine orders would allow him.

Ground signals, in the form of white canvas strips, were put out by these report stations, when H.A. were visible, to indicate their height and direction, but the pilots did not always know where to look for these signals, and often missed them. To overcome this difficulty Lanoe asked the report stations to make a permanent chalk circle, outside which the strips could be placed; thus the pilots came to know the positions of the circles, and quickly did a round of them to see if any signals were out. The first sample circle was made on the aerodrome at Bertangles, and can be seen in the photograph.

Lanoe was very proud of his squadron, and liked the Generals to visit and encourage his pilots. He was keen on his inventions and improvements, and took great pleasure in showing them to authorized visitors. General Trenchard, in his B.E.2c, paid several visits to the squadron, and his appreciation added to the keenness of the pilots and to his own popularity; few senior officers realized so well that a few well chosen words of encouragement from them, marked them as an object of respect and affection, and increased the enthusiasm of those serving under them, whereas a noisy scolding induced anything but these sentiments.

Lanoe's inventions were so numerous and diversified that it is not possible to describe them all, in fact many were taken into

use without it being remembered that they originated in his
fertile brain.

By far the most important of Lanoe's inventions, was
mentioned at the beginning of this chapter and was called the
" Upward Shooting Sight ". It was considered so important to
keep it secret that, in the first instance it was only fitted to
aeroplanes flown in this country; later it was used by specially
selected pilots well behind our lines in France; in consequence
of these precautions, this invention remained secret throughout
the war and for many years thereafter.

And yet, once thought of, how simple, how very simple it was,
only it needed some spark of genius to think of it. No one need
suffer from an inferiority complex if he could not think out the
answer, as Lanoe did, for the Germans saw, again and again,
their own aeroplanes being shot down behind our lines by the
pilots of our machines flying well below them; yet never guessed
the secret, nor could they counter its deadly effect.

Let us follow Lanoe's usual train of thought; his first two
steps, recognition of the need and definition of it, have already
been mentioned. As the next step, he would analyse the problem
into separate parts and study known facts about each part; he
knew already from experience the facts concerning the aeroplanes
and their relative positions and speeds. Next he studied the
facts concerning the machine gun; there are range tables for
every service firearm giving, amongst other statistics, details
of muzzle velocity, range, trajectory and the effect on the line
of fire of cross winds of different velocities.

Lanoe studied the range tables of the Vickers machine-gun
with the greatest care and thoroughness; the trajectory of the
bullet could be plotted in the form of a parabola, distorted into
a steeper descent due to the retarding effect of the atmosphere;
there is, of course, a differently shaped curve of trajectory for
each angle of elevation of the gun. The data for very high
angles were lacking, but Lanoe was able to exterpolate curves
for these, and he plotted several at the high angles needed to
shoot upwards at his foe above. He also studied the horizontal
deflection of the bullet due to strong cross winds and he was
able to exterpolate curves for wind velocities equivalent to the
speed of his aeroplanes in flight.

One can almost hear his teeth suddenly clenched together as

he gripped his jaw in that characteristically determined manner and see the eager glint in his eyes, followed by that glassy stare, as he suddenly noticed that one of the curves of trajectory and the curve due to wind pressure were almost identical; here must be the key to the problem. If one curve could be made to cancel out the other, then the bullet would travel in a straight line and no calculation nor allowance need be made for the speed of the aeroplanes (wind pressure) nor for the range between them (trajectory) within the limits of the co-incidence of the curves.

There were many more minor problems to be worked out, such as the method of using the discovery, the effects of altitude on the trajectory and air pressure, and so on, but these could be solved by the logical progress of a well trained and imaginative brain, such as Lanoe's. Thus he saw that the fighter pilot below had only to fly at the same speed and in the same direction as his enemy above, read off the velocity on his air speed indicator, set his sight at the corresponding elevation to the coincidence of the curves of trajectory and wind velocity, aim his machine-gun, pull the trigger and his bullets would fly in a straight line for about 2,000 feet. There was no need to allow for relative speeds, since both aeroplanes were flying in the same direction at the same speed; no need to allow for range, nor deflection by air pressure, as the one cancelled out the other. The name of this invention came naturally—" The Upward Shooting Sight ", the most deadly and effective invention, during the whole war, given to the defending aeroplane.

Millions of our citizens, without ever knowing it, owed at least their tranquility, often their property to the total value of millions of pounds, and many their lives to the genius of this modest, courageous and intensely patriotic young officer. His resourcefulness was remarkable in finding a practical and simple solution to what had seemed an insurmountable difficulty. One might think that some special care would have been taken to preserve such an ingenious brain, even if not to reward it, but no one thought of this and Lanoe gave to his country his inventions without expectation of reward, nor would he seek safety whilst danger threatened England.

Thus was lost an inventor, invaluable, irreplaceable.

27

Work and Play

WHILST Lanoe was training his pilots, with the help of his inventions, he was also busy with the organization and work of his squadron. The first of its kind, this scout squadron required of its commander constant initiative in deciding points of detail, many of them vital to its efficiency. The day was a long one, even in March; reveille was at 6 a.m. and lights out at 9 p.m.; the men worked in two shifts, but Lanoe was on duty all day. To economize time, when the days grew longer, the quarters and mess were moved to huts on the aerodrome.

On the 19th, 20th and 31st of March the first engagements with the enemy, including a double fuselage aeroplane known as " Two-tails ", took place during patrols and escorts behind the German lines. The escorts were successful in protecting our reconnaissance machines, but owing to incomplete training of Lanoe's pilots no casualties were inflicted on the enemy.

On the 25th of March the squadron suffered its first war casualty through Lerwill landing in " Hunland ". He had just escaped from a nasty accident due to his aileron control snapping, which caused his machine to spin into the ground. Like the other pilots in the squadron he took his harrowing experience as a great joke, and Lanoe encouraged them always to laugh off the effects of their terrifying escapes.

Sibley also had a narrow escape, and Tidmarsh received a direct hit from an Archie shell, which passed through the nacelle, narrowly missed his shins, and burst harmlessly further on.

Cowan, too, had a remarkable adventure driving a H.A. down, forcing it to land and shooting at it on the ground, but when he tried to recover his engine he found that the thumb switch had jammed, and his engine would not come on again. Scrabbling feverishly at the switch with his nails, he was forced to land in enemy territory beside his victim. Fortunately the jolt of landing released the switch, and he got safely home.

There were many other narrow escapes, some of them terrifying, especially those from " cylindritis ", when departing cylinders just missed cutting the tail booms or main spars, and the unbalanced engine nearly shook the aeroplane to pieces in the air. Hughes-Chamberlain escaped twice by the narrowest of margins, and Wilkinson was saved only by being close to the ground when one of his cylinders flew off. Unfortunately several good pilots were killed by this deplorable malady. The engine gave so much trouble that there seemed to be a devil smouldering within it, ready to destroy at any moment its gallant pilot. Far from trying to hush up these appalling defects, Lanoe hung outside the office a cracked-off cylinder as a gong and the twisted connecting rod as a knocker, useful to warn the stand-by patrol that hostile aircraft had been sighted, and, at the same time, a quixotic challenge to this fiendish engine to do its " damnedest " that all might see and know that he and his pilots faced this terrible danger with fearless hearts.

But if Lanoe expected his pilots to accept these hazards cheerfully, he also did all that was possible to minimize their risks; when a corporal mechanic carelessly failed to secure the Lewis gun on one machine so that the pilot was unable to use it in a fight and was nearly shot down, then Lanoe was relentless. The corporal, despite an unblemished record, was court-martialled; filled with remorse he admitted that this severity was perfectly fair and faced his punishment uncomplainingly. When these too frequent accidents were not attended by a fatality, Lanoe treated them lightly and his pilots gallantly followed his example.

Mr. W. Beach-Thomas, famous war correspondent of the *Daily Mail,* wrote an article which greatly added to the merriment of the mess. Lanoe pinned it up on the notice board to the delight of his pilots and the amusement of all visitors to the squadron. The facts were accurate enough to be easily identified with No. 24 Squadron, but the quaint prosaic wording appealed particularly to pilots whose sole object in life was to seek out and fight the enemy aeroplanes.

" 27.5.16.
A screamingly funny article called ' Thrills of the Air ' deals exclusively, as far as I can see, with the exploits of my squadron."

Somehow a piano was procured, Wilkinson thumped out the latest popular tunes and Lanoe led the singing, still "yards off the note", but his lack of ear only added to the general hilarity. He initiated rags to celebrate victories, promotions, the award of decorations, perilous escapes and, as the battle progressed, there were even rags designed to forget, or at least to try and forget casualties, especially those due to accidents. These latter rags placed the greatest strain on Lanoe's self-control, for no one ever felt the loss of a friend more acutely than he did; yet to dwell on the harrowing death of a gay and lovable comrade could not bring him to life again. Above all, the morale, the good spirits of the squadron must be kept at pinnacle height, for as the year wore on and the Germans brought more and better machines to the Somme front, so the inferiority of the D.H.2 with its defective engine and its one unreliable gun, became more and more apparent.

In his efforts to keep the pilots cheerful, Lanoe was greatly helped by his neighbours, No. 11 Squadron till the beginning of April and after that No. 22 Squadron, who replaced them and who flew two-seater pushers, F.E.2b's, under the command of Major Barry Martin. No. 22 was one of the hardest fighting two-seater squadrons in the R.F.C.; the squadrons worked and ragged together; the D.H.2's provided escorts for the F.E.2b's who never felt happier nor safer than under the protection of the pilots of No. 24 Squadron.

On returning to the aerodrome the pilots sometimes "shot up" the "Boche" belonging to the other squadron; this was considered an outrage calling for immediate reprisals in the form of an air counter-attack, hangar-zooming, or a land expedition to secure hostages for future good behaviour. The scraps were many and good-natured, the weapons varied and ingenious, and the battles often quite well organized. Armoured cars (cane armchairs), bombs (tennis balls), flammenwerfer (soda syphons), chemical warfare (a large size Flit fly-spray, a great casualty producer and useful as a mace-in-hand at close quarters) and the infantry with any weapons that came handy; these, with raids and counter-raids on No. 22 Squadron, became the chief squadron recreation.

No. 24 moved its mess into a large hut on the edge of the

aerodrome; the principal feature of this hut was a wide panel of the wall hinged at the top to swing outwards; at the height of an after-dinner scrum in the mess the struggling mass would be steered towards this panel which, under pressure, would swing open momentarily, leading to a drop of two or three feet on to the dark aerodrome, to the surprise and dismay of the visitors. The brigade commander, General Ashmore, who sometimes dined with No. 24 Squadron, thoroughly enjoyed the fun.

Inter-squadron visits were fairly frequent, averaging once a week to dine, with occasional intervening rags. No. 24 visited and was visited by the officers of brigade and wing headquarters, the two other D.H.2 squadrons, No. 29 at Abeele and No. 32 at Treiziennes, and most of the other squadrons on the Fourth Army front. They also visited the famous French Nieuport Squadron No. 3 at Cachi; there the English pilots could hardly keep their eyes off the boyish Guynemer, the greatest French " ace " silent and sombre; they noticed a strange likeness to their own leader in his large eyes which he kept fixed on Lanoe. Expeditions were made to Les Gobberts, Josephine's and other restaurants in Amiens. Thus the pilots were kept from thinking too much of the dangers they had to face each time they went up, and of the fate of those of their comrades who would never face these dangers again.

On one of these visits to a neighbouring squadron, recently arrived from England, Lanoe was royally entertained, and then his hosts produced with pomp and pride an exceptionally fine model of a new aeroplane due to be issued shortly, but already known to be a poor performer. Some of the pilots, who had made the model, were conspicuously pleased with their work and expected Lanoe's admiration and praise. Instead, a puzzled look spread over his face and, as he peered closely at the model, he tilted his head to one side and stroked his chin as if in grave doubt about something; this was not at all the enthusiastic reception which they had expected for their fine work. " What's the matter? " they asked. " Something missing," Lanoe said. " What's missing? " they asked indignantly. With a wide grin, Lanoe pointed at the model and replied " A Hun on it's tail."

There were roars of laughter and they all danced and romped to an improvised ditty, each verse of which ended with " A

Hun on his tail ". So the night wore on, singing and ragging till at last it was time to turn in. What a jolly evening, what a Squadron Commander! All care and fear forgotten for the moment, they retired to bed, well content with the success of their party.

Soon after arrival in France, during one of the romps in the mess, Lanoe received a bang on the head and became unconscious; his pilots tried the usual restoratives without effect; thoroughly alarmed, Andrews said he would fetch the doctor, upon which Lanoe revived. Some days later he told Andrews that he had been aware of all that went on, and laughed at the fright he had given them. In August or September, on the way back from a merry dinner " ragging " in the car, Lanoe again received a knock on the head and " passed out ". This time Andrews was determined not to be the victim of a hoax; Lanoe was lifted out of the car, his boots removed, his feet tickled, barley grass thrust up his nose, but all in vain; he remained completely limp; so he was left to lie on the edge of the aerodrome whilst his companions walked home to bed. The next morning Lanoe's batman, greatly perturbed, came to Andrews to tell him that the major could not be found and had not slept in his bed; Andrews became anxious again, but at breakfast time Lanoe turned up in an uncommunicative mood. It was never known where or how he passed the night, though some days later he reproached Andrews for having poked grass up his nose. Whether these trances were the consequence of the slight concussion Lanoe had received from an Archie burst in No. 6 Squadron, or whether by some means he had the power of throwing himself into them is not known; he had always possessed an abnormal power of concentration, and could withdraw into himself regardless of activities around him, but these trances went far beyond concentration. The mystery was never solved, and Andrews remained somewhat unhappy at having left Lanoe to lie out on the aerodrome.

To give his pilots sufficient exercise Lanoe borrowed horses from the cavalry for them to ride, but there were never enough to satisfy him; he considered riding not only good exercise, but excellent training for a pilot's nerves. He also started bumble-puppy, and later made a tennis court on the aerodrome.

The pilots smuggled out a couple of walking stick guns, and

practised " marksmanship " with these on the local partridges, and indulged in further " shooting practice " with small bore rifles and revolvers on chimney pots and other tempting targets; Lanoe was obliged to exercise a certain amount of restraining influence on these practices.

The pilots lived a life of vivid contrast; for most of the time they were warm, comfortable, well fed and enjoying themselves royally, the best and jolliest of friends; then suddenly they would be subjected to a tremendous strain; freezing in winter, though not too uncomfortable in summer, they were put to the acid test of courage and endurance. Sitting in an armchair, it is difficult to imagine the nerve strain imposed upon the pilots of those days. Without the companionship of an observer they flew a machine that might at any moment tear itself to pieces in the air and hurl them to death, perhaps a flaming death; each time they went up they " went over the top ", facing not only the alarming and often accurate fire of Archie, but the streams of bullets, some incendiary, some explosive, directed with accuracy and determination by their skilled and courageous opponents who had the advantage of fighting on their own side of the lines with better weapons. Not for one second whilst on patrol could they relax from extreme vigilance, for at any moment one or more hostile scouts might dive down upon them with their machine-guns rattling out flaming death.

Engine failure, serious damage to the aeroplane in combat, a dangerous wound, each meant inevitable capture if not death, the risk being greatly increased by the prevailing westerly wind. Once the fight started there could be no breaking it off unless the enemy were willing; the sole defence of a D.H.2 was its ability to whip round and attack. In the middle of a fight drums of ammunition had to be changed, during which time the D.H.2 was defenceless; the enemy could fire continuously twice as fast and many times as long. The D.H.2 not only ran out of ammunition first, but owing to its unreliable engine it was apt to run poorly or peter out at a critical moment.

Courage, efficiency, confidence in themselves and in each other and in their ability to outfight the enemy constituted the chief assets of these pilots. Underlying their *esprit de corps* was an ever-present realization that their final objective was to help and protect the infantry, whose plight in the trenches drew their ready sympathy; they were determined to make a great name for their squadron, and live up to the reputation of their leader; by their confidence in him, in each other, and in themselves, they had already won half the battle against the dreaded Fokkers before they had met them; their courage and skill completed the victory. Each pilot took the air thirsting for a fight, never counting the odds; each was convinced that there was no other unit equal to Hawker's Squadron.

28

The Fokker Defeated

TOWARDS the end of March, T. moved down to the Somme front with the 8th Division, early arrivals of the Fourth Army, in preparation for the impending battle. Up to this time, air activity had been negligible owing to bad weather.

> " 28.3.16.
>
> This is a very dull place, I quite regret Flanders, for which I am developing a post impressional! affection—such is the human mind, always displeased with its present surroundings and fancying the thing it can't get is preferable.
>
> T. hints at joining me, which would be very pleasant.
>
> I am well but rather bothered with that continual sub-conscious feeling that something is wrong—partly responsibility I think, but largely liver."

Lanoe was suffering from what the Spanish appropriately call a " palpito ".

> " 1.4.16.
>
> Feeling much better now, thanks, and have traced the cause of my " something-was-wrong " feeling; Mrs. Bayly was very ill for a day or two, and Beatrice's moods always appear to react on me.
>
> Great thing happened day before yesterday—T. rolled up, looking very fit, having moved down this way, very pleasant indeed for both of us."

The meeting was certainly a most joyous one. T. arrived with his horses, and Lanoe dropped into the saddle as if he rode every day; thus mounted they did a quick tour of the aerodrome; Lanoe's many inventions were put through their paces, and eagerly discussed. He and his lads were all in great form, the weather had suddenly cleared, the engines seemed to be behaving better for the moment, there had been no accidents recently, and the pilots had gained confidence in their machines and in their

162

ability to shoot straight through practice with Lanoe's training devices.

On the 1st of April Andrews, on morning escort to No. 15 Squadron, had chased away old " Two-tails "; this was the first day on which the three escorting machines had flown in formation, and it had turned out highly successful, with promise of great improvement in the tactical use of the squadron in future. The next day Tidmarsh and Sibley shot down and crashed an Albatros over Grandcourt, thus drawing first blood for the squadron. To end a perfect visit Lanoe and T. found that they were both due for leave next month, and arranged to take it at the same time.

The following summary is typical of a quiet day's work :

" No. 24 Squadron Summary of work.		14th Wing. 8th April, 1916.	
Patrol	Andrews	6.00— 7.50 a.m.	Successful
,,	Sibley	6.25— 8.15 a.m.	,,
,,	Hawker	6.50— 8.15 a.m.	,,
,,	Ker	7.00— 7.10 a.m.	Engine trouble
,,	,,	7.30— 8.10 a.m.	landed at Baisieux
,,	,,	9.45—10.00 a.m.	machine damaged
,,	Wilkinson	8.00— 9.50 a.m.	Successful
,,	Breen	9.00—11.00 a.m.	,,
,,	Chamberlain	10.30—12.55 p.m.	,,
,,	Wilson	12.05— 1.50 p.m.	,,
,,	Cowan	1.30— 3.30 p.m.	,,
,,	Tidmarsh	3.05— 5.00 p.m.	,,
,,	Mitchell	3.40— 5.40 p.m.	Successful. Suzanne salient patrolled during artillery shoot.
,,	Morgan	3.45— 5.40 p.m.	Successful
,,	Andrews	4.50— 5.10 p.m.	Engine trouble
,,	Ker	4.50— 6.25 p.m.	Successful
,,	Andrews	5.35— 6.40 p.m.	,,

Pilots available 12
Pilots flying 12

Aeroplanes serviceable 7
Aeroplanes unserviceable 5

Total war flying time 21 hours 45 minutes
Total test flying time 15 minutes
Total time in air 22 hours

Very hazy and cloudy in the early morning, improving later.

(signed) L. G. Hawker."

Our hopes were high at that moment; in the air Lanoe had an aeroplane which, with bold and skilful handling, was a match for any German machine of that period; the pilots had greatly improved through training, and could not have been keener; they knew they had a leader who would give them every possible help, encouragement and opportunity. On the ground we had men, guns and ammunition in plenty, courage, confidence and optimism, the essential elements we thought, for a great victory, not realizing that bad generalship would ruin all.

April was a busy month for the squadron; besides the continuous patrol of one machine, which, failing a combat, collected information over the German lines, and two machines standing by in case of a hostile incursion, frequent escorts of three or four machines accompanied the two-seaters of Nos. 4, 9, 15 and 22 Squadrons, which were chiefly occupied on photographic work. The latter was not a popular job, as the D.H.2's had to follow closely the slow and steady flight of the photographic machines, and came in for a large share of well directed Archie fire.

Formation flying now became the recognized method, and on the 16th of April Andrews carried a streamer on his strut to distinguish him as the patrol leader. Each fine day a flight of D.H.'s escorted the reconnaissance or photographic machines. Lanoe took great trouble in arranging these escorts. To begin with he went himself to see the commander of the squadron for which he was to supply an escort, and agreed with him the exact rendezvous so that there should be no possibility of the two-seaters going off alone, a mishap fraught with grave risk of disaster, which occurred more frequently than might be supposed, unless arrangements had been made with the greatest care. Lanoe also discussed and settled the exact procedure of the escorted machines and the escort in case they were attacked, in case one or more machines had to turn back and so on; nothing was left to chance that could possibly be foreseen. On subsequent occasions he sent the flight commander of the escort to make these arrangements; no trouble was too great to take in a matter where Lanoe felt the lives of our airmen and the reputation of his squadron were at stake.

The Fokkers, who lately had kept at a respectful distance from the compact and well-ordered force consisting of the reconnaissance flight and its escort, at last decided to put an end to these long and leisurely inspections of their defences. On the 24th of April five B.E.2's of No. 15 Squadron went out under a close escort from No. 24 consisting of Andrews, Cowan, Manfield and Wilson; the two-seaters flew steadily eastwards, whilst the faster D.H.2's twisted and turned a few hundred feet above them; around and amongst these aeroplanes " Archie " jabbed his black shell bursts, which successively swelled into curling smoke-puffs, and then slowly melted into the air. Soon in the distance a group of specks appeared, and in a few minutes could be distinguished as a dozen mosquito-like monoplanes, the famous Fokkers, climbing rapidly and circling to cut off our machines should they decide to retreat; but the two-seaters had work to do and trusted the D.H.2's to deal with the Fokkers. At first it looked as if the Fokkers would attack immediately, but they held off and climbed till they were in a favourable position above and behind, and waited till our machines had reached their furthest point from home. The D.H.2's could not leave the machines they were escorting to chase away the enemy, but kept close to and just above their charges, anxiously awaiting the attack. Suddenly the Fokkers chose their moment and all came diving towards the two-seaters from behind; round whipped the D.H.2's and made straight for them, a manoeuvre which appeared to surprise the German pilots, for instead of continuing their dive they broke formation in some confusion; the D.H.2's were soon amongst them, twisting and turning as they fired first at this one, then at that one, then climbed out to change a drum, and darted back again into the dog-fight. Two or three Fokkers, apparently damaged, dived down out of sight, and the remainder drew off greatly disconcerted by the un-expected ferocity of these new opponents. The D.H.2's could not pursue the enemy and leave the two-seaters which were continuing their work as if nothing had happened, and in any case the Fokkers could escape easily as they dived much faster than the D.H.2's. Some of the Fokkers remained shyly in the air at a respectful distance, but none would renew the attack; they were beaten and they knew it.

The victory gained by Hawker's Squadron, though not spectacular, was a vital one; it was the first stand-up encounter with the Fokkers, and on the result depended who should rule the air, the Fokkers as heretofore, or the D.H.2's henceforth.

The Fourth Army commander made special mention of the four D.H.2 pilots for their gallantry.

The real significance of this victory was recognized when it was realized that a complete change had taken place in the air, suddenly and surprisingly; Hawker's Squadron had broken the " Fokker Scourge ", and the terror of their power was exploded. Lanoe's pilots knew that they could beat the Fokkers at any time, anywhere and in any numbers; the jubilation of the pilots was so great, and they were now so keen for a fight, that Lanoe feared they might disobey orders and leave the machines they were escorting to follow the Fokkers down to the ground, but he impressed upon them their sacred trust, and they never let him down, though continually exasperated by the pin-pricking tactics of the enemy machines. Upon their return from these encounters the pilots discussed their fights with Lanoe, and he always made some helpful suggestions and gave them a few words of encouragement.

One of the difficulties our pilots were to experience throughout the war became very apparent now; although there were many further successful combats, it was difficult to be sure that the H.A. had been shot down and crashed, for our pilots, having forced one machine to dive, were too occupied with the other H.A., to watch their victims till they reached the ground; owing to the fact that all fighting took place well over the enemy lines, they could seldom tell what damage they had done to their opponents. A skilled German pilot would fall, apparently out of control, only to fly home safely; on the other hand a badly damaged H.A., or wounded pilot, might fall or land behind his own lines without our pilot being aware of having registered a hit. It would have been a very different matter had the fighting taken place over our own lines; the German pilots could not then have escaped by diving, but would have been forced to stand and fight, or land as prisoners.

The result, however, of the escorts was highly satisfactory to the accompanied machines. Before they had been escorted, they had lost machine after machine on their distant reconnaissance and photographic work, which they only continued owing to their remarkable courage and perseverance; now they never lost a machine and they completed their tasks undisturbed. The Fokkers were engaged before they could reach the two-seaters and driven off by the D.H.2's, or more frequently the enemy abandoned the idea of attacking machines that were protected by one of Lanoe's escorts; the escorted reconnaissances not only became comparatively safe, but much more efficient; they could give their full attention to their work and take their time.

The object of the R.F.C. at that time was to reconnoitre enemy territory, report movements of troops and trains, photograph defences, trenches, ammunition dumps, and gun positions, and range our guns by wireless on to suitable targets, or bomb and machine-gun them; all this work was designed to help the infantry forward to victory; fighting in the air was incidental to this work. The German scouts tried to prevent our machines from accomplishing their tasks; the main object of our scouts was to protect our two-seater machines by driving the German scouts away. It was not essential to the success of our scouts that they should shoot down the Fokkers; they achieved their object if they enabled our machines to do their work unmolested. There is no record or mention of the loss of one of our reconnaissance machines whilst being escorted by No. 24 Squadron; on the contrary each squadron commander enthusiastically remembers the immunity of his machines and the confidence of his pilots when protected by these escorts.

Much importance was given later to the numerical score of successful scout pilots, especially in the case of German aces, who mostly had the comparatively safe and easy task of shooting down a number of inexperienced English pilots on inferior machines far over the hostile lines. From a military point of view such victories achieved little of material importance, though the moral effect of these spectacular feats was considerable; but our machines continued to reconnoitre, photograph, bomb and register targets. On the other hand the German machines seldom crossed our lines in 1916, their scouts never escorted them, and their few incursions were short and furtive, or at such great heights that our scouts could not reach them; they gave little help to their troops, who suffered heavily in consequence. This aspect of the war in the air was recognized by our H.Q., who accepted our heavier air casualties in return for the invaluable help given by the R.F.C. to the troops on the ground.

Each day, following the successful engagement of the 25th of April, a number of Fokkers would appear when our escorted machines crossed the lines, and hang like minnows in a stream, but they would not fight the D.H.2's again, though often superior in numbers. The success of No. 24 Squadron in defeating the Fokkers was fully realized at H.Q. when they found that they were now able to obtain, without loss, photographs of the enemy defences on the Somme front, which were an essential preliminary to drawing up the plans for the impending offensive.

Sir Henry Rawlinson, commanding the Fourth Army, wrote on the 23rd of May :—

" It was about the first week in May (actually the last week in April) that we sent out our reconnaissances over Bapaume escorted by the de Havilland machine. Up to that time we had been carefully training our young pilots and it was not till then that Ashmore thought them sufficiently expert to take on the Fokkers. In carrying out the reconnaissance they were attacked by the Fokkers and rendered a good account of themselves for they reported that on the first occasion they sent two Fokkers to earth in a damaged condition and on the second they destroyed another which fell in the town of Bapaume and was smashed amongst the houses. All three of these machines fell of course in the enemy's lines so we have no certain information of what actually happened to them. But the fact remains that since this occurrence we have successfully photographed the whole of the enemy's trenches in front of the Fourth Army, the first line, intermediate line, second line and third line, over a front of more than twenty miles without being once attacked by the Fokkers. This was done on the 15th, 16th, 17th and 18th May, and clearly shows that for the moment at any rate we have command of the air by day on the Fourth Army front. I cannot speak too highly of the work of these young pilots, most of whom have recently come out from England, and the de Havilland machine has unquestionably proved itself superior to the Fokker in speed, manoeuvre, climbing and general fighting efficiency." (V. II, p. 160.)

Encouraged by the success of No. 24 Squadron, the other fighter squadrons also attacked the Fokkers, whose supremacy, which had never extended beyond their own lines, was now completely broken.

29

Death of Mitchell

MITCHELL, who commanded " A " Flight, had been on leave during the recent fighting, and on his return he wished perhaps to show his squadron commander that he was as keen and daring as any of the other pilots; without telling Lanoe, who, he feared, might forbid it, he decided to loop the loop in his D.H.2, a machine that so far had not been looped.

Just after 7 p.m. on the 29th of April he was up stunting over the aerodrome when Lanoe, apparently seized with a premonition of impending disaster, came out of the office and looking up saw Mitchell, in a steep dive, pull his machine suddenly back; the left wing collapsed, the gravity tank fouled the propeller, and the machine came roaring and flaming down to crash on the aerodrome, the fire made brilliant by the dusk; it was a terrible sight.

To Lanoe, who loved Mitchell, it was a nerve-shattering shock; knowing it was useless, yet he ran over to the wreck; Mitchell had jumped clear and was killed instantly; he was not burnt; it was Lanoe's only consolation. Quietly he returned to the office, arranged for Mitchell's burial, the disposal of his effects, and with a shaking hand wrote the casualty report. He then retired to his billet to collect his thoughts.

" Bim " Mitchell, Mitchell the handsome, the debonnair, the gay, who had saved him from collapse at Hounslow, whose joyful laugh had been with him all these months of trial and training, now had left him just when all that work was about to bear fruit. Always before Lanoe's eyes was that haunting, terrifying sight of the flaming plane carrying his beloved friend to certain destruction; he sat late into the night trying to see the reason of it all. He took up his pen, and with still shaking hand wrote to Beatrice; he knew she would understand, and he longed for her sympathy.

" 29.4.16.   In the field.
Dearest,
   Just as my pilots have done well—remarkable well, and
earned the congratulations and thanks of the other squadrons
for their protection—when the days were fine and the weather
warm—when everything seemed splendid and I was cheerful
and happy, we
   It was a terrible accident—one of my flight commanders,
the one I had first at Hounslow, who helped me so much when
I nearly broke down with over-work.
   He was in a practice flight, dived steeply and pulled his
machine up much too suddenly—no machine could have stood
the strain—and it collapsed in mid-air.
   Nothing could have saved him, but it caught fire and crashed
to earth in huge flames, an awful and terrible sight.
   It was merciful tho' and I knew at once all was over—
   And we had been doing so well and thought our luck had
changed.
   We met the Fokker for the first time, and thoroughly bested
him—we drove him down over his own country and he hasn't
dared attack us since."

   Lanoe took his usual nightly walk round the sheds where
his men were working late, the sinister silhouettes of the machines
throwing fantastic shadows in the lamp light.   Gone for the
moment were his usual cheerful manner and brisk walk as he
moved about the aerodrome; he hardly heard the sergeant's
progress reports, for his mind was still struggling to find some
divine reason for Mitchell's fate.   The mechanics, who by now
were deeply attached to their major, paused in their work and
muttered sympathetic remarks as unheeding, unseeing, he passed
on into the darkness.
   Early the next morning, very tired, but in a steadier hand, he
added another page to his letter, telling Beatrice all she meant
to him, and then :—

   " What's happened to the white violets?   Are they over?
   They seemed to get bigger and bigger each time, they must
   have been beauties."

When Beatrice wrote to Lanoe she used to send him a few
flowers between the pages of her letter; they carried their
fragrance to him, and with it the sweet thoughts of home life of
which he now saw so little.

But though Lanoe was deeply affected by the death of Mitchell, he did not allow it to depress his pilots, and they were quick to equal up the score with the enemy. The very next day Tidmarsh whipped suddenly round on a Fokker that had dared to come close behind him. The Fokker pilot lost his nerve, and, diving away steeply, could not regain control and plunged vertically into the middle of Bapaume.

" 2.5.16.

This last week has been glorious weather, with corresponding activity, in which this squadron has made itself felt, four of my chickens earning a special ' order of the day ' expressing the General's appreciation of their work—this was chiefly ' straffing the Fokker ' who now can't stand the sight of a D.H.

In fact one of my chickens so terrified one of those terrible monsters that he dived straight into the middle of a town, completely out of control.

And in the midst of all this, which of course is very gratifying to me as their major, as I can only do things by proxy now-a-days, we had another sad accident that robbed me of my best flight commander.

It is such a pity that our first success should be marred by such a regrettable and sad accident, but these things will happen, and we can only steel our hearts and carry on with the job in hand.

Spring is really here at last and the woods are lovely, but I am a little weary."

Lanoe was trying to work out the philosophy of this tragic business.

" 4.5.16.

Truly one learns only by sorrow; it is the only education the soul gets, and it requires a terrible grief that shakes the very foundations of one's being to bring the soul to its own.

It probably explains the existence on this world of ours, of all the terrible suffering that seems to deny the existence of a loving God.

People who have done no wrong, who have always lived a blameless, sinless life (according to our moral code) suffer disaster after disaster in apparently the most unfair manner, whereas down right evil doers appear to be happy and prosperous.

The explanation must be that their goodness is too material, and they have failed to learn the lesson of their soul. They are probably more advanced than the 'downright sinner' who at least does not lie to himself and may be really doing well on his very limited opportunities.

We should therefore thank God for our sufferings, and pray for enlightenment, so that we learn our lesson and so do not have to repeat our sufferings for the same reason.

I know the landmarks in the education of my soul are all periods of suffering.

When Dad died, I learnt the existence of the soul as opposed to the material mind.

Gordon taught me to see life in death; at first I wished for death and really did not mind the idea of being killed, but I learnt that was wrong, for it was not till I decided I wished to live that I perceived the reality of Gordon's continued existence, from which I drew ultimate comfort.

This last accident was a terrible blow, as I was very fond of this charming lad, but I do not yet know what it is I have to learn.

Perhaps the great truth that suffering is sent for our own good, to educate our souls."

T., visiting the squadron again, found Lanoe quieter than usual, his large eyes troubled, his mouth set in a firm line, and he seemed to have lost his gay laugh. At first he could not talk about Mitchell, then, when they were alone, he quietly described what had happened. " If only he had asked me," Lanoe said, " I would not have forbidden him to loop, but would have told him how to fly the machine carefully round instead of pulling it back violently."

Somehow he felt that he should have divined that Mitchell might want to loop, and should have warned him in time.

T. mounted Lanoe on his favourite charger, and the brothers galloped across the aerodrome, through the wood and down the gully to the machine-gun range, thence to the quarters in the village. The exhilaration of the gallop, the anticipation of going on leave with his brother and many a laugh over T.'s foolish questions in the mess, did much to revive Lanoe's usual cheerfulness.

Leave came at a most opportune moment. The complete change and rest were just what Lanoe needed, and it was remarkable to see how quickly he regained his joyous spirits. He spent most of the time with the family in Weymouth, where he saw Prideaux, and had long discussions with him on the progress of the disintegrating machine-gun belt.

" 17.5.16.
I have several important transactions in town, but hope to call in at Wycombe on Saturday afternoon."

The important transactions had to do with his inventions, and he asked at the War Office for the double drum for the Lewis gun to be made and sent to him for trial. He then spent a day with Beatrice and her mother at High Wycombe.

By the time he was due to return to France he was again the well known and well beloved " Jolly Old Hawker ".

30

Sweeping the Sky

" 23.5.16.

Nice comfy journey with large cabin at my disposal (O.C. ship I was) which I shared with T.

Smooth as a mill-pond but rather hot in the train.

Great news when I got here. Two of my lads have been given the Military Cross and the squadron has downed two more Huns.

One shot down in flames over the lines and one frightened to death this side.

Also many scraps in which the D.H.2 did well, but just didn't *get* the Hun.

The G.O.C. R.F.C. in the field [General Trenchard] came round the other day and was very pleased with the squadron, and said he had brought it to the notice of Sir D. Haig!

So naturally I am feeling very bucked."

Tidmarsh and Cowan had been awarded the M.C. for their early successes against the Fokkers, and Wilson was awarded the M.C. shortly afterwards.

On the 20th of May, Tidmarsh and Wilson, starting before dawn, had each caught a German machine trying to avoid trouble by completing their reconnaissance before sunrise. Both were shot down in flames, one falling just inside our lines. These were the first fruits of Lanoe's intelligence system.

General Trenchard again visited the squadron, in his B.E.2c, and boomed out his congratulations for all to hear. Andrews fired at " the Boche " for his entertainment; the whole squadron was in high spirits.

Lanoe's pilots had noticed the frequent letters in a girlish hand, the eagerness with which he read them, the flowers in his hut, his many replies; nothing was missed by their sharp, young eyes. They spoke of matrimony as being more dangerous than the Hun, and poked gentle fun at their major, who smiled indulgently at their sallies.

" My chicks are always very suspicious when I come back off leave, and anxiously enquire if I have ' done anything rash ' as they put it. Bar a newcomer, they are all bachelors and confirmed woman-haters of twenty years experience.

As the colonel truthfully remarked, it's a school I run and not a squadron—there is only one older than myself and the majority are not yet of age.

They are a splendid lot tho' and I am very fond of them."

He was also extremely proud of them.

Lanoe took Hughes-Chamberlain with him on an expedition to the trenches to see the wreck of the aeroplane shot down in flames by Wilson, and discover whether there was anything worth salving. It was not an enjoyable expedition ; they crawled about, a good deal in the open, with the stench of the roasted pilot in their nostrils. After examining the machine, and deciding that a few trophies might be salved, they had a drink with some infantry officers, due to make a raid on the German trenches that night, who said it was a case of " a military cross, a red cross or a white cross ! "

On the way back Lanoe called on T., who was adjutant of an artillery group in front of Albert, and recounted his experiences. T. scolded him for exposing himself unnecessarily to snipers, who were deadly in some parts of this sector. However, after dark, two machine guns and a 160 h.p. Mercedes engine, all badly damaged, were recovered from the wreck.

Lanoe's intelligence service did not always yield the fruits of labour for which he hoped. On one occasion he noticed from the reports of an Anti-Aircraft Section at Albert that a German L.V.G. reconnaissance plane came over every third morning at the same time and height, crossed the lines at Thiepval, flew south to Albert, where, being directly over the A.A. guns he was safe from their fire, and then turned due east and dived for his own lines. His total incursion was only seven miles and took less than five minutes to complete. It was most important to put an end to this repeated reconnaissance before our preparations for the battle became obvious.

Allotting this " sitter " to a pilot, who had become restless from missing the fighting so far, Lanoe gave him careful instructions which would bring him over Albert just above his opponent at the moment when the latter reached his furthest point from his own lines. Lanoe went by road to the A.A. section to watch the fun, and proposed afterwards to have breakfast with T. to celebrate another victory for his squadron.

To start with, everything turned out according to plan. With Teutonic regularity the L.V.G. kept the appointment, the D.H.2 was in place and dived on the intruder. What Lanoe had not foreseen was that the H.A. might be carrying bombs; he carried three, though for what reason remains a mystery, and his first act was to dump them at once. They fell uncomfortably close around the A.A. section, and Lanoe admitted that their shattering explosions frightened him horribly. The L.V.G. then fell like an autumn leaf, and when low down recovered control and dived across to the safety of its own lines, whilst the inexperienced D.H.2 pilot, who had assumed too soon that his opponent was dead, stunted his machine above Albert to express his joy at such an easy victory.

Lanoe was so angry, first at being bombed and then at his pilot allowing himself to be fooled, that he cut his breakfast appointment and hurried back to the aerodrome to accord the unfortunate lad a suitable reception on landing.

In May the strength of the squadron was raised from 12 to 18 pilots and D.H.2's.

In the middle of June three Bristol Scouts and two Morane Monoplanes with their pilots were withdrawn from the corps squadrons of the Third Wing and attached to No. 24; these aeroplanes were not considered as good in a fight as the D.H.2's, but Lanoe had a high opinion of the Bristol Scout now that it was fitted with a synchronizing gear allowing the machine-gun to be fired straight ahead; unfortunately this gear was disappointingly unreliable. The Third Wing Scouts were not replaced when they became casualties, and their numbers dwindled away till, by the end of July, they ceased to exist.

It now became more difficult to bring the Germans to action; their chief effort was at Verdun, and they were not inclined to dispute the air with pilots who showed such an aggressive spirit. They had on the Somme front about thirty single-seater fighters, but these kept at a respectful distance when the D.H.2's flew over; the work of our reconnaissance, photograph and artillery machines proceeded unmolested. With the object of bringing home to the enemy our complete ascendency in the air Lanoe flew to Cachi and arranged for combined offensive sweeps with the friendly French crack squadron, now known as the " Storks " ; whilst there he put the D.H.2 through its paces for the benefit of a group of French officers assembled for the purpose, but it could not compare in speed and climb with the French Nieuport Scout.

The weather during the first half of June was wet and stormy, and air activity was at a minimum. Lanoe took the opportunity to move the squadron's quarters from the village to huts on the edge of the aerodrome; he preferred the squadron messing under one roof, and it was a great economy in time having everyone close at hand; there was a large hut (already described) for the mess and a neat row of small Armstrong huts for the officers' sleeping quarters. Lanoe had a hut to himself, divided it into bedroom and sitting room, and later added a bathroom. Most of the other huts were shared by two officers in each; all these smaller huts were moved by their new owners into a nearby shady copse, each one choosing and clearing his own site; cane chairs and other items of furniture were imported, so that the new quarters were soon comfortable.

Lanoe was fully occupied with the move, with the organization of his larger squadron, with training his pilots on his new devices, with obtaining his new machines, of which there was always a shortage, and with the arrangements for co-operation with other squadrons, which he frequently visited; he greatly preferred making his visits by air on account of the saving of time, but often a D.H.2 was not available, and he sometimes borrowed a B.E. from a neighbouring squadron.

On one of these visits in a B.E. Lanoe noticed a Nieuport Scout manoeuvring towards the sun; it was a common trick for some of our scout pilots to practice stalking and diving on to our B.E.'s (" quirks " they called them), and try and " put the wind up them ". They thought it a great joke; but in this case Lanoe was not caught napping and, when the Nieuport dived out of the sun, he whipped round on to its tail. Annoyed at the tables being turned on him, the Nieuport pilot attacked again, doing his utmost to get on to Lanoe's tail, but without the slightest success; Lanoe threw the B.E. round with complete mastery, and at last the Nieuport retired discomfited.

The pilot of the Nieuport was Ball; he returned to his

squadron furious and disgusted with his performance at being "bested by a miserable quirk". He naively recounted his seemingly humiliating experiences, and was well ragged by his fellow pilots, one of whom, out of curiosity, rang up the squadron to which the B.E. belonged, and discovered that it had lent the machine to Lanoe; Ball cheered up when he learnt who his opponent had been, for he felt it no disgrace to have got the worst of an encounter with so famous a pilot.

Ball gained his first success in a Nieuport Scout by crashing an H.A. on the 1st of July. He soon afterwards reverted to two-seaters for a month, and his next victim fell on the 22nd of August. He returned to England on the 3rd of October after shooting down a total of twelve German machines, mostly two-seaters in which he specialized. He came out to France again in April, 1917, to continue his meteoric career. (See *Captain Albert Ball*—R. H. Kiernan.)

Towards the latter half of June the weather improved, the enemy became inquisitive about our preparations for the battle, and activity in the air increased. On the 17th Gray forced a fast biplane scout to land and machine-gunned it on the ground. Wilkinson crashed another H.A., but received several bullets in his own engine during the fight.

On the 18th a reconnaissance in force at 8 p.m. by a German two-seater squadron led to a battle royal. Wilkinson, Wood and Morgan attacked a formation of nine aeroplanes and broke it up; Wilkinson crashed one machine and forced another to land; Morgan forced one to land intact on our side of the lines. The weather was cloudy on the 19th, 20th and most of the 21st, but on the latter date Tidmarsh had a hot fight with several H.A. and forced one to land.

Lanoe now increased his offensive patrols to five machines each, and pushed them far out over the enemy's lines so as to engage and keep the hostile machines well away from our territory whilst the final preparations for the battle were being made. He gave the order that under no circumstances was a German machine to be allowed to cross our lines and the pilots became so obsessed with the vital need of carrying out this order that they did not count the odds against them and were prepared to attack under any conditions. Lanoe made them feel that by using intelligence and courage the chances would always be in their favour and if outnumbered their success would be counted the greater. They were his Davids fighting the German Goliaths.

There were several "dog-fights" on the 22nd in which Chapman destroyed one H.A.; Wilkinson was slightly wounded and his machine hit and damaged; Hughes-Chamberlain forced one H.A. to land; Ker had a fight with nine H.A. and received twenty bullets in his machine, some of his control wires being cut, but he managed to return safely; Jenkins, in spite of his machine-gun being jammed, dived repeatedly on a Fokker and succeeded in driving it away from the reconnaissance aeroplane he was escorting; Knight and Chapman attacked a group of seven or eight L.V.G.'s; the 52nd Anti-Aircraft Battery confirmed two H.A. shot down in this fighting.

One morning the zooming and roaring of an aeroplane brought T. out of his dugout; there, to his surprise, he saw a D.H.2 dive steeply over the flood waters of the Ancre at Aveluy, just touch the surface like a swallow drinking and then zoom up again, do an Immelmann turn and repeat the stunt. He was in no doubt that Lanoe was the pilot and waved wildly to him; flying low over the dugouts Lanoe waved back; it was his method of finding out if T. were "at home", and a couple of hours later he turned up in a car. He had a look at the German trenches from the Command O.P. (observation post) and then took T. back with him to Bertangles. With Lanoe at the wheel, the return drive was a succession of hair-breadth and yet well-judged escapes from collision. The aerodrome was a buzz of activity, machines landing and taxi-ing in, others starting up and setting off, mechanics and riggers all busy at their work, pilots from neighbouring squadrons arriving to arrange escorts, telephone messages, flight commanders, equipment officer, flight sergeants, each requiring some point settled. A crowd of questioners greeted Lanoe on his arrival; he listened to each in turn and gave quick, definite answers; his decisions were clear, complete and satisfactory; no one needed further explanations; in a few minutes, in his quiet incisive voice, he disposed of what had seemed a mass of difficult questions. Then he led the way to the sheds, and, with his head on one side, watched the canvas being stripped from the fuselage of a D.H.2; when removed it disclosed both main lower longerons, which were split. Lanoe looked at T., and T. looked at Lanoe; no words were necessary;

the defect was clearly due to a fault which put the pilot's life deeper in jeopardy. Still without a word Lanoe led the way to another machine, also stripped; neat steel shackles had been fitted round the longerons preventing splitting. The brothers grinned at each other; it was such a typical example of Lanoe's resort to a simple and effective solution to what had seemed a very serious defect requiring a radical alteration in design; soon Lanoe's shackles were fitted to all D.H.2's in France.

Later in the day a patrol came in which had had a hot fight. Lanoe heard the account of each pilot, asking many searching questions; the pilots criticised each other freely, and equally freely admitted when they had been at fault; rank counted for nothing, and the discussion was remarkable for its good humour, and above all for the intense desire to co-operate more effectively the next time. Lanoe never failed to have some practical and helpful suggestions to make; this pilot should have made sure that there was no Hun within reach of his tail, or that a D.H.2 was protecting it before diving on what was likely to be a decoy; the leader should have attacked the nearer Hun flight more promptly so as to prevent both Hun flights joining up; when the Huns attacked from above the correct manoeuvre was to spiral upwards; and so on. There was no question of reproach; it was purely a matter of profiting by experience; the lessons learnt by one patrol were passed on to the others, and the general fighting efficiency of the squadron was thereby greatly increased. Mutual co-operation and confidence in each other forged the key to their success.

" 22.6.16.

I went and saw T. yesterday and brought him back here for a change. He slept in my domain and returned next morning. Very pleasant having him within reach, and makes a change for both of us. I went up to his O.P. and looked at the Hun trenches, and a battery commander dropped a dozen 4.5 shells into their trenches just to show how it's done, very nice for the man in the trench!

The weather is nice and warm, the mess is very comfy and the huts are nice and fresh in the wood. I have a nice little bathroom stuck on to mine.

Of course we are all worked to blazes in this fine weather, but the longest day is now over, and the days get shorter and shorter thank God. 4 a.m. to 9.30 p.m. are our flying hours! That leaves seven and a half hours for *supper* and bed.

My lads are splendid beyond belief and the Hun gets a poor time with the D.H.'s about. We got two on Sunday. Monday one of mine attacked eight close together and got one, three attacked nine and got one in our lines and two their side. Tuesday was dud, but we got one yesterday and two today, all t'other side. Some land successfully in fields, but they don't wait now.

You can imagine the pleasure it is to command such a splendid lot of youngsters.

But how I long for this straffe to cease! I do so want peace and quiet and home comforts."

The spirit in the squadron was ecstatic. The young pilots went out like a pack of hounds on the scent, yelping for the blood of a Fokker. Decorations and mentions in despatches were the natural rewards of their exploits, and were made the occasion for hilarious celebrations. Lanoe kept a strict rule in the squadron that no alcoholic drink could be had till all flying had ended for the day.

That night there was a " binge " in the mess, during which T. noticed that one of the newly arrived pilots had a medical dressing on his head stretching from the centre of his forehead backwards for about five inches.

" What's been happening to you? " he asked. There was an awkward silence as this pilot looked down at his plate, and T. turned enquiringly to Lanoe.

" Serves him right," said Lanoe a little grimly. " He didn't obey orders to keep his head down when passing through the gauge." The " gauge " was a French side-board, with a shelf beneath the usual cupboard which had ornamental finials, at each end. Newly arrived pilots, as part of their initiation ceremony were swung by their comrades and projected face down from one end of the shelf to the other to slide out in a heap if satisfactorily gauged. If the novice, to see where he was going, raised his head, his scalp was split by the sharp point of the finial at the far end, as this youngster's had been and it required a few stitches from the medical officer to repair it.

T. looked at him sympathetically. " I have learned to keep my head down without orders," he said. This produced a howl of laughter from the pilots who could imagine T. with his 6ft. 5ins., doubled up as he crept along the trenches.

And so the fun went on, but not for long, as the pilots had to be up early on morning patrols.

In the cool night air, standing outside Lanoe's hut in the sweet-smelling copse, the distant rumble of the guns could just be heard, and their flash clearly seen across the dark sky, mocking the summer lightning.

With such a complete command of the air, with so great a concentration of guns and men against him, could the enemy save himself from defeat? We did not think so then, and that night the stars were very bright with promise.

The next morning T. stopped in the entrance to the office, his attention arrested by a large notice board; there before him was a distilled drop of Hawker's spirit, pure as the clear air his pilots breathed on their lofty patrols; on the board was pinned a single sheet of paper, which started with the preamble :—

" Tactical orders by O.C. No. 24 Squadron, Royal Flying Corps."

and it was signed :—

"L. G. Hawker, Major, Commanding No. 24 Squadron, Royal Flying Corps."

The tactical orders consisted of two words only :—

" ATTACK EVERYTHING."

This was exactly what the pilots set about doing. There were not enough H.A. willing to fight for their liking; the few they met, when on offensive patrol, they drove down to the ground and machine-gunned the German airmen if they showed any signs of life; they chased trains and punctured the locomotives, chased cars off the roads, bolted carts so that they overturned, chivvied horsemen, shot up infantry and any other moving targets. The German aeroplanes dared hardly show themselves, and soon their infantry would not shoot at our low-flying aeroplanes for fear of drawing fire upon themselves. This was the " mastery of the air almost undisputed " which General von Hoeppner admits existed on the Somme front. The change for the better in the situation in the air was so conspicuous that General Rawlinson was frequently sending messages of congratulations to Lanoe's pilots.

Our general bombardment started on the 24th of June, and this marked the opening phase of the Battle of the Somme. On the 25th No. 24 Squadron supplied escorts for a balloon strafe in which Lanoe took part. Three enemy balloons on the Fourth Army front were shot down in flames, and Manfield shot a Fokker to pieces in the air. From the morning of the 26th till noon on the 29th of June the weather was " dud " with low clouds and rain, making flying impossible. This gave the Germans a valuable respite at a critical moment. On the evening of the 29th, McNamara gallantly attacked four H.A. far over the enemy lines, but was himself shot down.

On the 30th, the eve of the infantry assault, at 7.30 p.m. Cowan and Prothero had a successful fight with five H.A., driving them down well behind their lines. At 8.20 p.m., when our troops were filing up to their assembly trenches for their attack on the morrow, and if seen by the enemy would give him warning, a squadron of hostile two-seaters, flying low to avoid our offensive patrols, made towards our lines ; it was an anxious moment. T., who was at the group observation post, saw them approaching and telephoned direct to Lanoe, asking him to chase them away ; they seemed to be trying to jockey each other a little nearer our lines, but were too timid to fly boldly over. In an incredibly short time three D.H.2's arrived, and the hostile machines scurried off like a lot of school girls ; the Germans had an excellent system of look-outs and ground signals, which they appeared to use to enable their airmen to avoid a fight should they so desire.

" The engine is the heart of an aeroplane, but the pilot is its soul. They succeeded so well that at the opening of the Battle of the Somme on the 1st of July, 1916, the Royal Flying Corps held the mastery of the air, that is to say, they held a predominant position in the air, and were able to impose their will upon the enemy." (V. I, p. 414.)

So successful were our machines in keeping the hostile airmen from prying over our lines, that the German generals were misled concerning the front on which the attack would be launched, and took no steps to reinforce the threatened divisions before the attack fell on them. (See *Military Operations, 1916*, pp. 318 and 485.)

31

The Sky Swept Clear

ON the 1st of July the attack on the southern part of the Somme front came as a surprise to the Germans, whose reconnaissance and photographic machines had been kept from discovering our preparations there, but the battle was lost before it started, for its success or failure depended upon the orders issued by the General Staff, and these orders took insufficient account of the realities of war.

" That greater success was not gained, was, however, as much due to faulty tactical directions from the General Staff, and to lack of experience in the higher ranks. . . . " (*Military Operations, 1916,* p. 491. See also pp. 485-9.)

All other conditions for a battle were in our favour; we had mastery in the air, more complete than at any time before or after; this meant a mastery too of the German artillery, for our guns could be ranged by wireless from our aeroplanes on to the enemy guns, and yet themselves remain undetected and immune from hostile fire. We could cut the German barbed wire entanglements, shell their trenches, their trench mortars, their ammunition dumps and all their vulnerable spots without risk of interference. The Germans dared not retaliate; if a German battery, bolder than the others, disclosed its position by opening fire whilst one of our constant aeroplanes was in the sky, it was soon spotted and silenced by an overwhelming concentration of our guns.

Our infantry were in fine condition, their morale never better and, with their stiffening of veterans, they were sufficiently trained if well directed from above. Failure was due to the system which led to our staff officers remaining far behind the lines, and thus becoming increasingly out of touch with the war. If the staff officers responsible for formulating the operation orders had gone over the top with the infantry, they would either have taken a greater interest in the dispositions they made so as to insure the success of the attack, or they would quickly have become casualties and made way for better men. Also they would have earned the confidence and respect of the officers and men in the line if they had shared their dangers, instead of the contempt with which those who did the fighting so often regarded the staff officers whose " out-of-touch " orders too frequently led to undue casualties amongst our own men.

The 1st of July seemed to No. 24 Squadron the culminating point of their training and preparation; each pilot was ready and eager for the fray, fully confident in his ability to beat whatever forces the Germans might put into the skies, for it was expected that the enemy would make a big effort to regain control of the air, at least over his own lines.

After several weeks' work, Lanoe had just completed the drawings of his latest invention, the " Hawker Fore-sight ", to which he attached some importance, and now felt free to take part in the battle; henceforth he paid no attention to the order forbidding him to cross the lines, judging that the risk was justified during operations of such magnitude, nor did his seniors appear to disapprove of his action. He carried out reconnaissances, supervised his patrols, often joining them in a fight, and when the pressure of work became heavier, and his pilots tired with the constant strain, he took the place of one or other of them so as to give him a rest, sometimes doing two patrols of two hours each in a day.

In this work he suffered from the disadvantage of flying strange machines, the peculiarities of which might be embarrassing in a fight; for instance, on his own machine each pilot knew by some private marks the best settings of the petrol valve under varying conditions of height and temperature; it took time and experience to find these settings and every pilot disliked borrowing a strange machine, the idiosyncrasies of which had to be learnt afresh. Lanoe was not deterred by these difficulties; he had great confidence in his ability to fly any machine under any conditions, and took over a D.H.2 at short notice without the slightest hesitation.

One of the most nerve racking moments of a pilot's life was his last patrol just before going on leave. Too often this had proved the fatal moment. Lanoe was aware of this apprehensive feeling and frequently made a point of taking such a pilot's place at this moment, so that he could depart on leave with a light heart.

However, the occasions on which he flew behind the enemy's lines were, of necessity, far fewer than those of a pilot whose sole duty was to go on patrol regularly every fine day, and sometimes twice a day; thus Lanoe lacked the constant practice and experience of his pilots, and this became a greater handicap when the Germans brought out new and better machines. Realizing this handicap, he usually took the place of another pilot and refrained from displacing the patrol leader.

On the 1st of July he began a daily system of offensive patrols of six or seven machines each which, according to the Air Ministry " Short History of No. 24 Squadron ", " were to gain for the R.F.C. early in the Somme Battle such a complete ascendency over the German Air Service."

These patrols sought out the enemy wherever he was to be found, and chased him down so that the air was kept clear for our reconnaissance, artillery and contact machines to do their work unmolested.

Lanoe did two reconnaissances over the enemy lines on the 1st of July, one at noon and the other in the evening, giving in detail the positions of our and the enemy infantry and the movements on the roads. Both Cowan and Bayetto had successful combats, the latter with Sibley also attacking a balloon. Bayetto repeated his attacks on balloons, but lacking rockets or incendiary bullets he could not succeed in setting them on fire.

On the 3rd the squadron extended the field of its activities southwards to take in the area in front of the French Sixth Army. On this day Gray was shot down by an anti-aircraft shell, a grim reminder that Archie could bite as well as bark. The weather then became cloudy for a week with few bright intervals, and Lanoe had time to visit the trenches again.

" 6.7.16.

I've been up and had a look at the various bits of war-on-the-ground on days when the weather's been dud.

Our fellows were splendid, but the Hun was very tenacious in one or two places. We examined some of their trenches, and they were a sight, beautifully deep and tidy at one time I suppose, but now all blown to pieces and the dug-outs in a horrid mess, tho' most of them held up all right.

We've been fairly busy of course, but the Hun is very much under-dog this end and doesn't give us much trouble, except to find him."

Lanoe again ventured too far forward, and this time was "ticked off" by some infantry officers for exposing himself.

T. by then had left the Somme front with the shattered remains of the 8th Division, the artillery of which was employed to support a holding attack on a "quiet" part of the line southwest of Armentières. But here the German airmen held their own, and our reconnaissance aeroplanes were unable to spot the enemy guns and prevent them from inflicting heavy casualties on some of our batteries. The position in the air was an unpleasant surprise to our gunners, who had expected the same protection as on the Somme, and now longed for the aggressive pilots of No. 24 Squadron to chase the German machines away.

On the 6th the weather was a little better, and the Germans began to dispute the tenancy of the air over their lines on the Somme front. They appeared with new two-seater machines firing one M.G. forward, either over the propeller or through its sweep, and another gun backwards operated by the observer. These machines were faster than the D.H.2's, both on the level and climbing, and had a higher service ceiling. This was not surprising, as it was now over a year since the first D.H.2 had been tested, and in the meantime the Germans had been busy developing bigger and better engines and more efficient aeroplanes; these new German machines, manned by picked pilots and experienced machine-gunners, could give a good account of themselves, and though the D.H.2's succeeded in driving them down, their own machines were often hit in the fight, Manfield and Cowan, amongst others, having very narrow escapes, but Wood managed to shoot down one of them.

About this time two N.C.O. pilots arrived, both courageous fighters, but on principle Lanoe did not like having other than officer pilots in his squadron; so much of No. 24's success was due to his personal influence, the optimistic atmosphere he was able to maintain, and the spirit of attack with which he imbued his pilots, that he felt he could not obtain the same results from those who, unable to share the mess life, did not come under his influence to the same extent. The squadron contained a number of naturally brave and dashing spirits, and Lanoe blended all who came under his command into a happy gallant band.

Numerous combats took place every fine day. Honnet, Pither, Prothero and Chapman each shot down an H.A., but on the whole the German machines kept well back over their own lines and avoided close encounters, despite the fact that they were receiving strong reinforcements. Lanoe was up occasionally supervising the patrols, but the H.A. were sufficiently shy for him not to feel any anxiety about his pilots, who attacked without hesitation everything they could see.

As air targets were becoming scarcer, Lanoe gave orders for the offensive patrols to " straffe troops on the ground whenever seen ". He also obtained some tracer ammunition with which to " straffe the balloon which does a great deal of harm to the infantry ".

On one of his expeditions to the trenches Lanoe collected from a captured dug-out some German field postcards as souvenirs. He wrote home on them without realizing the momentary shock they would administer to his startled mother who, on first sight of the German printing, imagined that he had been taken prisoner.

" Feldpostbrief.   15.7.16.
We have been having rather a hard time lately, and one or two of my chickens are feeling the strain, but the result has been well worth it.
Looking through our records, I see we have crashed a total of twenty, which isn't so bad.
How do you like my new style of paper? purchased from a Hun dugout. Nasty smelly one too, due, we discovered, to 'half a dead-un' someone had left behind. I don't mind meeting dead Huns s'long as they aren't too old, but I do hate seeing some poor Khaki."

The first phase of the Battle of the Somme, which had given us a six thousand yard footing on the main ridge, came to an end with a spell of bad weather, which prevented the essential air co-operation; our scout pilots had been completely successful in preventing the German aeroplanes from maintaining adequate reconnaissance across the lines, or from interfering with the work of our corps machines.

" On no single occasion were the co-operating aeroplanes prevented by the enemy aircraft from doing the duty allotted to them. Furthermore, although it was impossible to seal the air so that no hostile aeroplane could break through, the offensive patrols over the enemy's back areas kept the German airmen so occupied that the assistance which they were able to give to their own artillery and infantry in the first phase of the battle was negligible." (V. II, p. 234-5.)

The moral effect of our mastery of the air was immense; our infantry felt safe to move and our guns to fire without fear of enemy aeroplanes watching from above. On the other hand the German infantry and artillery were under the constant observation of our machines, and in continual apprehension of being shelled as a consequence; they dared neither move nor fire. This complete mastery of the air had only been won by a concentrated effort against the enemy's aircraft, especially his scouts, by fostering the spirit of attack, and by the careful training, hard work and undaunted courage of the pilots, all of whom did two and sometimes three patrols of two hours day after day. Some of Lanoe's pilots were feeling the strain, but not one would miss a patrol, if he could help it, so long as the battle continued. Each felt that victory depended on the unremitting work of Hawker's Squadron.

32

German Reinforcements

On the 19th of July the German First Army was revived under the command of General von Below and occupied the Somme front opposite the British. It took over from the Second Army 74 aeroplanes, and received reinforcements of 66 two-seaters and two new single-seater fighter squadrons of 12 machines each. From now onwards the German air service on the Somme was consistently strengthened. (V. II, p. 236-7.)

On the 29th of August General von Falkenhayn was succeeded as Chief of the General Staff by Field-Marshal von Hindenburg, who ordered the immediate suspension of the Verdun offensive, and began a defensive concentration on the Somme front. A thinning of the German Air Force at Verdun and on all other fronts began at once, and, by the middle of October, 1916, when the German air concentration reached its peak, more than a third of their air force was opposed to the British and French on the Somme. (V. II, p. 251.)

On the 8th of October a complete re-organization of the German air service was begun under General von Hoeppner who was, by his enthusiasm and administrative ability, well fitted for his new command. By the 15th of October the number of aeroplanes with the First Army had increased to 333, including 45 single-seater fighters, which latter were " more effective than anything we could oppose to them ". (V. II, p. 304-5.)

The Fokker monoplane, which had proved so successful from the autumn of 1915 until the spring of 1916, was replaced in August by the faster Halberstadt and D type Albatros scouts, which had as armament two fixed machine-guns firing through the propeller. " As fighters they outclassed every contemporary British aeroplane opposed to them." (V. II, p. 281-2.)

These single-seater fighters were grouped into " Jagdstaffeln " each consisting of 14 aeroplanes. Seven were formed in August, eight in September, and nine in October. " These Jagdstaffeln, whose sole duty was fighting, were intended to overcome the superiority of the enemy in the air on the Somme. . . ." (V. II, A. VII.)

The pilots were ordered to fight in strong formations of as much as a whole " Jagdstaffel ".

" The personnel of a ' Jagdstaffel ' was chosen with particular care. Only such pilots whose airmanship had already been proved reliable when with the reconnaissance flights could be recommended for training as fighter pilots. After a short course of practical training at the Grossenheim (Saxony) and Paderborn (Westphalia) single-seater fighter schools, these pilots passed for special training to the ' Jagdstaffeln ' school near Valenciennes, which training was concluded in the ' Jagdstaffeln ' at the front." (V. II, A. VII.)

This methodical care contrasted vividly with the British extravagance in sending inexperienced and untrained pilots into the furnace of the Somme.

" Boelcke, who had been empowered to organise one of the new pursuit squadrons for the Somme, had a free hand in the choice of his officers, and invited Manfred Freiherr von Richthofen to join his new unit, an invitation which was readily accepted. The new unit, known as Jagdstaffel 2, was formed on the 30th of August, 1916, at Lagnicourt, where the pilots impatiently awaited the arrival of their new aeroplanes. Meanwhile Boelcke made occasional patrols alone. The first batch of new aeroplanes arrived on the 16th of September." (V. II, p. 282.)

Lanoe and Boelcke had much in common and their squadrons had frequent encounters, in which, in the end, both of these leaders were destined to lose their lives.

The German reorganization and reinforcement of their air service found no counterpart, as yet, in ours. Whilst we improved our two-seaters and manufactured some efficient engines for them, little progress was made in improving the scouts for the R.F.C., and we were largely dependant on the French for their engines. The only up-to-date scouts available in the summer and autumn of 1916 were either the French Spads or Nieuports or the Sopwith Pups and Triplanes. The French needed the Spads for themselves, and the navy absorbed most of the few Nieuports which the French could spare us. The navy also monopolized the output of the Sopwith factory, and used these scout machines for operations near the coast. The naval officers were not to blame for doing their best for their own service; the fault lay with the muddled system of competition for the output of the British aircraft industry between the services, which should have been remedied by the Government. Mr. Asquith's weak policy of appointing committees without executive authority prolonged the trouble.

The few Nieuport Scouts, which had been obtained by the R.F.C., with difficulty, were used in August to re-equip a squadron withdrawn from the line owing to its heavy casualties. It is doubtful if this policy was sound, and it may fairly be argued that better use could have been made of these efficient machines by experienced fighter pilots in a successful squadron.

It seems certain that had No. 24 Squadron been re-equipped with Nieuport Scouts in the late summer of 1916, it would not only have held its own with the latest German machines, but would have continued to be the terror of the German air force right into 1917, instead of being, as it inevitably was, steadily worn down by casualties due to its obsolete aeroplanes.

The Nieuport Scout had a superior performance to the D.H.2, had a more reliable engine and, as it was a tractor bi-plane, the Lewis gun could be aimed upwards as well as forwards, a valuable feature.

The following figures are taken from *War in the Air*, Appendix XXVI.

Aeroplane and engine	Speed in m.p.h.		Climb in minutes		Service Ceiling
	at 6,500 ft.	at 10,000 ft.	to 6,500 ft.	to 10,000 ft.	
D.H.2 100 h.p. Mono Gnome	86	77	12	25	14,000 ft.
Nieuport Scout 110 h.p. Le Rhone	107	101	$5\frac{1}{2}$	9	17,400 ft.

Of the British single-seater squadrons sent as re-inforcements to the Somme front, only No. 21 (B.E.12's) joined the IVth

Brigade on the Fourth Army front, and its machines were too clumsy to be of any use and were withdrawn in September. This was unfortunate for Lanoe's pilots, who would have been very glad of help in the heavy work of keeping the air clear over the Somme battlefield.

Eventually, but after Lanoe's time, our worst deficiencies were remedied. The two flying services were amalgamated into the Royal Air Force, we produced greater quantities of efficient scout machines, notably the Bentley Camel and S.E.5, with more reliable engines and improved armament, outnumbering the enemy. Our scout pilots received special training and squadrons were concentrated on vital battle fronts.

That the German pilots fought on, outnumbered, short of essential supplies, with small hope of victory, and yet denied us the same mastery of the air that we won on the Somme, must invoke our admiration for their courage and tenacity.

33

Attack Everything

THE second phase of the battle, a tense struggle for the main ridge, was marked by the arrival of substantial German air reinforcements opposite the British front. The German squadrons had orders to put a stop to our incessant incursions far over their lines, and, feeling more confident in their new machines, were prepared to stand and fight when in superior numbers. This led to continual heavy fighting.

Lanoe did everything possible to keep up the strength of his patrols, sometimes taking part in them himself. There was no time to train newly arrived pilots, nor could they serve an apprenticeship in comparative safety behind our lines, since all fighting took place the German side. Lanoe sent them out with the experienced pilots, warning them not to become involved in ' dog-fights ', and above all to avoid presenting an easy target by diving the slow D.H.2 when there was a H.A. behind it. He taught them to spiral upwards, a difficult manoeuvre to perform, but very effective in avoiding the enemy's fire.

On the 19th of July in a fierce fight Chapman and Tidmarsh drove three enemy machines down, one of which appeared to be firing shells from a small gun. A few hours later Wilkinson, Wilson, Knight and Sibley were hotly engaged in a long fight with four Rolands, two Fokkers and several biplanes of different types. Wilson shot down a Fokker, and the D.H.2's fought on till compelled to return owing to lack of petrol. Shortly afterwards Tidmarsh and Chapman attacked five L.V.G.'s and six Rolands, which they forced to retire. In consequence of the increased German strength, escorted machines were asked to keep in close formation so that the D.H.2's could be more certain of giving them all adequate protection.

Lanoe was faced with a difficult problem. He had to supply escorts each fine day, provide army patrols at fixed times on a line roughly above the Bapaume-Peronne road, and in addition send out offensive patrols to seek out and fight the enemy well behind the lines. Each of these tasks demanded a strong formation of experienced pilots; he was not in a position to supply them at the same strength as the newly arrived German squadrons.

On the 20th the weather was misty, and the German machines left the escort alone after Bayetto drove one of their machines down, but in the evening, when the weather had cleared, an offensive patrol by " B " Flight met twelve H.A. willing to fight, and the battle that followed lasted twenty-five minutes. A copy of the combat report hangs today in the mess of No. 24 Squadron in memory of its glorious days in the war.

" COMBATS IN THE AIR.

Squadron : No. 24.   Date : July 20, 1916.

Type and No. of aeroplane : de Havilland   Time : 8.20 p.m.—
   Scouts. Nos. 5992, 6010, 5924, 7842.   8.45 p.m.
                               Duty : Offensive

Armament : 1 Lewis gun each.   patrol.

Pilots : Capt : R.E.A.W.H. Chamberlain,   Height : 10,000 ft.
   2/Lt. A. E. McKay, Lieut. C. M. B.
   Chapman, 2/Lt. H. C. Evans.

Observer : ——

Locality : FLERS.

     Remarks on hostile machine : Type, armament, speed, etc.
     8 type A (5 L.V.G's and 3 Rolands).
     3 type F.

NARRATIVE

The eight machines flying S. were joined over BAPAUME by three Fokkers, and Capt. Chamberlain led his patrol to the attack. Diving at an L.V.G., which immediately dived E., Capt. Chamberlain saw a Fokker underneath, attacked it, and fired half a drum. The Fokker went down in a nose-dive but flattened out very low down.

Attacked from behind by a Roland, Capt. Chamberlain, turning on a climb, out-manoeuvred and attacked it, firing the remainder of his drum. The Roland went down, but Capt. Chamberlain was too busy changing drums to see what became of it. Meanwhile Lt. Evans closed with a Roland, and fired half a drum at a range of only 25 yds. The Roland went straight down apparently out of control, and Lt. Evans was attacked from behind by two Fokkers, but these nearly collided and Lt. Evans escaped them and attacked an L.V.G. firing the remaining half of his drum.

Lt. Chapman attacked an L.V.G. which turned off, he was attacked from behind, but he escaped the H.A. by turning sharply and attacked another machine.

A Fokker and an L.V.G. attacked Lt. Evans, whose gun jammed, but were driven off by Lt. Chapman. Lt. Evans cleared the jam and attacked an L.V.G. which dived E.

Lt. McKay's engine was running badly, and he could only reach 8,500 at which height he followed under the patrol. A Roland dived at him from in front, but Lt. McKay out-manoeuvred it and attacked, firing the remainder of his drum. The Roland ceased fire and fell in a spinning nose-dive. Lt. McKay was now attacked by a Fokker, which he could not out-manoeuvre owing to his engine being shot, so to escape its fire, he descended in a steep spiral. Lt. Chapman, observing this, dived to the rescue, and attacked the Fokker at 1,000 over HIGH WOOD. The Fokker fell in a spinning nose-dive, hit the ground at S3b7.6 and burst into flames. Capt. Chamberlain was attacked by a Fokker which dived straight at him firing continuously from 400 yds. Capt. Chamberlain flew straight at it firing from 100 yds. till it passed just over his head. The Fokker went down, but Capt. Chamberlain did not see what happened to it, as he immediately attacked an L.V.G.

Meanwhile Lt. Evans attacked and drove off an L.V.G. and a Fokker.

All H.A. had now been driven off retiring down E., except one Fokker, which tried to manoeuvre on to Capt. Chamberlain's tail. Capt. Chamberlain, however, climbed in a spiral to attack and the Fokker climbed away East.

Capt. Chamberlain and Lt. Evans remained on patrol for another quarter of an hour, but did not see any more H.A.

The A.A. batteries reported 1 de Havilland and 3 H.A. driven down. The de Havilland was Lt. McKay, but he managed to return low down though his engine was badly shot about.

An observer of No. 9 Squadron who saw the fight reports three H.A. were shot down and crashed, one of them bursting into flames. Probably the following were responsible for the three H.A. brought down.

1. Lt. Evans, who fired half a drum into a Roland from 25 yards.
2. Lt. Mckay, who attacked a Roland which ceased fire, and was seen to fall in a spinning nose-dive by several pilots.
3. Lt. Chapman, who attacked a Fokker, and saw it crash and burst into flames.

(sgd.) L. G. Hawker,
Major,
Commanding No. 24 Squadron.
Royal Flying Corps."

From evidence which came in later Lanoe added to this report :—

> " 4. Capt. Chamberlain, 1 Roland or 1 Fokker or perhaps both seen to fall out of control by observer on ground.
>
> 4. N.B. 4th Army observers from the ground saw :—
> 1 machine fall in flames.
> 1 burning on the ground and 2 or 3 falling out of control.
>
> It is therefore probable that 1 Roland or 1 Fokker or both were brought down by Capt. Chamberlain."

In the whirl of those hectic days there was little time to bother about the details in a report and apparently this correction did not reach the headquarters' file.

This was a very important combat, for the German Air Force, with the help of reinforcements, was making its first attempt to wrest back the mastery of the air from us. Had one of 'B' Flight pilots lost his nerve, or had its gallant commander retired in the face of what might well have seemed long odds, the day would have been lost and the enemy encouraged to fresh efforts. As it was the German airmen, after suffering severely, retired precipitately to their aerodrome, convinced that the D.H.2 pilots were too good for them.

General Trenchard knew of German reinforcements arriving on his front, and was particularly pleased at this early sign that our pilots could cope with them. He sent them the following message :—

> " Well done No. 24 Squadron in the fight last night. Keep it going. We have the Hun cold."

No. 24 Squadron was jubilant at having got to grips at last with the enemy, and at beating him despite his numbers.

It had been exasperating to such keen pilots that the German machines, with their greater speed, dived easily home. Now if they were going to stand and fight there would be a chance of showing what could be done with the careful training and practice Lanoe had given them.

The squadron was, therefore, in high spirits on the 21st of July, and eager for all comers. Its first patrol of five D.H.2's led by Andrews, in company with two F.E.'s of No. 22 Squadron, went off at half past six, and was in its first fight, with five

Rolands and five Fokkers, an hour later over Roisel. One of
the Fokkers was shot out of the fight by Andrews, and went
down to crash its under-carriage as it landed in a field. Pither
followed it to the ground, and scattered with his fire a group of
men who had run to the wreckage. In the meantime a general
fight was in progress above, and eventually all the enemy were
dispersed, three Fokkers having gone down, but under control.
Honnet's D.H.2 and the two F.E.'s, hit many times, were compelled to return. The remaining four D.H.2's closed up and
continued their patrol towards Peronne, where Lanoe joined
them. They soon discovered below them four two-engined
machines flying towards the British lines. Lanoe led his formation down and fought the Germans back to their aerodrome.

In describing this offensive patrol he wrote.—

> " I joined the O.P. at 8 a.m. S. of Peronne, but could not
> see the F.E.'s. Observing four type G flying W. underneath
> in open formation, I waved to the nearest D.H., dived and
> attacked the near machine, which was lower than the others.
> I opened fire at about 100 yards, but my gun came loose in
> the mounting spoiling my aim. I attacked about four other
> machines at various times, but had great difficulty with my
> gun. The double drums worked perfectly and were easier
> to change than the single. Having lost a lot of height I
> retired to climb and then rejoined the fight. The H.A. retired
> E. I chased one to YPRES but was only overhauling him
> very slowly, so finished my drum at a range of about 150-200
> yards."

The defective gun mounting was exasperating, but Lanoe
suffered, as usual, from the disadvantages of flying someone else's
machine.

The midday patrol met and drove back east first seven H.A.
over Martinpuich, then five H.A. over Morval. Some H.A.
kept up at 15,000 feet, a height the D.H.2 could not reach. At
5 p.m. the squadron provided an escort for a balloon strafe, but
though they " sat " for twenty-five minutes over the balloons the
attacking aeroplanes failed to turn up.

" The squadron's next fight came in the evening when three
pilots, flying with two from No. 22 Squadron, joined a Morane
Parasol pilot of No. 3 Squadron in an attack, lasting half an
hour, on fifteen German aeroplanes over Bapaume. One enemy
machine crashed near Warlencourt, another fell into the village

of Combles, and a third dropped to earth at Beaulencourt. Two others were forced to land in a field, after which the remaining aeroplanes in two's and three's flew away east leaving the air to the British formation which had inflicted its defeat without loss to itself." (V. II, p. 263.)

It had been a busy day for Hawker's Squadron.

Extract from The Fourth Army Intelligence Summary of the 21st of July, 1916 :—

" Hostile aircraft were very active but did not interfere with our artillery machines which engaged 36 targets."

That was the true measure of success.

Copy of message to O.C. No. 24 Squadron, dated 22.7.16 :—

" General Trenchard has telephoned his congratulations to No. 22 and No. 24 Squadrons on their excellent work accomplished yesterday and on the evening of the 20th. He has informed the Commander-in-Chief of the work done.

From O.C. 14th Wing."

During numerous offensive patrols in the following week of dull weather few H.A. were seen, and these mostly scurried home again.

Lanoe, well aware of the importance of this fighting, which he referred to as " obstinate fleet actions ", and greatly cheered at the success of his squadron, nevertheless was feeling the strain. Divisions, when tired, were moved to a quiet part of the line, the infantry were rested at regular intervals, but for No. 24 there was no respite, for it was the only scout squadron in the Fourth Army.

" 25.7.16.

I am getting a little war worn and want a rest, but don't see much chance of one just yet awhile. . . .

The Hun may think he now has our offensive well in hand, but slow and sure is our motto, and he'll be disagreeably surprised. Verdun'll be nothing to it."

" 29.7.16.

I am not getting as much leave as I did last summer I regret to say ; in fact I don't see a reasonable chance of any before September : Sad, is it not ? I do so miss my visits to you ; I wonder when the war will end ?

The Bosch seems to be getting a bad time all round, but he does hold on marvellously. We are getting a lot of our own back, now we've got the shells, and I suppose we'll just go on pounding away till he breaks to pieces."

The flower of the German army was being steadily destroyed by our shells directed by wireless from our artillery aeroplanes, working for long hours under the protection of the patrols from Lanoe's squadron.

The offensive patrols, five or six strong, frequently met German formations of from five to twenty machines, and drove them off east.

Then on the 30th the D.H.2 again killed one of Lanoe's best pilots and a dear friend. Lanoe was watching Wilson leave for the front and saw the machine catch fire and crash down into a barn which it set alight. He rushed to the spot and plunged recklessly into the flames in an attempt to drag the pilot out, but Wilson was already dead. Lanoe returned to the sheds, his cap burnt and his eyebrows singed off, very distressed at the accident. This was the only time that any of his pilots saw him badly shaken.

" 14.8.16.
I lost one of my lads the other day in a terrible accident. He had just been promoted and was going out on his last flight here ; when at 2,000 feet his machine suddenly burst into flames and fell like a stone, burying him in the debris of a barn which burnt down. Very sad and very dreadful as there was no obvious reason why the machine should have done that."

Lanoe was feeling tired and depressed, but on the last day of July, Saundby,* who had only arrived on the 25th, shot down a Fokker, though himself wounded in the arm, a staunch deed that greatly cheered Lanoe.

" 31.7.16.
The fine weather has been giving us a lot of work ; but we have earned much cudos straffing the Hun. Rather amusing today as we were photographed or rather cinematographed from the air. If it's a success it ought to be very interesting.†
Any news from T.? Where has he got to?

* Author of *Flying Colours,* and writer of the foreword to this biography.
† It would interest the writer to know what became of this film.

Rather difficult time just now as all my lads are being promoted in turn and heaps of new people coming, they do very
well though; it must be the atmosphere they find when they
arrive; my newest shot down a Fokker today and was wounded
himself—just a slight graze on the elbow—if they all carry on
as he did we'll keep up our reputation, which is pretty good
just now."

On the 6th of August Evans wounded the observer of a
German two-seater, and indicated to him that he must fly back
with the D.H.2, but as he did not comply with this invitation
Evans was reluctantly forced to shoot down the machine. On
the 7th Lanoe went on escort to a balloon strafe, but again the
attacking machines failed to turn up, much to his disappointment. On many offensive patrols Andrews, Evans and Cowan
were conspicuously successful. As a reward for their strenuous
fighting Andrews and Cowan received the M.C. and Evans
received the D.S.O. The latter was a very gallant officer who
had been gassed at Ypres, but, despite the permanent injury to
his lungs, he refused to go sick and, after much fearless fighting,
was finally killed in action in September.

Fighting was now continuous against superior numbers and
better machines. In such circumstances casualties were inevitable. On the 16th of August Hughes-Chamberlain was delayed
fifteen minutes by plug trouble, and had the mortification of
seeing his patrol go off without him. Fuming with impatience
he reached the lines at last, but could not see his flight. Coming
towards Albert with the obvious intention of crossing the lines
were eight German two-seaters in close formation. Chamberlain,
without the slightest hesitation, dived into the middle of them,
shooting left and right, and breaking up their formation. They
concentrated their fire on him and after a few minutes of a
whirling dog-fight he received a severe wound in his right foot.
His very gallant action had gained valuable time and as he
dived out of the fight the rest of his patrol arrived on the scene,
drove off the German machines and escorted him to safety. His
departure was a severe loss to the squadron; his calm courage
had been invaluable; he was an experienced pilot, a most capable
flight leader, a determined and skilful fighter, typical of those
who built up the magnificent reputation of No. 24 Squadron.

Several of Lanoe's best pilots were on the point of being

promoted, and some of his veterans were due for a well earned rest. He dreaded losing them, for in the mess they were such a happy family, and in action they were staunch and completely reliable, with divine confidence in each other. Moreover the squadron was three pilots below establishment, the Third Wing Scouts had dwindled away, and the newcomers were untrained.

With his new machines the enemy now could, and often did keep out of reach of the D.H.2's.

> " 19.8.16.
> The squadron continues in excellent form, tho' the Hun is very wary and nowadays it is extraordinarily difficult to get to close quarters.
> We raked in two more decorations the other day, making a total of one D.S.O. and five M.C's.
> The D.S.O. was a fairly new man, ex-observer, also ex-Boer War, who has shot down no fewer than four Huns in about a month.
> Leave, I'm afraid, is very problematical, but it ought to fructuate some time in Sept.
> I do hope it will, as I do so long to be with you again, even if it's only for a few short days."

The lack of leave had a serious effect on the efficiency of pilots. When they were too tired their reactions became slower and their perceptions less acute. It was a false economy to keep them at work too long.

In spite of his weariness, Lanoe continued to keep up the morale of his pilots and there were frequent evening visits from and to other squadrons and between these there were sing-songs and romps in the Mess which, if anything, became more frenzied than before.

These parties were always a great success and took the pilots' minds off the perils and trials of their work. But too soon the next day would break grimly to the portentous noise of the engines being warmed up for the dawn patrol. Once more they and their beloved friends in turn would take the air on their perilous patrols, once again they would be torn relentlessly, if sometimes unconsciously, by great anxiety. Only those who have experienced this strain day after day can understand what it cost to keep a cheerful face and a keen spirit to fly and fight without apparent end.

It was astonishing then, and seems even more so after careful thought, that these young pilots never faltered and always went up eager for a fight.

What a relief it was to forget these gnawing anxieties and fears, if only for a few brief hours, in the jolly companionship and good fun of these evening romps and rags.

On the 16th of August, Capon was posted to the squadron. The following account of his experiences gives a vivid picture of a gallant, but inexperienced and almost untrained pilot joining the foremost fighting squadron which was at grips with an enemy who had an ample supply of picked and well trained pilots in the latest and best machines : —

> "I took my ticket about May, 1916, and went to Joyce Green in July for instruction on single-seaters (D.H.2 and F.E.8).
>
> I arrived at Bertangles in the early hours of the morning and went to bed in comfortable quarters. I was awakened by a batman who said 'A fine morning, Sir, and Mr. "A" has been shot down and Mr. "B" crashed in flames in the village'. (I think "A" was Hughes-Chamberlain and "B" came from another squadron.)
>
> I inherited 'A's' flying coat.
>
> I was sent up by Hawker to demonstrate that I could fly. I gave him of my best. When I landed I was ticked off for showing off and told that I would have to learn to do my turns without losing height.
>
> I had arrived in a squadron of veterans. I felt very inexperienced, the more so as I had never seen a Lewis gun."

To those who imagined that Lanoe's success was due to his picking his pilots, it will surely come as a revelation to learn that a youngster was posted to him, who had never before seen a machine-gun.

Lanoe's rebuke to a newcomer may have seemed harsh, but it was all-important that he should not lose height on turns, and he was so impressed by Lanoe's words that he remembered them after twenty years. Capon fought with the same courage as the rest of Lanoe's pilots, but he was wounded before the end of the month.

The fighting continued to become heavier and more difficult. No. 24 Squadron took steady toll of the German machines, but now suffered more and more casualties as the D.H.2 became further outclassed, and the veteran pilots were replaced by inexperienced and untrained ones.

Evans, Sibley, Knight, Cowan, Wilkinson, Byrne, Andrews, Glew and others all took part in successful fights, and Lanoe joined some of these offensive patrols.

The German scouts dived in formation on the D.H.2's, raking them with a short burst of fire as they flashed past, continued their dive in an easterly direction, climbed again when out of range and repeated the manoeuvre. The German two-seaters, keeping at a respectful distance, poured in a steady fire from their rear guns, and broke off the fight by side-slipping or diving if they felt in danger, returning to the attack if they were so inclined. With greater speed, more rapid climb and higher ceiling than the D.H.2, the new German machines could fight or not as it suited them. As the fighting took place over German territory, the enemy machines could always escape with ease by diving. They then climbed again, gathered in strong groups, and came forward for another tip and run fight.

In this way No. 24 Squadron was kept hard at work all day, for if the sky had been left vacant by our scouts at any time the German machines would have attacked our corps' aeroplanes and interrupted their work, which was indispensable to our progress on the ground.

" 27.8.16.
A record three days ago, in fact 81 hours : of which I did 3 hrs. 5 mins., which is a record in itself for our small beasties. The shooting isn't nearly as good as it used to be ; I went out myself to see how they were working, and was able to correct several errors.

The birds are very shy and I couldn't get near them, even single-handed.

I flushed a covey of five and got in a few long shots just as another covey came down wind overhead, but of course they were out of shot before I could reload.

I got a bit closer to three stray birds later on, and managed to wing one, but he got away.

Our bag for August is regrettably small compared with July —2½ brace instead of six—our total being 12½ brace."

During the fighting on the 25th Sibley's D.H.2 was wrecked by " cylindritis ", the vibration of the unbalanced engine partially breaking up the machine in the air, and dismounting the gun, which hit the pilot on the head, wounding him slightly. The machine crashed, and was a complete wreck; it was amazing that the pilot was not killed.

Sibley received some kind of concussion from his loosened machine-gun and could not remember what followed, but he staggered into a neighbouring squadron mess, stark naked and streaked all over with blood from his head wound, a startling sight to the officers and men of that unit.

The only thing he had not taken off was his identity disc and, after giving him every attention, they were able to discover his unit and report his whereabouts to Lanoe, who went over at once to see him and then to search for his crashed plane. This was eventually found in a tangled heap in a wood, which may have broken Sibley's fall and saved his life. The D.H.2 was a complete write-off.

Lanoe was sorry to lose Sibley and he to leave the squadron, but casualties were inevitable in these unreliable machines and all were thankful that Sibley was still alive to fly again.

On the 26th of August, as a reinforcement to the Fourth Army Air strength, No. 21 Squadron arrived at Bertangles with 17 of the clumsy B.E.12 single-seaters. All these machines were housed next to No. 24's sheds in one large Bessonneau hangar, which was blown over by a gale on the 29th of August, and the aircraft bundled into an ignominious tangle. It was no great loss, as the B.E.12 proved useless as a fighter, a disappointment to No. 24 Squadron's pilots, who would have been glad of a fresh scout squadron, which could share the strenuous air fighting now going on. However, they tried to console themselves by quietly " borrowing " some of the timber and canvas from the wrecked hangar to make extensions to their living quarters. Half the lorries sent to remove the damaged hangar for repairs failed to find a load, and official correspondence about this phenomenon continued for months.

On the 31st of August the D.H.2's had a number of fights with fast scouts of a new type which gave small chance of getting to close grips. Fighting was now almost continuous, and the squadron reported as many as twenty distinct combats in one day. Langan-Byrne, a dashing Irishman, dived into the middle of every hostile formation he saw, shooting left and right, scattering the German machines by his impetuosity. Only the limited performance of the D.H.2 and his lack of training prevented him from piling up a much larger score of victories.

On the 6th of September Lanoe went out with " A " Flight on evening patrol, and was engaged in fighting for an hour. The German machines, as usual, dived away east when closely engaged.

The second phase of the battle ended with a sad period for No. 24 Squadron. The heroic Evans fought three of the new German scouts until at last he was shot down. Glew, an excellent pilot, was killed by " cylindritis ", the tail booms being cut by the departing cylinders, leaving him no chance of controlling his machine. Manfield, a veteran pilot, was killed in a hot fight against heavy odds. Two newcomers, Briggs and Bowring were taken prisoners. But as a fighting unit the squadron remained conspicuously successful.

" 6.9.16.

How time does fly! September already, and the days getting shorter and shorter thank goodness.

I find I can't possibly get leave in September as I had hoped ; the battle is going too well.

I wish I could give details of our work, as really it's very interesting, but that would hardly do.

I have just been compiling our records, and find we have shot down 28 up to the end of August, and a further four on Sept. 2nd.

We've got one D.S.O. and five M.C.'s and I hope to get another two D.S.O.'s soon and two more M.C.'s a little later on.

No wonder the Hun is a little shy down here! I see they have been publishing extracts from prisoners' letters saying what the Hun thinks of his own Corps.*

I'm so glad the R.F.C. collared the Zep. as they've put an enormous amount of work into the job.

Talking of sights I made one myself in my own workshops and it's just going home to be taken up I hope. I am very proud of this one, as it has turned out a very neat job."

" In spite of the German air reinforcements, now making their presence felt, the corps' pilots and observers continued to do their

* A page of extracts of the laments of German soldiers on the measure of our superiority in the air on this front is given in *War in the Air,* Vol. II, p. 269, and an extract from General von Below's famous memorandum giving a clear idea of the material and moral effect of our domination of the air is given on the next page.

work with no effective interference whilst the fighting pilots continued to dominate the situation higher up." (V. II, p. 268.)

In a preface to *Flying Colours* by Captain R. H. M. S. Saundby, now Air Marshal Sir Robert Saundby, General Ashmore wrote :

" The artist of these pictures was one of a very gallant band of pilots who fought under the late Major Lanoe Hawker, V.C., during the Somme offensive of 1916.

The dash and skill of our scout pilots on that historic Front produced the nearest approach to command of the air that has been experienced up to the present time (September, 1918). For months on end no single aeroplane crossed our lines ; our contact patrol and artillery machines did their work unmolested, so far as the German air service was concerned. . . ."

Our success on the ground was dependent on the effective co-operation of the R.F.C. This co-operation was in turn contingent upon the protection afforded to the corps' machines by our scout pilots.

Lanoe fully realized the importance of the work being carried out by his squadron, and his policy continued to be :—

ATTACK EVERYTHING

34

Aeroplanes and Engines

BEFORE the war the R.F.C. had been starved for money, and depended on the French for engines and the Germans for magnetos. At the beginning of the war all available personnel and machines were sent to France, which handicapped expansion at home. Moreover skilled mechanics enlisted in the army, and so were lost to the R.F.C. and the R.N.A.S. Since the Admiralty had priority in all supplies, they obtained the best aircraft, but there were no means of allocating them to the most important tasks. (V. III, C. IV.)

The French, however, manufactured successful engines, especially of the air-cooled rotary type, but could only spare us a small supply.

The Germans found their water-cooled engines for airships easily adaptable to aeroplane use, and produced quantities of these, the most successful of which, the 160 h.p. Mercedes, was claimed by Fokker to be better than the Hispano-Suiza or even the Rolls-Royce. This Mercedes engine was first used in scout machines in the late summer of 1916 with great success. The German air force also designed and manufactured for its own use reliable machine-guns, and fitted two of these to each scout at an early date.

Both French and Germans concentrated their chief effort on producing a series of the best possible single-seater fighters, realising that all other air work depended upon the success of their scouts. Having carefully picked and trained their scout pilots they took care to supply them with a succession of these machines with the minimum of delay.'* In contrast to this policy, during the first two years of the war British designers and manufacturers concentrated their efforts on two-seaters. This

* Guynemer and Bert Hall made constant reference to the new and improved machines put at their disposal.

led to our scouts being completely out-classed in the autumn of 1916.

German H.Q. gave Boelcke, Richthofen and other leading fighter pilots far more practical support and freedom to use their initiative than did the higher command of the R.F.C. Also in the autumn of 1916 Boelcke's Staffel had the advantage of practising mock fights with a captured D.H.2, so that he and his pilots became familiar with the weakness of this machine, and confident in their ability to out-fly it.

" It has often been revealed in this history that technical superiority, not necessarily of great degree, is a dominant factor in air warfare." (V. VI, p. 445.)

Taking this into account, the full significance will be realized of the following table giving for comparison the performances of the Albatros D.II, the D.H.2 and our more modern scouts that came into service in the R.N.A.S. in 1916.

COMPARATIVE PERFORMANCES

Aeroplane and engine	Speed in m.p.h. at 6,500 feet	at 10,000 feet	at 15,000 feet	Time in minutes to climb : 10,000 feet	15,000 feet	Service ceiling in feet
D.H.2 100 h.p. Mono Gnome	86	77	—	25	—	14,000
Nieuport Scout 110 h.p. LeRhone	107	101	—	9	—	17,400
Sopwith Pup 80 h.p. LeRhone	106	104½	94	14.4	30	17,500
Sopwith Triplane 130 h.p. Clerget	116	114	105	10.5	19	20,500
Albatros D.II. 160 h.p. Mercedes	Speed :— 200 kilometers per hour (equivalent to 124 m.p.h.)			Climb :— 5,000 meters in 20 minutes (equivalent to 16,400 feet in 20 minutes.)		

Note :—Figures for the Albatros D.II supplied by the Reichsarchiv. For the other figures see *War in the Air*, Appendix XXVII.

The Albatros D.II, a well designed tractor biplane with its excellent stationary engine and two synchronized machine-guns, was a revolutionary advance in scout design, and the Fokker D.VII, the outstanding machine at the end of the war, still retained these basic characteristics and the same engine.

The D.H.2 was a back number compared with the Albatros D.II, and the saving grace was that few German pilots realized the markedly superior performance of their new machines over our old pushers. This was largely due to the courage with which the D.H.2 pilots continued to attack though out-classed. Boelcke and Richthofen, having practised with the captured D.H.2, became aware of the advantage they held, and, by their aggressiveness, set an example of success that gave confidence to the pilots in their squadrons. Boelcke was the first to contest the British mastery in the air, which Lanoe had established on the Fourth Army front in the summer of 1916. When Boelcke was killed Richthofen carried on the tradition. Both were exceptionally keen and capable pilots, but they remained over their own territory where No. 24 Squadron's offensive patrols were always prepared to fight them.

After Lanoe's death our offensive spirit waned for a time, and the German pilots, gaining confidence, crossed to our side, and shot down a substantial proportion of our machines in the British lines. Out of 27 machines lost in December, 1916, 17 fell in the British lines. (V. III, p. 320.)

It is interesting to notice that during Lanoe's lifetime not one of his pilots was killed by the enemy on our side of the lines, and that only two pilots of the squadron were so killed in the whole war, an indication of the way in which this squadron consistently fought over the enemy's lines.

35

Morale versus Material

THE 15th of September, which marked the opening of the last phase of the Battle of the Somme, again emphasized the vital importance of air co-operation with our artillery, our infantry and now with our tanks which went into action for the first time.

No. 24 Squadron was busy throughout the day keeping the air clear of German aeroplanes. There were many combats in which Knight crashed an H.A., Langan-Byrne brought down one in flames and crashed another. Going back to the aerodrome for more ammunition he entered the fight again, attacking repeatedly every H.A. he could see. He then joined Wilkinson in ground-strafing, the risk of which was many times multiplied by the unreliable engine which at any moment might deliver them as helpless prisoners into the enemy's hands. Wilkinson was apparently celebrating his receipt of a well earned D.S.O. by shooting at motor lorries, horsemen and troops at close range. The 16th and 17th also saw heavy fighting, and in a lively combat with seven H.A. Cowan shot down one in flames and drove another to earth, whilst Langan-Byrne accounted for a third.

" 19.9.16.

Very bad weather these last few days, pouring rain and decidedly cold.

We had a great time on the 15th and 16th, two of my people bagging no fewer than five Huns between them.

Bad time for the enemy just then, as I see by the papers we claimed no fewer than 22 put ' hors-de-combat '."

In spite of the substantial air reinforcements which the Germans had received, General Trenchard was able to report that in the last week " only 14 hostile machines crossed the line of the 4th Army area, whereas something like 2,000 to 3,000 of our machines crossed the lines during the week. Also the

artillery and contact machines have practically not been inter-
fered with at all for the last three days." (V. II, p. 284.)

No. 24 Squadron, by heavy and continuous fighting, kept the
H.A. busy over their own lines so that our Corps machines were
free to help our infantry forward. Casualties on the ground
were not measured in two's and three's, but by thousands, and
effective co-operation from the air enabled our guns and tanks
to crush the enemy defences, destroying his best soldiers, whom
the German commanders admitted were irreplaceable.

On the 16th of September Jagdstaffel 2 received its first batch
of new fast scouts. The next day Boelcke led five of them with
their specially selected and carefully trained pilots, including
Richthofen, into action for the first time, and each shot down
one of our two-seaters on a bombing raid. This remarkable
success gave Boelcke's fighting squadron immediate prestige and
proved the efficiency of the new German machines.

From now on Lanoe's pilots frequently reported combats with
" very fast enemy scouts ". Fighting in the air became increasingly severe on each fine day, Langan-Byrne plunging recklessly
into every combat. On the 23rd four H.A. concentrated their
fire on him at thirty yards, and shot through his engine, a tail
boom and the main spar. His machine-gun, ammunition drums
and undercarriage were shaken off, and his D.H.2, out of
control, drifted towards our lines with two German machines on
its tail. Tidmarsh dived to the rescue and drove the Germans
off, but Langan-Byrne was observed to crash in our trenches,
and great was the sadness in the squadron that evening. However, that night he turned up smiling at what he considered a
great joke. Langan-Byrne was out every flying day and, if
targets in the air were lacking or too high for him to reach, he
shot at troops, horsemen, transport, trains, anti-aircraft batteries,
in fact anything and everything hostile. His machine, as might
be expected, was constantly hit and several times he was forced
to land with his engine shot through. It was impossible to.
imagine a more dashing pilot, but he lacked the careful training,
both in flying tactics and in shooting, that Lanoe had given the
pilots who came out to France with the squadron. Now there
was no time for preliminary training, as the air was full of
German machines which had to be fought back unremittingly
to protect our two-seaters. Langan-Byrne was eager to fight any

numbers under any conditions, trusting to his own impetuosity and a great measure of luck to carry him through.

The month ended with Roche being wounded in the back by a very fast scout, probably from Boelcke's Staffel. He was rescued from amongst a pack of H.A., and escorted back to the aerodrome by Cowan and Saundby. This team work, typical of No. 24 Squadron, gave the pilots great confidence in each other.

These were anxious days for Lanoe, though he concealed his feelings from his pilots. He knew perfectly well that his machines were out-classed and out-numbered, but the moral factor was ever uppermost in his mind. With hidden apprehension he sent his young pilots out, some of them almost untrained. Each time he counted the returning machines with seeming unconcern, but when the last one landed safely, what a relief, what a relaxation of taut nerves! His " chickens " were safe—safe for one more day—and to such young and hazardous lives in these fantastic times one day might seem eternity.

The evening patrol was often the critical one and nerves were tense till all planes were safely back; both officers and other ranks would wait anxiously for the last man home. The mess became quiet, the gramophone silent and most of the pilots were reading or writing or seeming to do so, all with ears cocked, but pretending not to listen, for the familiar drone of the Gnome engine which would signal safe return.

Every now and then one of the pilots would get up and, feigning nonchalance, would stroll out of the hut and scan the distant sky, still light, as the land beneath faded into the night; his unconcern was denied by the fury with which he smoked his cigarette. Lanoe, pretending to read, made little progress; his jaw was firmly set and his mouth held in a straight line.

A shout outside, a cry from inside as everyone looked up, but the excitement was caused by the precautionary routine lighting of the flares along the landing path, just in case the missing pilot might return for a night landing.

No, he had not been seen.

The atmosphere in the mess became painfully tense and Lanoe was just about to move when the telephone buzzed. Many jumped up to answer it and the nearest pilot grabbed the receiver; after a short pause, as all held their breath, he shouted excitedly: "He's all right, his engine was shot up, he landed at Guillemont, and the Frogs are sending him back in one of their cars."

There were whoops of joy, everyone started talking at once, drinks were ordered, the gramophone turned on; it was all right.

Only Lanoe remained quietly seated; he was looking down unseeingly at his paper, his mouth now relaxed, quivering a little at the corners, as if he found it hard to smile. Too often it had not been all right, and the strain on him each time was taking its toll; it was agony waiting in doubt each time, and his vivid imagination made him realize what those at home must suffer, always waiting anxiously and wondering.

Suddenly he got up smiling, thrust his hands deep into his pockets and strolled over to the others to join in their conversation. He had not only the ability to concentrate completely on one subject, and then another, but also, by sheer will power, he could switch his mind from one mood to another, and this he did now. Anyone walking into the mess at this moment would never guess the strain from which he had been suffering a short time ago; there he was, calm, confident, smiling and talking without a tremor in his voice, and yet it had probably been a big effort to restrain his tears of relief a few minutes before.

That night, when the missing pilot turned up, there was a royal binge and romp to celebrate his safe return and Lanoe joined in with as much zest and fun as any of them.

One more day had passed and all his beloved young pilots were safe. It would not always be so, and as he lay in bed he wondered how many more days before this pitiless war would end?

Lanoe kept a watchful eye on his pilots and knew better than they did themselves the condition of their nerves. He had recommended two of his flight-commanders to be sent home as instructors—Wilkinson who, intensely keen, always dashed into action, though knowing well the danger, and Tidmarsh, the grand and gallant Irishman. Nine months was the maximum that could be expected at one stretch from these hard-working and hard-fighting pilots. It was a mistake to keep them too long in the line, and though they were glad of a respite they were most reluctant to leave 24 Squadron. Lanoe was very loath to lose them, but he was glad to feel that they would be safe for a while. He counted on filling their places by promoting some of his veteran pilots who knew his ways, and could be counted on to keep up the reputation of the squadron. His dismay was therefore intense when he learnt that one of the best of them, the naturally dashing Cowan, was to be posted as flight-commander to No. 29 Squadron, also flying D.H.2's.

" 2.10.16.
Not much luck with Huns this last fortnight, as tho' several have been chased off or down in a violent hurry none were seen to crash tho' three or four landed.

Other people, however, have been more lucky, so the enemy has by no means had a slack time.

Our quarterly bag is 23 brace, making a total of 55 birds, not bad on the whole, but they average 70 to 80 hours a piece.

Awful blow yesterday, as my best pilot was promoted and moved to another squadron. He came to me in Sept., 1915, so had been with me over a year. A nice boy and an extremely clever pilot—he got the M.C. last May and a bar to it this month.

Dreadful loss as I am moving two of my three flight commanders home for a rest and was counting on him to replace one of them.

One of my best youngsters, [Roche] too, was hit in the back, nothing serious but most annoying as he was a stout lad and only just trained. However these things will happen.

October; how time does fly! and yet two years ago I was still an unfledged pupil at the C.F.S.!

Very annoying putting the time back again—summer time was much nicer. Now we have to get up one hour earlier, and it's too dark to play tennis after tea!"

Sometimes, in spite of running out of ammunition, a pilot continued in an offensive patrol, diving on the H.A. so as to drive them off the tails of other members of the patrol. Lanoe wrote the following account of one of the offensive patrols in which he took part:—

No. 24 Squadron Record Book.

" 10th Oct., 1916.   8.5 a.m. to 10.25.   Offensive Patrol.
As the O.P. reached BEAULENCOURT Andrews dived so followed and saw H.A. doing contact patrol over

EAUCOURT. Dived inside him to cut him off and gave him a drum from 75 to 100 yards as he crossed chased by Andrews.

Changed drums and gave him a second at 2,000 feet over Bapaume but at too great a range. Returning climbed above the patrol and saw H.A. diving on an F.E. The F.E. dived straight and I could not get within range, but chased him towards BAPAUME and gave him a drum at about 150 yards.

Patrol followed Andrews back to Albert and I was left alone on the lines for some time. Picked up Kelly and dived on a Hun over ROCQUIGNY firing half a drum at 100 yards but he walked away from me. Saw two D.H.'s flying from SUZANNE to ALBERT so flew in and picked them up and went back beyond the BAPAUME-PERONNE road. A Nieuport type H.A. came overhead without seeing us, so turning I raised the mounting and fired a few ineffectual shots as the mounting was very wobbly—this finished my ammunition. Saw Nieuport type H.A. dive on a D.H.'s tail, and dived after it, but the D.H. went down too quickly for me to catch up, the H.A. however dived East.

Andrews rejoined the patrol so followed him. Some rough-house with several Nieuport type H.A., dived on three or four, frightened them off D.H.'s tails but could not do much without ammunition. The H.A. all retired East and climbed and probably came back as soon as the D.H.'s left the lines.

(signed) L. G. Hawker."

On the 10th of October Middlebrook was shot down by a member of Boelcke's staffel and taken prisoner; Sergeant Cockerell was wounded by Boelcke himself and counted by him as his 32nd victory, but Cockerell was rescued by two of his companions who drove Boelcke off, and he landed safely in our lines. Promoted to second lieutenant, he rejoined No. 24 Squadron on the 11th of November, 1916.

The 13th of October saw the departure of Wilkinson and Tidmarsh, followed by Morgan on the 16th. The squadron "threw" one of its most hectic dinners, inviting friends from nearby squadrons.

Question to one present in the mess : —

" Do you remember that dinner ? "

Answer : " God help us, that was a night."

Q. : " Can you give me a description of it, or were you too far gone ? "

A. : " Much too far."

Like all Lanoe's pilots, these two carried with them the

Hawker tradition for efficiency, courage and co-operation, and took a fierce pride in living up to his maximum standard. Early in 1917 Wilkinson and Tidmarsh were specially chosen, together with Robinson, V.C., to command the three flights of No. 48, the first squadron equipped with Bristol Fighters which had Rolls-Royce engines (" Oh what a relief ! ").

Wilkinson's squadron commander noted his strict devotion to duty, when rather than make some excuse for delay, when his newly married bride arrived on the tarmac belatedly, to say goodbye, perhaps for the last time, he waved away the chocks without hesitation and took off for France.

Tidmarsh after accounting for several German machines, went to the rescue of a companion in distress in spite of the hopeless odds against him, was shot down and taken prisoner. This was the spirit of devotion to duty which Lanoe inspired, and once his pilots were animated with it, nothing could make it fade. Space does not allow a description of the career of each one of his pilots, but all took with them the determination to live up to his standard. What was it he had said one day in his quiet, steady voice?

> " There is but one task for all,
> One life for each to give.
> Who stands if freedom fall?
> Who dies if England live? "

If these were his colours, they would carry them too.

One of General Hoeppner's first tasks was the reorganization of the German anti-aircraft artillery. The pilots of No. 24 Squadron were constantly under Archie's fire and only avoided heavy casualties by their manoeuvrability.

On the 15th Nixon was hit on the head by a fragment of shell, but kept on with the patrol and refused to leave the squadron. Unfortunately he was injured in a forced landing on the 21st and had to be sent to hospital.

Little has been said recently of the constant trouble with engines and machine-guns experienced by every pilot of a D.H.2. To repeat each record of these troubles would be intensely monotonous. Nevertheless, these defects constituted a serious handicap to the pilots of No. 24 Squadron who were fighting against more reliable German machines and guns. Forced landings due to engine trouble were alarmingly frequent, and several pilots had very narrow escapes. In addition the single Lewis gun often jammed at the critical moment causing exasperating disappointments. The mechanics were indefatigable, and worked long hours into the night, never disheartened under Lanoe's encouraging leadership.

The 16th of October was another sad day for Lanoe. The stop-at-nothing, incredibly gallant Langan-Byrne, who had just succeeded Tidmarsh in the command of ' B ' Flight, led his patrol with his usual hair-raising élan straight into the middle of the twelve machines of Jagdstaffel 2, and Boelcke, in his vastly superior Albatros Scout, shot him down after a short dog-fight in which the D.H.2's were hopelessly out-classed. Langan-Byrne had recently been awarded the D.S.O. for exceptional gallantry. His gay laugh and his fearlessness will be remembered by all who knew him. His flight was taken over by von Poelnitz, who arrived on the 18th. New pilots were passing rapidly through the squadron now, and few of the veterans were left. Of the original pilots, Andrews alone remained. Knight, Wood and McKay, who joined in June, were the only other pilots who had been with the squadron through the battle of the Somme.

Forty-two pilots, including six flight commanders, had left the squadron through casualties, accidents, sickness, promotion, etc. Of these, twelve had been killed, three of them flight commanders. It was inevitable that casualties should be high in a squadron that constantly sought out and fought the best of the enemy machines, whilst themselves flying obsolete aeroplanes, but it was sad for Lanoe who loved them all dearly, and counted each as a personal friend, one of his " chickens ". These casualties were not incurred without exacting a fitting return from the enemy, including Jagdstaffel 2, and Richthofen recorded in *The Red Knight of Germany* on the 3rd of November :—

> " In the last six weeks we have had out of twelve pilots, six dead, and one wounded, while two have suffered a complete nervous collapse."

German writers have frequently paid tribute to the sporting and combative spirit of the British aviators. One of the most striking is that written by General von Hoeppner in *L'Allemagne et La Guerre de l'Air* " : —

> " Whereas the English aviators gave proof of an eminently combative spirit, it is incontestible that the French aviators adopted an appreciably more timid attitude. It is for this reason that from the battle of the Somme, we were obliged to have the greater part of our scout squadrons opposite the English."

To which le Comt. de Castelnau, the translator, replied in a footnote.—

> " It cannot be denied that the English airmen, by reason of their heredity and education, were more combative than the French or German airmen."

This combative spirit was the soul of No. 24 Squadron, but the obsolete D.H.2 was responsible for heavy casualties.

In depressing moments Lanoe's thoughts turned to home and those he loved. The realization that he was fighting for them gave him fresh courage.

> " 22.10.16.
> The violets were lovely and still smell sweet. I love getting your letters—they give me a glimpse of ' Blighty ', which is very welcome out here.
> I am feeling very depressed as I hardly know anyone in my own squadron now. Three or four went home for a rest, including two flight-commanders. I had two good lads to replace them, but one was taken for another squadron as I told you, and I got a stranger instead. The other however, was a splendid fellow—just got the D.S.O., a charming Irishman and brave as a lion. He had done more in two months than most of my people did in six months, and I relied on him to found the ' New 24 '. Unfortunately he was shot down two days after he was made flight-commander, and I haven't recovered from the blow of losing him, he was such a nice lad as well as the best officer I have ever met."

Lanoe's reference to the " New 24 " was due to one of General Trenchard's staff officers telling him that he was shortly due for promotion to command a wing of scout squadrons, of which No. 24, equipped with new machines, would be one.

Mr. C. G. Grey wrote in *The Aeroplane* of the 11th July, 1917:—

"So highly was Hawker esteemed by his seniors that it was generally recognized, just before his death, that he was to take command of the next wing to be formed, and had he lived there is little doubt that in little more than a year he would have had a brigade."

Lanoe's letter of the 22nd of October was his last one home for he was shortly due for leave. T. had returned to the Somme with the 8th Division, and was with his brigade H.Q. near Ginchy. The division was having an exhausting time in the sea of mud and waterlogged shell holes that now constituted the Somme battle ground. At last on the 1st of October he was given a warrant for ten days leave from the 16th, and managed to get to Bertangles to arrange with Lanoe that they should go on leave together. T. lunched with Lanoe's pilots again, but although they were in excellent spirits there had been so many changes that he hardly knew any of them.

The tactical orders " Attack everything " had given place to detailed instructions for co-operation and for raising the gun to shoot at any Germans overhead to whose level the D.H.2's might be unable to climb.

In the mess was a newly arrived pilot with a bruised face. T., thinking to be funny, asked him if he had been tackling the Huns with his fists. The question caused an awkward silence. The pilot turned pleadingly towards Lanoe, who flushed and looked down at his plate; the subject was changed. Later one of the senior pilots explained to T. that this newcomer, for a hoax, had pinned a notice on the board asking for volunteers to join a squadron of Spads, the latest French scout machines of vastly superior performance to the D.H.2, and the envy of all British pilots. The hoax had been adjudged " heresy ", and without Lanoe's approval the newcomer had received a rough handling. The pilots of No. 24 were too loyal to Lanoe to allow even the thought of leaving him to enter their minds, especially at such a moment.

On the 20th of October Lanoe was up for two hours twenty minutes on offensive patrol, repeatedly attacking and driving the H.A. eastwards. There were 50 or 60 in the air at once.

On the 26th Knight, McKay, Crawford, Lewis and Pashley had a fierce and prolonged fight with about 20 H.A., mostly the new fast scouts.   The D.H.2's gave such a good account of themselves that they damaged and drove off at least eleven of the H.A., it being impossible to ascertain their fate during the battle. Running short of petrol they fought their way back to the lines where the remainder of the H.A. left them.

On the 28th of October, at the head of Jagstaffel 2 Boelcke attacked Knight and McKay of ' C ' Flight, who had ventured far over the German lines.   Following their usual tactics, these two pilots circled sharply, confusing the German attackers. Boelcke, in striving to shoot down Knight, came into collision with another Albatros, glided down, but crashed on landing and was killed.   The other German pilots, discouraged by their lack of success, allowed Knight and McKay to regain our lines. Boelcke's death was learnt by our H.Q. at once, probably through the German wireless news, and Lanoe was told to send in full details of the fight.   Our pilots did not then know the name of the Albatros and described it as a " small Aviatic Scout ".   Lanoe questioned Knight and McKay, and drew up the following detailed report :—

" 28th Oct., 1916.   No. 24 Squadron.   14th Wing.
Combat Report.

D.H. Scouts—A2594, A2554. 1 Lewis gun each. 3.40 p.m.
Lieut. A. G. Knight, M.C., Lieut. McKay. Defensive Patrol.
POZIERES—BAPAUME. Height—8,000 to 5,000 feet.

---

12 H.A. Halberstadters and small Aviatic Scouts.

Lieut. Knight was at 8,000 feet and Lieut. McKay, who had been delayed by engine trouble, was about 1,500 feet lower down.

Six H.A. fast scouts (Halberstadters and small Aviatics) appeared at about 10,000 feet over POZIERES.

They hesitated about five minutes before they attacked. One then did a side-slipping dive under the top D.H., but Lieut. Knight did not attack as he was suspicious of this manoeuvre.

The H.A. then all dived at Lieut. Knight, who promptly spiralled to avoid their fire.

During the fight six other scouts joined in, making a total

of twelve against two D.H.'s, and some went down and attacked Lieut. McKay.

The H.A. dived in turn on to the D.H.'s tail, but the D.H. promptly turned sharply under the H.A., which usually switched on and climbed again.

The D.H.'s were very careful to avoid diving straight at any H.A. that presented tempting targets, but fired short bursts as H.A. came on their sights.

It was after about five minutes strenuous fighting that two H.A. collided. One dived at Lieut. Knight, who turned left handed. The H.A. zoomed right handed, and its left wing collided with the right wing of another H.A., which had started to dive on Lieut. Knight.

Bits were seen to fall off; only one H.A. was seen to go down, and it glided away east, apparently under control, but was very shortly lost to sight, as the D.H.'s were too heavily engaged to watch it.

The fight continued for another fifteen minutes, drifting East during which time Lieut. Knight came down and joined Lieut. McKay. The D.H.'s were about 5,000 feet just East of BAPAUME, when the H.A. broke off the engagement and allowed the D.H.'s to return unmolested.

(signed) L. G. Hawker, Major,
Commanding No. 24 Squadron,
Royal Flying Corps."

Oswald Boelcke's death was a serious loss to the German air service. " In less than two months' air fighting in the Somme battle he had shot down twenty British aeroplanes. The aeroplane on which he did so well was handier, faster, and more effectively armed than anything flying against him, and all his combats were offered to him in the air above his own troops. Nevertheless he proved a determined, resourceful, and gallant foe, and his successes inspired the members of his own squadron and put heart once again into the whole German air service." (V. II, p. 312.)

The R.F.C. respected him, and chivalrously dropped a laurel wreath on a parachute over the German lines with the inscription " To the memory of Capt. Boelcke, our brave and chivalrous foe. From the British Royal Flying Corps." Every officer of No. 24 Squadron would far rather have welcomed him to their mess as a prisoner than have him killed in this manner, but it was nevertheless a feather in their cap that they had been responsible for eliminating the most redoubtable German pilot.

The command of Jagdstaffel 2 was taken over by Kirmaier, of whom more later.

German headquarters, placing a practical value on tradition, ordered that Jagdstaffel 2 should be renamed " Jagdstaffel Boelcke ", and so it remains for all time, honouring the man who created and led it, an incentive to others to emulate his fine example.

Fighting continued on an active scale into November, Andrews, McKay and Pashley being particularly successful.

On the 5th of November Lanoe went on leave at long last. Alas for T.'s hopes of leave at the same time ; the wheels of war were grinding exceeding fine, and H.Q. had little consideration for those junior officers and men who did the fighting for them. Their leave was cancelled on the slightest pretext, and so it came about that T. was never able to use his leave warrant, and Lanoe went to England alone.

The battle of the Somme had died down, smothered in mud, and the most strenuous efforts of our infantry could now have but small results. This was all the more disappointing in that they had won a dominating position on the main ridge, which threatened the entire German defences right up to Arras. Now that wet weather had set in no substantial progress was possible, and it would have been sensible to close down active operations at once, put the lines into a state of defence for the winter, and withdraw for training and re-equipment those squadrons which had fought so strenuously and so continuously. But the French Commander-in-Chief demanded that we should continue our attacks during the winter, and the willing squadrons like the willing troops, were called upon to continue what had become an impossible and futile effort.

36

Lanoe's Last Leave

WHEN Lanoe reached Boulogne he found the cross-channel service suspended whilst a German submarine was being hunted down and its mines swept up. He was greatly disappointed that T. had not been able to join him after all. In this hope he had delayed his leave till the last moment, and had made no arrangements for spending it other than attending as best man the wedding of Capt. E. N. Clifton, familiarly known as " George ", who had flown and fought as Lanoe's observer in No. 6 Squadron, and had been one of his pilots for a short time in No. 24 Squadron. The wedding took place on the 8th of November and Lanoe won praise from Clifton as being " the only one present to remember that even bridegrooms get thirsty ". Immediately afterwards the press photographers were busy.

That night Lanoe went to the Empire Music Hall in Leicester Square, expecting to meet at their usual haunt some of his wartime friends, but he was disappointed. Heavy casualties had depleted their ranks and he found it disconcerting that there was not a single familiar face there. He missed his friends, especially he missed his brother's gay care-free company and, above all, he missed Beatrice. He wired to her and her mother and to his sister Siola to join him at the Redbourne Hotel. He planned to have a gay week-end before joining his mother at Weymouth.

The next day, as a record of the wedding, there appeared in the *Daily Mirror* a large photograph of Lanoe buying a souvenir handkerchief, wrongly described as Capt. Robinson, V.C. In a small medallion was a wee photograph of the married couple smiling grimly. On Thursday the 9th Lanoe wrote to Andrews :

" Redbourne Hotel,
Great Portland Street, W.

Dear J.O.,

According to instructions I was in at the kill and saw George unconditionally spliced—you probably saw the photo in the *Mirror* and I enclose one of the souvenirs which I (not Robinson as there stated) bought—the victim, as usual, occupying a very minor corner. I'm glad they had their mouths shut.

We were delayed two days at Boulogne, so I don't return till Friday—please break the news gently to von P.

Went to the Empire on Wednesday, and didn't meet a sole I knew—shocking—what is the world coming to.

So I'm collecting own party for tomorrow and Saturday— shan't be had again.

George sends his love.

I hadn't time to get a present before, but will do so tomorrow—if I remember.

So long, good luck.

Yours,
L. G. Hawker.

P.S.—We weren't the only ones who thought George was hedging—I stood by while he received their condolences—

I told them we nearly wired to him to come out to France as being much safer——"

Lanoe's spelling was typical; when disgusted with the dirtiness of his apparel he spelt it " cloathes ", and so here he didn't meet a " sole ". It is easy to see from his good-natured banter that he was in excellent form, and the week-end was a great success. On Saturday he collected his party and took them to a lunch at the Regent Palace Hotel, then to a matinée, then back to a quiet tea at the Redbourne Hotel where Siola amused them by telling fortunes by palmistry.

" It's a funny thing," said Lanoe, " but the lines seem to have gone out of my hand." Sure enough Siola found that the line of fate disappeared into a smooth patch in his palm which was ascribed to the pressure of the joy-stick, but Siola concealed her apprehension; twice before she had seen the same thing, and those two boys had not come back from France.

Lanoe next took his party out to dinner to which the Cliftons were invited. Beatrice, for the first time, wore the garnet brooch which Lanoe had given her ages and ages ago, or so it seemed to him, but really it was no earlier than January, 1913. Lanoe noticed the brooch at once, admired it with his head on one side, a characteristic attitude of his, and then gave Beatrice a beaming smile of understanding. He knew then, for certain, that his patience was to be rewarded.

The party went on to another theatre, and after that to supper at Hatchett's, to which Wilkinson and his fiancée were invited. Enjoying themselves to the full, they were reluctant to leave, and finally had to be " drummed out ".

On Monday Beatrice saw Lanoe off to Weymouth. Just before the train went out he said—" In three months' time I'll be a colonel and will be home on leave again and we'll have a great time," and Beatrice promised to get leave from her war work.

The last few days of his leave Lanoe spent quietly in Weymouth with his mother, whose calm and unfaltering courage was an inspiring example to her three soldier sons. All too soon this last leave came to an end. He returned to France greatly refreshed and cheered, bringing with him the breath of life from " Blighty ".

No man could have had higher hopes or more pleasing prospects than Lanoe at this moment; Beatrice had worn his brooch; he was due for promotion and, though he would not count it, this inevitably meant reducing the risks of flying and fighting. His heart and mind were already projected into the organization and training of the new wing.

Yet his squadron was very dear to him, and he returned to it fully realizing and accepting the inevitable danger of flying and fighting in obsolete machines. But he was at peace with himself and had conquered fear, putting his trust in the wisdom of God.

37

An Eye for an Eye

DURING Lanoe's absence on leave No. 24 Squadron fought on under the capable leadership of Andrews whom, since Langan-Byrne's death, Lanoe hoped he would be allowed to appoint to the command of the " New 24 ". Von Poelnitz, however, was the senior flight commander, and a somewhat similar position existed in the Boelcke Staffel, where Richthofen was the acknowledged leader in the air, though Kirmaier was in command of the staffel.

Fighting was almost continuous on fine days in which three H.A.'s were set on fire or crashed and at least ten others driven down damaged by the squadron. On the 16th Lanoe lost little Jerry Knight, one more of his best pilots, so gallant, so skilful, so loyal, promoted and posted to another D.H.2 squadron to fall at last, on the 20th of December, Richthofen's thirteenth victim. Then on the 17th he learnt of the death of Cowan, another of his favourite lads who, whilst leading a flight of No. 29 Squadron, was killed in collision with one of his own machines in the same manner as Boelcke. It seemed such waste, and there were moments when the war was very bitter for Lanoe.

Of two H.A. destroyed on the 17th, one was an Albatros D.II from the Boelcke Staffel. Saundby escaped from the fight with a shattered engine, but W. Crawford was killed, probably by an Albatros Scout. Thus these two squadrons on opposite sides of the lines, each the leading fighter squadron of its air force, took regular toll of the other.

Lanoe's return to France was followed by three days of stormy wet weather. Unable to reach T., on the far side of the sea of shell holes and mud, over which the battle had slowly advanced, he sent word asking if he could give any comfort or help. Promoted captain of a battery now bogged in the mud near Ginchy, T. was easily spared, and by the favour of his general's car, spent a few happy hours with Lanoe, who was in excellent form, though still showing signs of the heavy strain of the protracted fighting.

It was remarkable to find the same cheerful optimism in the mess despite the recent heavy losses. The squadron had its tail well up even though it was clear that the D.H.2 was now hopelessly out of date. Moreover, the engines were worn out and again giving much trouble, though at no time had they been in any way reliable. But Lanoe confidently expected, now the battle was ending, that his squadron would be given a well-earned rest.

He was greatly concerned for his brother who was completely exhausted, and would have liked to have kept him at Bertangles for a few days rest, but this was impossible. He was much cheered by the news that the 8th Division was to be relieved shortly and that he would be able to see T. again very soon; but T. never saw that relief. It was the last time the brothers were to meet.

The 22nd of November was comparatively fine, and Lanoe's patrols were out all day, Pashley shooting down an H.A. north of Flers. The following note in the squadron diary gives some indication of the enemy's tactics at this time :—

" During the whole of the patrols there were twenty or thirty H.A. overhead, but the D.H.'s could not reach them and they refused to come down and give fight."

This day Andrews, on his way back from a fight in which his engine had been damaged, was dived on by a flight of H.A. scouts which, however, did not fire at him. Dexterously he turned on to the tail of the lowest machine and emptied a drum into it at short range. It was Kirmaier's Albatros, and it crashed heavily just behind our front line trenches near Flers. K. Crawford, who had been forced by engine trouble to land nearby, recovered from the wreck the two machine-guns with a 500 round belt for each. This was the first and possibly the only Albatros D.II Scout brought down within our lines.

As bad luck seemed to dog the leader of the Boelcke Staffel when promoted from within the squadron, the next commander was chosen from another unit. Major Walz was the third officer to command the Boelcke Staffel within little over a month. The other two had been lost in combats with Hawker's Squadron.

Although casualties on both sides were heavy, probably heavier in the Royal Flying Corps than in the German air service owing to the advantageous conditions under which the latter fought, there could be no doubt that the British effort had been fully justified.

The success of our armies was dependant on efficient support from the air and on depriving the enemy of a similar support from his air service, but the fruits of this success were not all apparent at the time. It was known at once that the French had been saved from General von Falkenhayn's attempt to " bleed them white " at Verdun, but only later was it realized that by winning a key position on the ridge, turning the German defences as far as Arras, we obliged the enemy to retire to the Hindenburg Line early in 1917. This retirement proved fatal to his great offensive in March, 1918, for, instead of capturing territory of vital strategic value, the German troops spent their strength on recapturing the ground they had given up in 1917.

It was not till after the war that it was fully realized how heavy a blow had been dealt to the German army and its morale, how vital the part taken by the Royal Flying Corps in inflicting this defeat, how the German regiments never again fought so staunchly, and how they dreaded the thought of another " Somme ".

With better generalship we might have persuaded our enemies to sue for peace in 1916. As it was, the Battle of the Somme ruined their highly trained army, prevented them from winning the war, and paved the way to their ultimate defeat.

38

The Last Fight

THE following description of Lanoe's last fight is based on the personal accounts of the two pilots of No. 24 Squadron who were with him on patrol when he met Richthofen, also on their combat reports, the records they made in their log-books, the Squadron Record Book, on Richthofen's combat report, on his account of the fight in *The Red Airfighter,* and on the account of Major von Schönberg, who witnessed the fight from near Ligny-Thilloy and had a close view of its closing phases.

For copies of the above accounts see Appendix II.

Although the Battle of the Somme had been brought to a state of stagnation by the bad weather, nibbling attacks were still being planned towards Bapaume with the object of further outflanking the German lines. As an essential preliminary to these operations the defences had to be photographed and, during a comparatively fine spell on the 23rd of November, this was being done round about noon under the protection of the offensive patrols of No. 24 Squadron. 'C' Flight under Long returned just before 1 p.m. and reported the arrival of strong enemy formations and increasing activity in the air.

'A' Flight under Andrews was on the point of starting out and, owing to a shortage of trained pilots, Lanoe decided to join the patrol. Long and Pashley, both stalwart pilots, were told to get their machines ready again and reinforce the patrol at 2 p.m. Andrews leading, Lanoe on the left, Saundby on the right and Crutch behind, left the aerodrome at 1 p.m. Crutch had engine trouble and landed at No. 9 Squadron's aerodrome for repairs.

In spite of the patrol now numbering only three machines, it was in fact a strong and compact unit. Lanoe was the most skilled and determined fighting pilot in France; Andrews was the most experienced, having constantly flown and fought in the

D.H.2 for almost a year, and his cool leadership and extra-ordinarily keen eyesight were well established; Saundby had been four months in the squadron, had shown his fine mettle at the start, and had fought his way with distinction through the squadron's hardest battles. These three pilots had complete confidence in each other, and Lanoe started out with the determination of getting to grips with the enemy. He was confident in his ability to out-fly any German pilot, the only difficulty he anticipated being to find one that would stay and fight.

Mounted in up-to-date machines, this patrol would have been a formidable fighting unit; but the inferiority of the D.H.2 was now such a handicap that no amount of courage or skill could compensate for it when engaged with the pick of the German Air Force in their best and latest machines. These considerations, however, did not trouble Lanoe.

At 1.30 p.m. the patrol had gained a height of 11,000 feet over the lines, and seeing a fight between Nieuport Scouts and a formation of H.A. near Grandcourt, made straight to join in, but on their approach the German machines retired at once. At some time, probably on crossing the lines, Lanoe fired five rounds to test his machine-gun.

The patrol continued its flight towards Bapaume, and at 1.50 p.m. saw a couple of enemy two-seaters low down N.E. of that town. Andrews immediately dived down to attack them, with Lanoe and Saundby rather wide on his left and right respectively, so as to catch the enemy should he turn to either side.

The German aeroplanes, seeing the D.H.2's at once, dived away east, and a strong westerly wind carried the machines at high speed well behind the enemy lines, making it almost impossible for the D.H.2's to overtake them. Andrews scanned the sky quickly to make sure that these two-seaters were not a decoy, a ruse well known to all our pilots at this time. Sure enough, straight overhead were two little groups of German scouts, just black dots in the sky, but very menacing to an experienced pilot. Andrews at once put his machine into a wide right-hand turn, and Saundby, complying with the manoeuvre of his patrol leader, now found himself in front, heading for our lines.

Lanoe, however, kept straight on. Whether he thought that

Andrews had turned back owing to gun or engine trouble, or whether it was just another case of his seeing his enemy and going straight for him, the reader must judge for himself. Andrews saw him diving past and realized instantly that he was running into great danger. Continuing his turn in a complete circle, as being the quickest method of rejoining Lanoe, he saw the enemy scouts in two flights come diving down upon them. The leading scout made straight for Lanoe, but before he could shoot him down Andrews was able to get in a burst of twenty-five rounds at close quarters, obliging the H.A. to turn away. This not only saved Lanoe, but gave him warning of the new arrivals. At the same moment another German scout dived on Andrews' tail and sent a stream of bullets into his engine and petrol tank, putting the former out of action at once, so that he was compelled to leave the fight and glide against a contrary wind in the hopes of reaching our lines. The German scout, which had attacked him, followed closely, firing burst after burst of bullets into the helpless D.H.2. Andrews, crouching his economic form in the nacelle, owed his life to the protection of the engine and the stupidity of his enemy, who did not think of attacking him from the side. The German bullets tore the fabric of the wings, smashed cambox and cylinders, and it seemed inevitable to Andrews that he must soon be hit.

At this moment Saundby, who had been spiralling out of the line of fire of several of the other machines, which had dived down at him, finding himself clear of the fight, made straight for Andrews' aggressor and fired three-quarters of a drum into him at twenty yards range. The German machine turned quickly from side to side and then dived down vertically until out of sight. Andrews managed to reach a French emergency landing ground at Guillimont, whilst Saundby, after seeing him safely across our lines, continued the patrol.

On his glide back, and before the lower plane obscured his view, Andrews saw Lanoe at about 3,000 feet in a circling fight with a German scout. He could not go to his assistance as his engine was out of action, neither had he any means of signalling to Saundby to do so. But Andrews had no reason to feel any particular anxiety for Lanoe. He was well aware of his exceptional skill and resource, and of course could not guess that he was now pitted against the only pilot in the German Air

Force who stood any reasonable chance of shooting him down in a duel. Lanoe's formidable opponent had already accounted for ten English machines in his remarkable fighting career, and had shown his exceptional qualities of courage, determination, ruthlessness and cunning.

Richthofen had been specially selected by Boelcke and trained by him. He had tried out and discovered every weakness of the D.H.2 in mock fights with the one captured by Boelcke. He knew that he could stick closely to the tail of this inferior machine, no matter how well it was handled, for his Albatros Scout, with its 160 h.p. Mercedes engine, was a great deal faster and climbed much better. Moreover he knew that by staying closely behind and above the D.H.2 he was in perfect safety, since his opponent could not fire backwards. Further, as the fight had started well over the German side of the lines and the wind was in the west, there was every chance of obliging his opponent to drift further away from his base until, through the exhaustion of his petrol, he would be forced to land and surrender. Everything was in Richthofen's favour, and this was the type of fight he liked best, for to him war was a deadly and serious business, and not a sporting adventure.

Lanoe, having got into a steep dive at the decoy machines, was not to be put off by Andrews turning back; the weakness of the formation, in which Lanoe took a subordinate place, lay in the fact that he did not feel compelled to adhere to the judgment of the patrol leader, who was his junior. He was out for a fight and a fight he would have; to the devil with decoys and such-like tricks. He had yet to meet the German who would stay and fight with him; so far the whole difficulty had been to get to grips with them; they always eluded him by diving away over their own lines.

Lanoe shut off his petrol to prevent his engine choking in the dive, and his first intimation that he had to deal with other aeroplanes than the two-seaters, came in the form of a sharp crackle of machine-gun fire from behind and above. A kick to the rudder-bar, a movement of the stick and he was in a close spiral, now husbanding his height as much as possible, whilst he turned on his petrol and tried to 'get' his engine again. This he managed, but after adjusting the petrol valve for a few moments he realized that through some defect his engine would not give its full revolutions. This was a vital matter, for without full power the machine lost height in close turns, and he was now keeping a tight spiral whilst watching his opponent, who was doing the same on the opposite side of the circle.

Each tried to get behind and above the other. There was no doubt that in this contest Richthofen was bound to win in his greatly superior machine; however, Lanoe was not yet convinced of this. He suddenly changed directions and circled round the other way. In this circling position neither opponent could bring his gun to bear.

Lanoe made his circles ever smaller, ever sharper; Richthofen kept above and behind, but on a wider circle. The D.H.2 could still turn more sharply and thus keep out of the line of fire of the Albatros, which however, owing to its better climb and speed, could always stay safely above. Had the fight been over the British lines Lanoe would have been in no danger, but this circling could not continue indefinitely, as the D.H.2 would run out of petrol, and he would then be taken prisoner.

He was losing height owing to his engine running badly, and if he were not careful the wind would soon drift him far into Hunland. Each of his turns now became elongated towards our lines so as to gain a little ground, and his changes from one side to the other were also designed to this purpose, but he kept a constant look out for the chance of getting his sights on to his opponent. Richthofen never gave him this chance.

At last he realized that the D.H.2 was incapable of bringing him into a firing position against the Albatros, and that for the first time he had met a German pilot who was prepared to stay and fight on to the end; this fellow at least had the courage and determination to stick to him. Spontaneously he waved his hand to him and Richthofen waved back. The opponents were so close to each other, that but for their goggles and helmets they could have seen each other's faces. So the circling continued, twenty circles to the right, then thirty to the left, each opponent wondering how to bring the fight to a finish.

Richthofen felt it was time that his opponent realized he should break off the fight and make for his own lines and safety. Under similar circumstances he would have prudently darted home some time ago. Yet Lanoe kept on, always hoping for some change in the fight. He had seen Andrews glide back over our lines escorted by Saundby, but Saundby was still up there, also Long and Pashley were due out now. They might see him circling below, difficult though it would be to spot a machine so far beneath them; the possibility was always there, and then he would have the chance of letting off a drum at this audacious German, whom he now recognized as the most aggressive and capable enemy airman that he had ever met or heard of.

Lanoe imagined the three D.H.2's diving down suddenly to his rescue. Then there would be a bit of fun; but the fun never came. The three D.H.2's continued their patrol high above the fight, all unconscious of the deadly peril of their beloved leader, whom they thought safely home by now.

Gaining a little ground with each turn, Lanoe arrived at last over Bapaume at about 1,500 feet, and his opponent showed no sign of tiring of this circling contest. It seemed interminable, circling to the left, then to the right, then round to the left again; for over half an hour the struggle continued. The machines were so close together that neither Archie nor the infantry dared fire at them. With Richthofen's machine always a little above and a little behind him, continually losing height, but constantly gaining a little ground, Lanoe realized at last that he must make a dash for our lines that now seemed within easy reach.

What a rag there would be in the mess that night! He would pull the legs of the pilots of the patrol sitting up above whilst he fought the scrap of his life down below. What a laugh his lads would have when he told them how he had been chased all over Hunland by this bold Boche! Already he could hear their ribaldry, see their laughing faces in the mess at Bertangles.

Well, it was now time to make a break for it. He would first put the D.H.2 through a few stunts just in case the Hun above him was tempted to move out of place for a moment and give him the chance of getting in a few shots. The D.H.2 zoomed up into the air, looped, turned sharply to one side, then spun round to the other, but Richthofen gave no chance away. Within two miles of our front line and safety Lanoe chose his moment and made a sudden dash, zig-zagging towards our lines.

This was Richthofen's opportunity. Following the D.H.2 closely, at each change of direction he was at last able to bring his guns to bear, a difficult target, but nevertheless his opponent must cross his sights at each turn. Burst after burst he fired at the D.H.2 without effect, till at last he began to think that he would expend the whole of his 1,000 rounds of ammunition without result. His fellow pilots would then laugh at his poor shooting, and " that would be too bad ". To make matters worse both his guns jammed. His disappointment was acute, for he thought his enemy would escape, but a quick reloading of the guns started them firing again.

The machines were now within a thousand yards of the front lines and not 150 feet above the shell-torn ground. Richthofen finally fired a last carefully aimed burst. The D.H.2 stalled for a moment, then plunged obliquely to the ground from 100 feet, crashing and turning over in the water-logged shell holes. Out of 900 rounds fired by Richthofen one had chanced to hit Lanoe in the head.

A few more seconds and he would have been safe, for Richthofen, of all pilots, was not the one to take the risk of flying low over our lines. If Lanoe had survived another burst of fire, his opponent's ammunition would have been exhausted. Lanoe or his machine might have been hit in any out of a hundred other places without it being fatal, as many of our pilots and machines often were so hit and survived to fight again. He had every reason and every expectation of thinking that he would regain our lines in safety.

Fortune, never more fickle, deserted him at the moment of his greatest need. He required but some thirty seconds out of thirty-five minutes he had fought, a few hundred yards to safety, to escape one shot out of a thousand. Was this really a mathematical chance or was some great, relentless hand of Destiny stooping to pluck him from the war he detested, that he might fill some higher post?

He had believed implicitly in a merciful God, Who hurt us terribly that by our suffering we might learn the lesson of our soul and suffer no more. And now he was borne swiftly to that God on the soft dark wings of the Angel of Death.

So passed from the Royal Flying Corps a squadron leader, beloved, even worshipped by his pilots, as no other had been. With him they felt a confidence and inspiration which calm reason would have belied. No risk to take, no sacrifice to make seemed to them too great to win his ready smile of approval. He never asked them to do what he would not gladly do himself.   In his sharing of their danger and their toil lay half their love. But the passion which they felt for him was of a quality divine and undefinable.   No matter what the danger, what the discomfort, what the trial, with him they felt supremely happy.

None will ever forget the days he spent in Hawker's Squadron.

" In the Field,
28th Nov., 1916.

My dear Mrs. Hawker,
  I am writing to tell you how deeply sorry we all are that your son is missing.

He is a grievous loss to the country, the work he did was of the highest value.

From the reports I have I should say that there is a good chance of his being a prisoner and unhurt.   Capt. Andrews, who was near him, saw him at 3,000 feet under control, and I do not think he would have been so low as that so far over the lines unless something was wrong with the engine. . . .

We have dropped messages to ask for news, but the Germans do not often give us information now. . . .*

I needn't tell you how wonderfully brave your son was, his influence in the squadron is very largely responsible for our success in the air during this battle.
                    Believe me,
                        Yours very sincerely,
                            E. B. Ashmore.
Brigadier General, Commanding 4th Brigade, R.F.C."

In a foreword to *A History of 24 Squadron* Air Marshal Trenchard wrote :—

" No 24 Squadron came under my command about February, 1916.   This Squadron was commanded by that great leader, Major Hawker, V.C., and within a very short time of its arrival in France, it showed itself worthy of its leader and maintained a great reputation through the battles of the Somme in 1916. . . .

The loss of its Commander was a great blow, but the Squadron carried on in the way Major Hawker would have expected of it."

* It was not till July, 1917, that definite news of Lanoe's death was received from Germany.

39

T.

ONLY three miles to the south of where Lanoe lay dead, his brother, just promoted from adjutant, was in charge of six guns, deep in the shell-ploughed mud near Ginchy Telegraph, sharing with his gunners the utter misery and privations of the winter battlefield. In this respect he was no worse off than the thousands of men around him, but he was suffering from what he supposed to be a feverish cold and determined to get the doctor to give him some remedy for it. In his goatskin coat he struggled through the mud to the medical officer's dug-out. On the way he felt burning hot and into his mind came a great apprehension and fear, which he could not understand.

The medical officer took his temperature, hastily shook down the thermometer and tried again. He firmly ordered T. back to his battery, sending an orderly to accompany him. It took an hour to cover less than a mile through the heavy mud. In the meantime the M.O. had telephoned to the colonel, who sent his own horses at once to fetch T. back to brigade H.Q., where he was allotted a little hut he had made himself when adjutant and, on the recommendation of the kindly divisional doctor, he was given a warrant to England for the morrow, too late, alas, to share his leave with his brother, and he felt no pleasure in it, for that feeling of apprehension and anxiety was now taking shape and he begged and obtained leave to telegraph to No. 24 Squadron for news of Lanoe. The subalterns from H.Q. and the wagon lines gathered in the hut, each bringing his contribution to the last supper together. The meal finished, their gay chatter was interrupted by the shattering reply from No. 24 Squadron :—

" Hawker missing."

They filed silently out of the hut. Sympathy is not easily expressed, and theirs was very real. In the past, the marvellous brightness of the stars had been full of promise, and so, outside in the cold night air T., in despair, sought from them some flickering sign of hope, but they confirmed the fatal answer he already knew, for they had withdrawn behind a misty veil, never again to shine so brightly for him.

A dense soul-chilling fog shrouded the sodden battlefield; the exhausted armies lay silenced in its dark and paralyzing grip.

40

The Grave

BAPAUME, on the Somme front and well within the German lines, was a main point of focus for our airmen, and easily recognised by the roads radiating from it.   Two and a quarter miles to the south on the road leading thence to Flers, once stood Luisenhof Farm, reduced (by Nov., 1916) to a crumbling heap of ruins surrounded by a sea of water-filled shell holes.   In the cellars of this farm there sheltered, with his staff, Major von Schönberg, the commander of the 1st Battalion of the 100th Royal Saxon Reserve Grenadier Regiment, which held this part of the line.

On the 23rd of November, Major von Schönberg and many of his men witnessed Lanoe's fight with Richthofen, and saw his aeroplane crash 250 yards to the east of Luisenhof Farm. The area was under fire from our machine-guns in Gueudecourt.

The next morning Lieut. Bergmann reported to Major von Schönberg that the English officer was still lying under the wrecked aeroplane, and asked if he might bury him.   Major von Schönberg gladly granted this permission and said that such a brave enemy should be accorded the honours due to him.   Lanoe was buried beside his fallen machine.

Major von Schönberg's batman, Grenadier Paul Fischer, made a cross from the wreckage of the aeroplane, carved an inscription upon it, and placed it over the grave : —

"HIER RUHT DER ENGLISCHE MAJOR HAWKER
VOM BRITISH ROYAL FLYING CORPS,
GEFALLEN NACH HELDENHAFTEM LUFTKAMPF
Am 23.11.16."

Thus in the noblest traditions of military chivalry, these courteous and kindly Saxons, in spite of their intense sufferings during the Battle of the Somme, paid military honours to their fallen foe.   The Royal Air Force, when its turn came, buried

Baron Manfred von Richthofen with the honours due to him.

To these gentlemen, the comradeship of arms rested on a plane above the spite and deceit of politics. Had the British and German fighting men been able to carry on the war on these clean and generous lines, the Armistice would have seen the end of all bitterness, and we might well have found that our late enemies could be our staunchest friends.

Then indeed our beloved ones would not have died in vain.

41

Death of a Fighter Squadron

ON his return to the aerodrome Saundby expected to find that
Lanoe had landed before him. Then Andrews telephoned from
Guillemont that he had last seen the Major circling down near
Bapaume at 3,000 feet, engaged with a German scout. As each
machine came in, pilots and mechanics eagerly watched its
flight, hoping to see Lanoe's firm touch and direct, well-judged
landing near the sheds. Anxiety grew at dusk when no message
came from him, and landing lights were kept burning. It
would have been so like him to have hedge-hopped in after dark
on a half-crippled machine which he had somehow patched up
in no-man's-land. Ears were cocked for the sound of his
sputtering engine—in vain. Utter desolation descended upon
the squadron as all felt that he would never return after a day
of hoping against hope. Everything seemed to go out of life.
The mechanics went about gloomily and remembered the many
acts of kindness they had received at their major's hands. They
could hardly bring themselves to believe that they would never
again see his cheerful figure moving briskly about the aerodrome,
never again hear his infectious laugh. They had become used
to doing their best without supervision; they did it for love of
their leader. They would still work their hardest for his sake.
The pilots would fly and fight as he had done, all grimly determined to carry on as he would have wished. A casualty report
had to be sent in. Hawker was missing, but the war must go
on relentlessly; Lanoe was a man in a million, but his life was
but one of millions lost in the war.

Not yet was Hawker's Squadron to die; it was licking its
wounds after a fight it had won only at heavy cost. For a time
it seemed stunned; a combination of circumstances led to it
sinking into the background for a year; Andrews, the last of the
original pilots, did not fly a D.H.2 again; both he and Saundby

served with great distinction in other squadrons and continued their brilliant careers in the R.F.C. and the R.A.F.

The weather reduced flying to a minimum; activity on the Somme ceased for the winter; the German concentration in the air moved further north; in January, 1917, Richthofen left the Boelcke Staffel to command No. 11 at Douai, and with his departure much of the fire went out of the squadron he left.

The remaining pilots of No. 24 Squadron carried on gallantly with decreasing opportunities, but only one H.A. was destroyed in the next two months, and ten more were destroyed by May, 1917 when the D.H.2, acknowledged obsolete, was replaced by the D.H.5. Unfortunately this latest de Havilland product proved to be almost useless as a fighter, and with it only two H.A. were destroyed up to the end of 1917, when at last the squadron was re-equipped with an efficient scout, the S.E.5a. Then, rising like a phoenix from the ashes, proudly calling itself Hawker's Squadron, it exacted a terrible toll from the German Air Force, crashing and shooting down in flames well over 100 H.A. and 20 kite balloons before the armistice put an end to hostilities.

The end of the war led to a drastic reduction of the Royal Air Force, all fighter and bomber units being disbanded; to preserve the more famous squadrons from extinction they were given other tasks. During the Armistice the French authorities would not allow civilian aeroplanes to cross their territory. So that statesmen, politicians and senior officers might travel quickly between London and Versailles or elsewhere the Royal Air Force was called upon to carry them, and No. 24 was turned into a communications squadron for this important duty.

But as a fighting unit Hawker's Squadron died, mourned by the survivors who served in it during its glorious days; they longed for the moment when it would be revived as a fighter squadron and given a task suited to its great traditions.

When the time came to defend these Islands again from the German aggressor, our pilots fought with matchless courage; for though Hawker died, his spirit lived on.

42

War Memorial

23rd November, 1936

THE fields in Flanders are back under the plough, and little remains to show where once there were aerodromes at St. Omer, Poperinghe, Abeele and Bailleul. Most of the country near Ypres, which Lanoe knew so well, was devastated by the fluctuating battles, nearly all the buildings were wrecked and the tall trees destroyed. The houses and farms have been rebuilt on more modern lines, less high and more scattered; young trees grow now where the old ones stood.

Bertangles has hardly changed from the days in 1916 when Lanoe described it as a " funny little village ". Sheep graze on the aerodrome, and round it are large boards painted diagonally half red and half white, for this space is preserved as a military landing ground. The copse is still there, but the sheds and huts have gone. Listening one almost hopes to hear the echo of the gay laughter from that jolly mess, but the only sound is the distant drone of some civil air liner passing on its busy way.

Further up the line the Ancre has withdrawn within its banks, and the floods near Aveluy, over which Lanoe stunted in his D.H.2, have now receded.

The battlefields are dominated by lofty war memorials. In places so numerous as to remind one of the heavy sacrifices made by our armies, are to be found the war cemeteries, each the beautiful work of an architect, enclosing its serried ranks of white headstones in a garden of lawns and flowers most meticulously cared for.

Yet further east where once stood Luisenhof Farm is to be found a low heap of shell-torn bricks beneath a clump of young trees. A few rusty accoutrements lie half hidden in the weeds.

The once shell-torn, boggy valley where Lanoe fell is now neat and trim under well grown crops.

At Arras a large cemetery encloses in its central court of the memorial to the missing, the Air Services Memorial designed by Sir Edwin Lutyens. The memorial is in the form of a square obelisk surmounted by a globe on which appear, in a symbolic manner, the equator studded with stars and wings and the ecliptic with the signs of the zodiac. At the top of the obelisk are carved the badges of the air services. On the far side are inscribed the names of the missing in the Royal Air Force, on the right those of the Royal Naval Air Service, and on the left those of the Dominions.

On the side facing the main entrance are inscribed the names of the missing of the Royal Flying Corps, Lanoe's name heading the list. Many familiar and well-beloved names are here. So in the company of some of the lads he loved and inspired with his great courage Lanoe's name is engraved for all to see.

As the sun sinks towards the horizon it glints on the stars of the memorial giving them light, whilst the wings almost seem to flutter.

God grant that gentle wings bear our beloved ones now.

43

My Brother

TILL now I have sheltered behind an initial, because I felt it difficult to write in the first person a biography about my brother. I hope that in so doing I have given my readers an accurate description of his too-short life, and that I have not allowed my love for him to take undue charge of my pen, although that love is very deep. It could not well be otherwise, for he himself was most loving and generous, and was gifted with those human qualities which win enduring love.

In his unselfishness he would shield me, though I little deserved his care. As a child he pretended that a wound I caused him was no more than an accidental cut so that I should not receive the punishment that was my due. As boys in Geneva he not only fought in the forefront of our schoolboy battles, shielding me, but so contrived to share with me his victories that I gained confidence to fight for myself when he was no longer there; these were but early steps in the long stairway of his loving care. Later in life, when by his hard work, his mature and orderly mind and his great courage, he was achieving such marked success, whilst I, butterfly-like, was happily extracting the utmost pleasure from each passing moment without thought of the future, then he would contrive to shield me from the perception of the wide difference between us, taking my arm in his that I might share his triumphs, as if somehow I had helped to accomplish them; and then making the most of my small achievements, with generous praise, that I might not feel too far beneath his level.

There were strange moments when he sank into moods of dejection, perhaps due to the over-working of his brain, but I saw little of these, for then it was that I would take his arm in mine and with gay chatter and fantastic ideas would carry him to my world of carefree pleasure, and once he had broken from the dark spell of his mood he would not return to it till some fresh trouble beset him. Alone he would fight slowly to the surface, helping himself on by prayer, gaining strength each time.

At last when success lay within his grasp, his promotion due, his great love about to be rewarded, and he returned to France, he would not stoop to accept safety in the easy shelter of his rank and fame, but must needs tempt Providence, sharing the same risks, even taking greater risks than his gallant lads, and Providence carried him away.

By his death another lost more than I and endured that loss with greater courage, but when he left this world he took with him something which I had come to think my own, wrenching it from me and leaving there a gap which I dared not face, nor did time seem to fill the empty space. At last, after twenty years, I laid the records of those times before me, realizing that the gap will remain till we meet again.

I hope that my brother's life may be a help and an inspiration to others who would serve their country nobly.

That would be his wish.

It is my prayer.

THE END

Appendix I

By the 11th November, 1918, of a total of 1,168 V.C's about 645 were awarded during the War of 1914-18, and of these only 19 went to members of the R.F.C., R.N.A.S. and R.A.F.

Among these 19 V.C.'s, eight were awarded to scout pilots for combats in the air. Of these eight pilots three were killed in action, and three in flying accidents during or after the war. The courage and boldness which earned them the V.C. also led them to take such risks that their chance of survival was only a small one.

Date of Action	Date of Gazette	Air V.C.'s		Date of decease
26. 4.15.	22. 5.15.	Lieut. W. B. R. Rhodes-Moorhouse	D. of w.	27. 4.15.
7. 6.15.	11. 6.15.	Flt. Sub. Lt. R. A. J. Warneford	K.a.	17. 6.15.
25. 7.15.	24. 8.15.	Capt. L. G. Hawker (S.P.)	K.	23.11.16.
31. 7.15.	23. 8.15.	Capt. J. A. Liddell	D. of w.	31. 8.15.
7.11.15.	23.12.15.	Lieut. G. S. M. Insall		
19.11.15.	1. 1.16.	Sqn. Cmdr. R. Bell Davies		
1. 7.16.	5. 8.16.	Maj. L. W. B. Rees (S.P.)		
3. 9.16.	5. 9.16.	Lieut. W. Leefe-Robinson	P.d.	31.12.18.
7. 1.17.	12. 2.17.	Sergt. T. Mottershead	D. of w.	8. 1.17.
period	3. 6.17.	Capt. A. Ball (S.P.)	K.	7. 5.17.
30. 3.17.	8. 6.17.	Lieut. F. H. McNamara		
2. 6.17.	11. 8.17.	Capt. W. A. Bishop (S.P.)		
period	2. 4.18.	Maj. J. B. McCudden (S.P.)	K.a.	9. 7.18.
27. 3.18.	1. 5.18.	Lieut. A. A. McLeod	D. of w.	6.11.18.
30. 3.18.	1. 5.18.	Lieut. A. Jerrard		
10. 7.18.	26. 7.18.	Lieut. F. M. West		
period	30.11.18.	Capt. A. W. Beauchamp-Proctor (S.P.)	K.a.	21. 6.21.
27.10.-18.	30.11.18.	Maj. W. G. Barker (S.P.)	K.a.	12. 3.30.
period	18. 7.19.	Maj. E. Mannock (S.P.)	K.	26. 7.18.

K.—Killed in action.
K.a.—Killed in a flying accident.
D. of w.—Died of wounds.

P.d.—Taken prisoner and died.
(S.P.)—Scout Pilot.

Appendix II

COMBAT REPORT.

" No. 24 Squadron.   23.11.16.   1.50 p.m.
Major L. G. Hawker, V.C., D.S.O.   Defensive patrol.
Capt. Andrews, M.C.   6,000 feet.
Lieut. Saundby.   BAPAUME.
Walfish

About 1.50 p.m., two H.A. were observed at 6,000 feet N.E. of BAPAUME. Capt. Andrews diving from above, drove them east, and then seeing two strong hostile patrols approaching high up, was about to retire when Major Hawker dived past him and continued the pursuit.

The D.H.'s were at once attacked by the H.A., one of which dived on to Major Hawker's tail. Captain Andrews drove this machine off, firing 25 rounds at close quarters, but was himself attacked from the rear, and his engine shot through almost immediately, so that he was obliged to try and regain the lines. He last saw Major Hawker engaging one H.A. at about 3,000 feet. Lieut. Saundby having driven one machine off Capt. Andrews' tail, engaged a second firing three-quarters of a double drum at 20 yards range.

The H.A. fell out of control for 1,000 feet and then continued to go down vertically. Lieut. Saundby could then see no other D.H.'s, and the H.A. appeared to have moved away east, where they remained for the rest of the patrol.

(signed) J. J. Breen, Lieut."

Copy from Capt. J. O. Andrews' Log Book :—

" 23.11.16. 1 p.m. to 2.10 p.m. D.H. 5998. Bapaume.
Had a stiff fight with eight H.A. Scouts over Bapaume. Saw Major driven down but could not help. Machine badly shot about. Large hole in cambox of engine, also one cylinder shot thro', smashed piston, etc.

Got back to Guillimont with Huns on my tail."*

* This was Andrews' last entry before returning to England with a total flying time of 332 hrs. 50 mins.

Copy from Lieut. R. H. M. S. Saundby's Log Book :—

"23.11.16. 1 p.m. to 3.25 p.m.   D.H. 5925.
Violent fight.   Attacked by two lots of H.A. near Achiet.
Maj. Hawker missing.   Capt. Andrews shot down and landed
this side of the lines.   Got well into a Hun on Andrews' tail
which went down out of control (believed crashed).   Joined up
with ' C ' Flight later."

Copy from No. 24 Squadron Record Book :—

"23.11.16.   D.H. 5998.   Capt. Andrews.   D.P. 1 p.m.—2.10 p.m.
At about 2 p.m. I attacked two H.A. just N.E. of BAPAUME
and drove them E. when I observed two strong patrols of
H.A. Scouts above me.   I was about to abandon the pursuit
when a D.H. Scout, Maj. Hawker, dived past me and continued
to pursue.   We were at once attacked by the H.A., one of
which dived on to Maj. Hawker's tail.

I drove him off firing about 25 rounds at close range.   My
engine was immediately shot through from behind and I was
obliged to try and regain our lines.

When on the lines another D.H. came diving past me from
our side and drove the H.A. off my tail.   I last saw Maj.
Hawker at about 3,000 feet near BAPAUME, fighting with
an H.A. apparently quite under control but going down.
                                        (signed) J. O. Andrews."

Copy from No. 24 Squadron Record Book :—

"23.11.16.   D.H. 5925.   Lieut. Saundby.   O.P. 1 p.m. to 3.25.
At about 1.30 I saw a rough house going on over GRAND-
COURT.   We went down with engines on but were too late
to do much good, as Nieuports of 60 Squadron had arrived
and driven off the H.A.   At about 1.50 (or so) the patrol
dived on one H.A. just N.E. of BAPAUME.   No. 2 (the Major)
went far east after it, patrol leader and I following.   We were
dived on by a patrol of seven or eight Walfischs.

One followed by another, dived on me.   I spiralled two or
three times and the H.A. zoomed off.   Then I saw patrol
leader being attacked by a Walfisch, and went to his assistance,
diving on to the H.A.'s tail, I emptied three-quarters double
drum into him at about 20 yards range.   He suddenly wobbled
and dived so steeply with engine on that I could not follow
him, although I dived up to 130 m.p.h.

I flattened out and looked round but could see no other
D.H.'s and the H.A. appeared to have moved away east,

where they remained for the rest of the patrol. I turned to see if patrol leader was all right and saw him go down and land at the French landing ground behind GUILLEMONT.

I continued the patrol defensively, alone until two other D.H.'s joined me at 2.30 p.m.

(signed) R. H. M. S. Saundby, Lieut."

Richthofen's combat report :—

" 23rd of November, 1916. At 3 p.m.

In the district south of Bapaume with Vickers single-seater. The crashed aeroplane lies south of Ligny Sector ' J '. From the aeroplane was salved a machine-gun by the 100th Regiment.

The pilot is dead.

Name of pilot : Major Hawker.

Account of the combat :—

' I attacked in company with two aeroplanes of the squadron a single-seater Vickers biplane at about 3,000 metres. After a very long circling fight (35 minutes) I had forced down my opponent to 500 metres near Bapaume. He then tried to reach the front, I followed him to 100 metres over Ligny, he fell from this height after 900 shots.'

Witnesses of the combat :—Lt. Wortmann, Lt. Collins, Jagdstaffel 2. Other witnesses :—Hptm. Jacobi, Lt. Scheck, Lt. Klewitz, Lt. Merker.

(signed) Frhr. v. Richthofen,
Ltn."

Richthofen's account of the combat in *The Red Air Fighter* :—

" I was extremely proud when one fine day I was informed that the aviator whom I had brought down on the 23rd of November, 1916, was the English Immelmann.

In view of the character of our fight it was clear to me that I was being tackled by a flying champion. One day I was blithely flying, seeking a fight when I noticed three English-men who had apparently gone a-hunting. I noticed that they were interested in my direction, and as I felt much inclination to have a fight I did not want to disappoint them.

I was flying at a lower altitude,* consequently I had to wait until one of my English friends tried to drop on me. After a short while he came sailing along and wanted to tackle me in the rear. After firing five shots he had to stop, for I had swerved in a sharp curve. The Englishman tried to get

---

* Richthofen could not advertise his use of a decoy.

into position behind me while I tried to get behind him. So we circled round and round like madmen after one another at about 3.500 metres. With throttles wide open we circled first twenty times to the left, then thirty times to the right, each thinking by this means we might get above and behind the other.

I had quickly discovered that it was not a novice that I had to deal with because he never dreamed of breaking off the fight. He had a fine-turning box. However, my packing case was better at climbing than his. But I succeeded at last in getting above and behind the Englishman.

After we had dropped about 2,000 metres lower without any result being reached my opponent ought to have discovered that it was time for him to retire because the wind, favourable to me, drove us more and more towards the German lines until at last I came near Bapaume about one kilometre behind the German front. The gallant fellow was full of pluck, and when we had got down to about 1,000 metres he merrily waved to me as if he would say ' Well, well, how do you do?'

The circles which we made around one another were so narrow that their diameter was probably not more than 80 to 100 metres. I had time to take a look at my opponent. I looked down into his cockpit, and could see every movement of his head. If he had not had his cap on I would have noticed what kind of face he was making.

My Englishman was a good sportsman, but by and by the thing became a little too hot for him and he had to decide at last whether he would land on our side or fly back to his own lines. Naturally he tried the latter, after having endeavoured in vain to escape me by loopings and such tricks. At that time my first bullets were flying round his ears, for so far neither of us had been in a position to shoot.

When he had come down to about 100 metres he tried to escape to the front by zigzag flying, which makes it very difficult to aim. Now was my opportunity. I followed him at a height of from 50 to 30 metres, firing all the time.

The Englishman must fall. But a gun jam nearly robbed me of my success. My opponent fell shot through the head 50 metres behind our lines. His machine-gun was dug out of the ground and it adorns the entrance of my room."

Major von Schönberg's description of the air combat :—

" I remember the air fight between Major Hawker and Manfred v. Richthofen very well; I watched it closely with many of my grenadiers from Luisenhofriegel. There was no doubt that we were watching breathlessly a duel between two first-rate champions of the air. Without exaggeration never before nor after have I seen such an exciting duel.

At first each of them tried to get behind his opponent by flying in narrow spirals. In this way they came nearer and nearer to the earth, so that at about a 1,000 metres they were just about above Bapaume. Then the fight went downwards more quickly and more in the direction of the front line of trenches. At last Major Hawker tried to cross the lines by flying in zig-zags close to the ground.

From then on Richthofen kept on shooting, flying close behind him. I expected every minute to see the aeroplanes crash down on the earth as the ground sloped upwards in the direction of their flight. Major Hawker, who was shot in the head, did not come down steeply but rather slantingly. The aeroplane after it touched the earth turned a somersault."

RICHTHOFEN

For an excellent short biography of Manfred von Richthofen, see *War in the Air,* Vol. IV, pp. 394-97.

Richthofen was brought down three times in his own lines : — once on the 24th of January, 1917, with a broken wing, a second time on the 9th of March, 1917, with his petrol tank shot through, and a third time on the 6th of July, 1917, with a wound in the head. See *Red Knight of Germany*—Gibbons, pp. 124-5, 138-9, and 305-15.

He was finally killed on the 21st of April, 1918, by a single bullet from the guns of Capt. Roy Brown. By a strange coincidence Brown set out from Bertangles aerodrome, and Richthofen was buried in Bertangles cemetery.